Free Priests

Free Priests

The Movement for Ministerial Reform in the American Catholic Church

by William F. Powers

A Campion Book

Loyola University Press
Chicago

Loyola University Press
3441 North Ashland Avenue
Chicago, Illinois 60657

Library of Congress Cataloging-in-Publication Data
Powers, William F., 1934–
   Free priests: the movement for ministerial reform in the American Catholic
Church / William F. Powers.
      p.   cm.
   Includes bibliographical references and index.
   ISBN 0-8294-0729-4
   1. Ex-priests, Catholic.   2. Pastoral theology—Catholic Church. 3. Catholic
Church—Clergy.   I. Title.
BX4668.2.P68   1992
262'.14273—dc20   92-8492
                                                            CIP

The poem *Phoenix Bird* by Gerald Grudzen appears in his book, *New Age
Catholicism: A Life of Service in the World* (San Jose, Calif.: Privately published,
1979). Used by permission of the author. All rights reserved.

Acknowledgment
Cover and interior design by Nancy Gruenke

For Ann

When one finds a worthy wife,
her value is far beyond pearls.
Proverbs 31:10

Contents

Part I

Origins of the Movement for Ministerial Reform /1

Part II

Shaping a Vision, Issuing a Call /53

Part III

Transformation of SPFM into FCM and the Founding of CORPUS /119

Part IV

Experiments in Free Ministry and the Role of Women /181

Part V

The Emergence of CORPUS and Prospects for the Future /241

Foreword

When the Vatican II Council ended in 1965, a host of fresh "spirits," to use Ignatius Loyola's term, were on board in the Roman Catholic Church. They were hoping—with their emerging programs—to be "discerned" more or less promptly and made the order of the day. On the other hand, a phalanx of contrary-minded spirits was waiting in ambush, determined, as it turned out, to see that most such programs died at takeoff. Now, in 1992, the various causes have had their run, and some judgment is in place.

Thus, the new liturgy, the married diaconate, a more open relationship with the laity, and the ecumenical outlook are examples of new ground won. On the other hand, some issues, like birth control, seem to have lost outright, at least officially. And some issues still remain in tension, pending presumably the experience of further generations.

One issue that has apparently lost—whether a married clergy is acceptable in the American (Roman Rite) Catholic Church—is the subject of this book. An associated question, raised by the title *Free Priests*, concerns what shape the priestly ministry might have taken if the rule of celibacy had been made optional.

At this distance, it is hard to recall the enthusiasm and confidence among a good number of American Catholic priests in the sixties and seventies, namely, that a dispensation from celibacy was just around the corner. Among them were well-known priests, both religious and diocesan, such as Bernard Cooke, Eugene Kennedy, Daniel Maguire, James Kavanaugh, Eugene Bianchi, Frank Bonnike, and Anthony Padovano. Indeed, in 1966 a large national sampling of diocesan priests, conducted by a prominent Jesuit sociologist, Joseph H. Fichter, reported six out of ten (62 percent) to be in favor of the diocesan priest's freedom to marry.

One might quote, too, the confident judgment of the editors of *America* magazine in the first issue of 1970: "By the middle of the decade a new and volatile element will have entered the staid galaxy of ecclesiastical authority: the priest's wife. The Roman Catholic Church will decide to make clerical celibacy optional . . . ."

Meanwhile, a series of organizational moves by interested priests gave both theoretical and practical sponsorship to the movement. Witness an alphabet of successive groups—NAPR (1966), SPFM (1968), FCM (1973), and CORPUS (1974)—whose charters and strategies traced the evolution of the "free" ministry envisioned for a married priesthood. As author Bill Powers tells it, that ministry was at first conceived as working inside, then outside or, finally, alongside the official ministry of the Church herself.

But early on, the other shoe dropped. In 1968, Pope Paul VI issued an encylical *Sacerdotalis Celibatus*, reaffirming the requirement of priestly celibacy in the Roman rite. An immediate effect was to take the American bishops out of play in support of the new movement. With that, the movement in some part radicalized, splitting into factions marked by uncertain vision and failing energies.

By 1992, some twenty thousand American priests are estimated to have resigned from the priesthood. Given such numbers, not to mention their one-time ministry and the affection in which they were held, it seems appropriate to set forth this historic record while events and personalities are still close by. Indeed, some quarters would see the account as open-ended still, considering the aging of the present priestly corps and the low rate of replacement.

Sociologist Bill Powers—himself a resigned priest (Brooklyn Diocese, 1959–69) and married since 1970—is uniquely well-placed to chronicle the movement here described.

Joseph F. Downey, S.J.
Editorial Director, Loyola University Press
Chicago
May 1992

Acknowledgments

In June 1989, believing that the time was right for a history of the free ministry movement, Tom Durkin wrote to me suggesting that I undertake the project. One of the first people I contacted in an effort to test the waters was Eugene Bianchi, the first president of the Society of Priests for a Free Ministry (SPFM). As it happens, in May, Joseph Fichter, S.J., who was writing a book on married Episcopal priests, had requested information from Bianchi on SPFM. The query prompted Bianchi to suggest to Fichter that the two of them coauthor a book that would explore the movement "as it experimented with new forms of ministry" after Vatican II. However, upon learning of my interest, Bianchi immediately offered encouragement and sent me the extensive files he had kept since 1968.

A second major source of documentation from the early years was William Manseau, who shipped several cartons of records that he had preserved during his long tenure as a dedicated free minister. Initially, I had worried that it might be difficult to locate information. As it turned out, I was overwhelmed with material.

A third major resource was Gerald Grudzen. Not only did he provide access to his files, but as chairman of the Federation of Christian Ministries (FCM), previously called the Fellowship of Christian Ministries, he facilitated my request for a research grant from that organization. Originally, the FCM board wanted me to write a history that focused on their organization. It soon became clear to me that FCM was but part of a larger and much more vital story.

The other group that has been central to the movement is the Corps of Reserve Priests United for Service (CORPUS). I am deeply indebted to Frank Bonnike, Anthony Padovano, and Terry Dosh for their generous cooperation, including reading and critiquing the chapters of which they are the principal subjects.

Similarly, I am grateful to Carl Hemmer, whose records and recollections made possible the reconstruction of the story of the National Association for Pastoral Renewal (NAPR) and to Rosemary Ruether for her valued comments on the chapter that relates to her role in the movement.

Virtually every person mentioned in the text was interviewed. All were delighted that the book was being written and were candid in their responses to my questions. What I discovered to be a near universal characteristic of free ministers was an optimistic attitude toward life, coupled with a deep sense that priesthood, though cherished, needed revitalization.

The writing of the first draft of the text was done during the 1990–91 academic year while I was on sabbatical leave from Suffolk County Community College in New York. With my wife, Ann, who took a leave from her position as chair of the Child Study Department of St. Joseph's College, New York, I spent the year in St. Louis. As volunteers with Boys Hope, the Jesuit Program for Living and Learning, Ann and I served as house parents for six teenage boys from dysfunctional families. I am grateful to Boys Hope for providing me with office space and a work schedule that enabled me to conduct my research.

My main cheerleader and closest collaborator was my wife. Ann read every word of the manuscript and made countless valuable suggestions. To dedicate this book to her is not merely to recognize her editorial assistance but to acknowledge her priceless companionship for over twenty years.

William F. Powers
June 1992

Introduction

One of the products of Vatican Council II (1962–1965) has been a movement by resigned priests and others to obtain greater ministerial freedom within the Catholic Church. The movement embraces a broad spectrum of people from those wanting nothing more than the freedom to marry to those calling for a revolutionary restructuring of the Church, including a radical reconceptualization of Christian ministry.

Stages of a Movement

The quarter century that has passed since the end of the council is sufficient time to review what has happened. In fact, in terms of a social movement it is a considerable length of time. The sociological literature contains several formulations of what are variously called the "social history" or "career" or "life cycle" of a social movement.[1] These models identify stages through which movements tend to pass. They do not have point-for-point correspondence with actual events but can serve as a broad overlay through which the lives of individuals and groups might be viewed. Such a framework can be helpful in an examination of what some call the married priesthood movement but for which the term *free ministry movement* is more comprehensive.

Any social movement then has several basic components. First, a category of people in a society or institution feel discontented.

Something is wrong, but it is not clear what can be done, or even if anything can be done. There is a feeling of powerlessness and futility. For example, African-Americans lived for almost a century under the racial segregation system known as Jim Crow. There was little overt or organized opposition. They seemed permanently trapped in a discriminatory system.

Then there occurs a precipitating event that ignites in the hearts of many the hope and conviction that change is possible after all. Rosa Parks's refusal to move to the back of the bus in Montgomery, Alabama, was such an event. Similarly, the freeing of Nelson Mandela in South Africa energized the anti-apartheid movement. The August 1991 coup attempt against Mikhail Gorbachev accelerated the nationalist movement that fragmented the Soviet Union.

The third element is the emergence of individuals who can articulate the goals and dreams of the group experiencing itself as oppressed. These charismatic leaders often have no official position but are invested with authority by their followers. Dr. Martin Luther King, Jr., was such a leader in the civil rights movement, Mandela in the anti-apartheid movement, and Boris Yeltsin, the elected president of Russia, was afforded even wider authority because of his personal appeal in a time of crisis during the Soviet nationalist movement.

Frequently, such leaders attempt to link the agenda of the movement with the underlying spirit of the society or institution they are striving to change. King appealed to the Declaration of Independence. American Indian leaders call for justice based on treaties made with their forebears. They argue that their desire for fuller self-determination is not so much a rejection of the society as a summons to fuller fidelity to its fundamental values.

Fourth, organization takes place. While visionary leaders continue to provide the ideas that reshape consciousness, others, possessing more practical skills, mobilize large numbers of people into action groups. The anti–Vietnam War movement of the sixties and seventies generated numerous groupings that staged marches, rallies, lobbying activities, and civil disobedience events.

Fifth, the leaders negotiate with the people in power, attempting to get them to accept the proposals of the movement. Leaders of the women's movement, perhaps the most successful example of a contemporary social movement, lobbied members of Congress and other government officials in their effort to obtain legislation and policies that would afford equality to women.

Sixth, as movements agitate for change in the established structure, conflicts and divisions occur within the movement itself. Leaders disagree on goals and on tactics. Since only the most charismatic leaders have widespread legitimacy, those who wish to lead must show results or yield to rivals who promise that they will be more successful. For example, the movement for the unification of Ireland is split into factions that favor peaceful tactics and those that advocate violence.

Next, movements need victories in order to attract and hold a significant number of adherents who will support the continuing struggle. Movements on behalf of minority group members, women, homosexuals, senior citizens, the physically handicapped, and the homeless can point to laws and policies and court decisions that show that they are making progress. Other movements, such as those to protect the environment, ban the killing of baby seals, protect wildlife, outlaw handguns, eliminate smoking from public places, curtail pornography, and improve public education can also approach potential donors and volunteer workers with lists of achievements.

Finally, hypothetically, when a movement achieves its objectives, it dies. Its life cycle is complete. The anti–Vietnam War movement achieved its objective when the United States withdrew from Southeast Asia. In practice, however, a movement may resist its demise by reconceptualizing its objectives. For example, many anti-war activists redirected their energies from ending the war to eliminating nuclear arms.

The Free Ministry Movement

Religion, as well as society as a whole, has experienced numerous social movements. The fundamentalist Islamic movement has transformed Iran and other parts of the Arab world. The liberation theology and base community movements have had an impact on the Catholic Church in parts of Latin America as has the Protestant Pentecostal movement. In the United States, in recent decades, the liturgical movement, the Young Christian Workers movement, the Marriage Encounter movement, the ecumenical movement, the charismatic movement, the Catholic Worker movement, and the Pro-Life movement are but a few examples of the movements that have engaged the interest and passion of American Catholics.

Another of these movements is the subject matter of this book. Although almost every Catholic has an opinion on whether or not priests should be allowed to marry, not many are aware of the highly organized efforts by many married priests to bring about such a change. Even fewer are aware of the range of proposals, strategies, and actions that have emerged as such priests have labored for the past twenty-five years searching for a way to achieve their objectives.

Many of the elements of a social movement can be found in the free ministry experience. Although its most direct objective—a married priesthood—has not been achieved, it will be shown that the movement has not been without its successes. At the very least it has nurtured men whose talents and energy have not been completely lost to the Christian community. Through the instrumentality of the movement, they experience themselves as continuing to be of service to the Church that called them to ministry and ordained them to preach the Word and administer the sacraments.

Although much of the initial, youthful fervor has gone out of the movement, it is still very much alive and serves as a sort of loyal opposition, a faction that reminds the Church that the work of reform is not complete. There are even some faint indications that, as bishops admit that a critical shortage of priests is imminent, the message of the "free priests" will at last be heeded. [2]

Major Organizational Components

Two organizations form the heart of the free ministry movement. The first, the Society of Priests for a Free Ministry (SPFM), was established in 1968. In 1973, the group's name was changed to the Fellowship of Christian Ministries (FCM), reflecting the emerging consciousness that the original name was too clericalist. Then, in 1980, responding to the sexism some saw in the word *fellowship*, the name was changed once again, this time to the Federation of Christian Ministries, still using the acronym FCM.

The major organizational structures of FCM are its national board, its newsletter, *Diaspora*, which has been published continuously since 1969 and goes out quarterly to four hundred members and subscribers, and the national meeting or convention, which has been held without interruption, also since 1969. (See Appendix A.)

The other group, the Corps of Reserve Priests United for Service (CORPUS), was founded in 1974, by and for those who wanted to maintain a focus on optional celibacy in light of the more diffuse and radical agenda adopted by FCM. However, CORPUS remained little more than a list of people who subscribed to a statement in support of a married priesthood until late 1984 when an executive secretary was hired and the process of forming a bona fide organization began. In 1988, CORPUS held its first National Conference on a Married Priesthood, established a national board, and was distributing its publication *Corpus Reports* to about ten thousand people, including the American Catholic hierarchy. (See Appendix B.) The fact that CORPUS has more members than FCM suggests that the group viewed as more conservative, or at least with more clearly defined objectives, attracts the larger following.

Both groups have local affiliates and insist that the heart of the movement is organization and action on the local level. There is considerable overlap in membership. Many CORPUS members are certified for ministry by FCM, and many FCM members subscribe to the goals of CORPUS.

The Lives of Key Men and Women

Tracing the development of these two organizations will be central to the analysis of the free ministry movement. However, since movements are people, the unfolding of the story will be in the context of the lives of the dozens of men and women who shaped the movement and who struggled in a spirit of faith to be true to themselves and to Christ. That faith, though tested by frustration, has provided them with inner peace. Most have long since purged from their hearts any remnants of anger or bitterness.

It is estimated that there are over twenty thousand married priests in the United States.[3] Most of those who have moved to the other side of the altar seem content to remain there as lay members of the Church. Only a small proportion are actively promoting a married priesthood and hence are participants in the movement. The men and women highlighted in this book are either the primary leaders or representative members. Hopefully, the lives of these two dozen people will serve to communicate the hopes and dreams that animate the thousands who must go unmentioned.

A Note on Sources

Two publications are referred to frequently, *Diaspora* and *Corpus Reports*. Although they are the principal channels of communication within the movement, libraries do not subscribe to them and their contents are not indexed. Therefore, access to back issues is difficult. Copies of the publications or other information can be obtained from the groups' national offices:

FCM: P.O. Box 9123, Berkeley, Calif. 94709
Phone: 1-800-726-4445
CORPUS: P.O. Box 2247, Mill Valley, Calif. 94941
Phone: 415-383-CORP

Other material in the book is derived from the unpublished files kept by the organizations and their leaders: board minutes, correspondence, and an assortment of clippings and notes that, fortunately for historical purposes, some people preserve but are not readily available to the general public. Yet without these sources, the reconstruction of the story would have been severely handicapped. It is due to this lack of easy access that unpublished sources are not always footnoted.

Finally, most of the men and women included were interviewed during 1990 and 1991. These telephone and in-person conversations were taped. When no other attribution is given for information related, it is derived from these interviews.

Part I
Origins of the Movement for Ministerial Reform

1

The Roots of Free Ministry

If it was Vatican Council II that provided the spark that ignited the dry tinder of the free ministry movement, then it was a handful of prominent priests who fanned the flames. Their reputations provided legitimacy and their ideas a rationale for change to the advocates of ministerial reform. Certainly there were others, but the contributions of six such men supplied an adequate foundation for the movement. All six have continued to publish and to speak out on behalf of Church renewal. Two do so from within the canonical priesthood: Hans Küng and Edward Schillebeeckx. The others have resigned and married but remain respected contributors to theological dialogue. They are Bernard Cooke, Eugene Kennedy, Charles Davis, and Gregory Baum.

Charles Davis

In 1966, with the ink hardly dry on the final council documents, the English theologian Charles Davis resigned from the priesthood and, more shocking still, left the Roman Catholic Church. Davis had gained international prominence on two levels. As editor of the *Clergy Review*, he addressed professional churchmen. In books such as *Theology for Today* (1962) and *Sacraments of Initiation: Baptism & Confirmation* (1964), he communicated to a broader Catholic population the new thinking that was percolating in theological circles.

The defection of Davis was a powerful jolt to those who looked to him for guidance. Why did he leave the Church? His response was not long in coming. In 1967, *A Question of Conscience* gave a lucid and moving account of the process through which he had passed.[1] Although much of the book addressed issues of faith and of difficulty with ecclesiastical bureaucracy, his initial response to the question Why? was on the psychological level. He said that now he was happy. There had been a malaise, a sense that something was wrong in his life. Once he cut his ties with the institutional Church he felt relief.

Davis's unhappiness may have been similar to the phenomenon that Betty Friedan identified in her 1963 book, *The Feminine Mystique*.[2] Friedan described a set of symptoms widely shared by women, but which they could not explain or understand. On the surface, everything was in order. Yet an unrest suffused their lives. Friedan termed it "the disease that has no name." The impact of the book was so profound that it is considered the opening salvo of the women's liberation movement.

On a more modest level, it might be argued that Davis's book marked the start of the free ministry movement. It too described what might be termed "a disease that has no name," and it struck a responsive chord in the hearts of many readers, priests in particular. This is not to say that *A Question of Conscience* called for the new movement but rather that it articulated the issues that brought it to life.

Davis identified three reasons for his new-found happiness, reasons which encapsulate the transformation of consciousness that was a major, if unanticipated, consequence of Vatican II. He wrote:

> I have taken possession of myself by a radical decision; I have accepted the risk of a wider and receding horizon; and I have joined myself in intimate love to an individual person.[3]

Each of Davis's reasons uncovered a dimension of the psychological restructuring occurring within the lives of many Catholics. To understand the psychology of Charles Davis is to understand the spiritual soil from which the free ministry idea sprang.

First, "I have taken possession of myself by a radical decision." There was a need for autonomy, for unshackling self from an infantilizing straitjacket of authority. Davis felt intellectually and emotionally constrained by the Church. He did not want any longer to be motivated by fear of sin, hell, or rejection by a hierarchy that he felt had usurped the authority of God and imposed undue limits on human freedom.

Second, "I have accepted the risk of a wider and receding horizon." Here, Davis expressed the impact of an accelerating scientific age, one which rejected the absolutes and dogmatism of the Church. Truth is a search, not a possession. Pope John XXIII in convening Vatican II had urged that the windows of the Church be opened. The fresh air that rushed in was intoxicating. Davis and free ministers could no longer subscribe to a static and parochial understanding of truth.

The wider horizon included an openness to other religions, prompted by the council's *The Decree on Ecumenism*, *The Declaration on the Relationship of the Church to Non-Christian Religions*, and, in particular, *The Declaration on Religious Freedom*. The exclusive claims of the Catholic Church had been rescinded, and Davis and free ministers were eager to learn from other Christians and to explore and experiment beyond the limits approved by the hierarchy. Catholic priests were not unaffected by the "freedom movements" that dominated the sixties. Davis was linking himself and those who listened to him to the spirit of the age.

Third, "I have joined myself in intimate love to an individual person." Perhaps this is the clearest and most concrete of Davis's reasons for happiness. It is the issue of sexuality.

For many, the free ministry movement is essentially the call for optional celibacy or for a married priesthood. Priests were forced to ask themselves whether the solitariness of celibacy was a higher form of life than the companionship of marriage. Psychologists were teaching them that healthy human development included the ability to relate intimately to the opposite sex.

Research in Church history and biblical scholarship was revealing that priestly celibacy was not mandated by the Scriptures and had not been universally enforced by the Western Church until the eleventh century. For many priests, be they highly intellectual like Charles Davis or humble parish priests, the mystique of celibacy was collapsing.

Davis dedicated his 1967 apologia "to Florence." In 1990, he dedicated *A Spirituality for the Vulnerable*[4] "to my wife, Florence." The word *vulnerable* encapsulated the insight that the age of Catholic triumphalism was over and that a Christianity that would attract contemporary men and women was one that understood weakness, tenderness, and fragility. The only ministers who could heal wounds were those who knew themselves as wounded. And it is in the give-and-take of married love that for most individuals their vulnerability and their lovableness are revealed. Not that marriage is essential for growth or effective ministry, but it was becoming clear to many that, rather than being an obstacle to sanctification, marital love is the ordinary God-given context for confronting the mystery of existence.

Although he did not take an active role, Davis was aware of and supported the free ministry movement. In the very first issue of *Diaspora*, the newsletter of the Society of Priests for a Free Ministry (SPFM), in August 1969, the editor remarked, "We have received a note from Charles Davis commending the SPFM and its efforts."

Bernard Cooke

While in England Davis was explaining the spirit of Vatican II to clerics, religious, and educated lay Catholics, the American Jesuit theologian, Bernard Cooke, was engaged in a similar task in the United States.

In particular, Cooke drew attention to the idea of universal priesthood, which would have far-reaching implications in the arduous process of reconceptualizing the Church and reordering ministry. In *The Challenge of Vatican II*, Cooke said:

> . . . everyone in the Church has a priestly and prophetic role. The notion of the priesthood common to all baptized Christians is prominent in the documents of Vatican II, particularly in the Constitutions on the Church and the Liturgy; the development of the doctrine in those documents is an advance over the position found in *Mediator Dei*, Pius XII's encyclical on the liturgy, which up to that time had spoken most clearly on this subject. In *Mediator Dei*, which admits that the layman has an involvement in the Eucharist, the whole emphasis is on what the layman *cannot* do and what the ordained priest *can* do; it is not too clear, in short, that the layman has a real priesthood, which he exercises.[5]

Besides the stress on universal priesthood, this quotation illustrates the concept *development of doctrine*, which means, in simple terms, that the Church can change, that even popes may not have had the whole truth. By teaching this theological principle, Cooke was planting the seeds of dissent, skepticism, and experimentation in the minds of thousands of priests and religious.

Many of those flocking to Cooke's lectures and reading his books were members of the bumper crop of young adults emerging from the seminaries and houses of religious formation in the fifties and early sixties. They had been incubated in the pre–Vatican II Church and hatched into the euphoria of the postcouncil era. They were ready for action. They could identify with youthful, Catholic politicians like the recently assassinated John F. Kennedy and also with the inspiring young cleric who was leading the civil rights movement, Dr. Martin Luther King, Jr. They were convinced that a New Age had arrived, not just for freedom and progress in their country but in their Church as well. After all, the council was all about *aggiornamento*. They would be the ones to spearhead the updating.

Cooke was a pied piper whose deep spirituality, crisp and clear presentation, and fresh ideas captivated audiences. A page in *The Challenge of Vatican II* contains but one sentence in large type:

> To the extent that people are not genuinely free, you do not have Christianity.[6]

Some of those who read these words would call for a "free ministry," convinced that it was a necessary and inevitable implication of the council.

In December 1969, Bernard Cooke announced that he was resigning as chairman of Marquette University's theology department and had asked to be released from the priesthood. His formal statement was indicative both of his own thinking and the state of the free ministry movement at that moment. He said:

> It seems to me we are in a period of rapid and drastic social change and that in the present situation of the Church there is a need to develop new forms of Christian life and priestly ministry, not necessarily replacing the old but supplementing them. . . . rightly, many in the Church—especially in the hierarchy—must give more of their attention to safeguarding and developing the important elements of traditional patterns; but others of us must then assume the responsibility of helping develop the new,

exercising initiative for which officials in the Church do
not have to take responsibility.[7]

By this time, priests and religious had been leaving the official
ministry in large numbers. By joining their ranks, Cooke heightened
their expectations for change.

The January-February 1970 issue of *Diaspora* contained the brief
notice:

> Bernard Cooke, who recently resigned from the Jesuits,
> has joined SPFM. He will be a very valuable member and
> we look forward to him for leadership in making SPFM
> successful.

Although he never became part of the organizational structure of
the movement, Cooke lent his name to SPFM as a member of its
advisory board. For years his name appeared regularly on its stationery and in *Diaspora*.

In April 1971, Cooke submitted a paper titled, "On Community,
Ministry and Leadership" to be read at a Detroit SPFM meeting. In
the paper, which stresses the need for the Church to encourage new
leadership, he says of SPFM:

> The very existence of the Society testifies to the felt need to
> plan for the future of Christianity in a more imaginative
> and flexible manner.

Cooke suggested that SPFM could contribute to the Church by
"providing tomorrow with the kind of people who can cope with the
problems and potential of a new world."

On one occasion, in response to a request for greater involvement
in the movement, Cooke said that he had wrestled with the question
of how he could best serve the cause and had concluded that he could
be most effective by focusing on his theological writings and by not
assuming an activist role.[8]

His ministry as theologian reached its apex with the publication in
1976 of *Ministry to Word and Sacraments*, a highly regarded comprehensive analysis of priesthood.[9]

Ever the popularizer as well as scholar, Cooke's three-part article,
"The Eucharist: A Threatened Species," was published in May 1990
in the *National Catholic Reporter*. In the series, Cooke, a professor of

theology at the Jesuit College of the Holy Cross in Massachusetts, developed a step further the theology of the priesthood of all Christians, which twenty-four years before he had identified as one of the key insights of Vatican II. He suggested that, in the light of the centrality of the Eucharist in Christian worship and the increasing shortage of ordained priests, "it is not clear why an ordained celebrant is absolutely needed" for the celebration of the Eucharist.

Edward Schillebeeckx

Much of the momentum for change that followed Vatican II originated in Europe. The Dutch church, in particular, was seen as a model for a more enlightened ecclesiastical structure. It was in Holland that new theological reflections would attract the enthusiasm of free ministers and the censures of the Vatican. To be sure, some of these ideas had not been published in the late sixties, but are logical developments from the call for freedom, experimentation, and equality that led American free ministers to look to Europe for leadership and collaboration. All early issues of *Diaspora* had a section titled "International Scene." There was a feeling that American priests were sharing in a worldwide movement for reform.

In 1971, the Dutch theologian, Edward Schillebeeckx, O.P., gave a series of lectures in the San Francisco Bay area. He forecast that the Catholic Church of the future would be a community of smaller churches and that the "big hierarchy" of Rome would function in the background. He also predicted that "by this fall men who have already been married for a number of years will be able to be ordained priests."[10]

Seizing the moment, Thomas Durkin, SPFM vice president, immediately wrote to Schillebeeckx, sending him literature about the organization and inviting his participation in the movement. Perhaps because he had enough problems already, the eminent theologian did not respond.

Some of Schillebeeckx's subsequent books became classic texts for the theology of free ministry. *Ministry* radically reconceptualized the notion of leadership in the Christian community.[11] Schillebeeckx's work was subjected to close scrutiny and sharp criticism by the Vatican. In order to clarify, refine, and extend his thinking, he published *The Church with a Human Face.*[12] In this more fully documented work, Schillebeeckx did not back away from his call for a revolutionary reform of ministry. On the contrary, he added the idea, gradually emerging to center stage in theological discourse, that women could no longer be denied full equality with men in all forms of Church service. As will be seen, the question of women in ministry would become a central theme on the agenda of the free ministry movement.

One further idea from Schillebeeckx, an idea echoed subsequently by Cooke in his writings, suggested just how radical the call for "free" ministry could be and how thoroughly could be challenged the beliefs and practices of centuries: the idea that the Eucharist was not intrinsically linked to ordination and that it was possible to imagine lay people presiding at the central action of Christian worship.

The feature article in the summer 1989 issue of *Diaspora* was titled "Can Lay People Lead the Eucharist?" It summarized Schillebeeckx's ideas on ministry, including the suggestion, so dear to free ministry advocates, that experimentation with "alternative practices" in ministry is consistent with the will of Christ, even if prohibited by Church officials.

Hans Küng

While Schillebeeckx was stirring up the theological waters in Holland, Hans Küng in Germany also was challenging traditional Catholic understanding of everything from papal infallibility to divorce and contraception. Küng's voluminous writings on the council and its implications have won a wider audience around the world than the work of any other author. They have also deeply disturbed Church officials. In 1979, after a long and acrimonious struggle, the Vatican charged that Küng had departed in his writings from "the integral truth of Catholic faith." Rome declared that Küng "can no longer be considered a Catholic theologian nor function as such in a teaching role."[13]

By no means has this censure deterred Küng from writing and speaking, and it has enhanced his reputation as a champion of reform within the free ministry world. Immediately after the censure was announced, William Manseau, past president of FCM, wrote a letter of support to Küng. In a March 1980 response, Küng said that he had received six thousand letters and telegrams encouraging him to continue his work. In contrast with Charles Davis, who felt that the autocratic Roman bureaucracy necessitated his departure from the priesthood and the Church, Küng affirmed that he would not be forced out; that the Church was his birthright.

It might be noted that in a "Statement on Celibacy" issued in 1969, the National Conference of Catholic Bishops attempted to defuse the free ministry movement by urging that resigned priests be treated in a kindly fashion. The reason given was that such an approach would "reduce the temptation to exercise a priestly ministry apart from unity with the Bishop."[14]

While the bishops attempted to stamp out dissent, Küng has modeled and encouraged it. Further, he has served as adviser to FCM, written encouraging letters to leaders, and on several occasions met with FCM members in conjunction with speaking tours to the United States. As recently as 1989 he assured the FCM president, Joseph Ruane, of his continued support for the movement.

Rare is the meeting of FCM or CORPUS at which the name of Hans Küng is not invoked to support a position. His work has been highlighted in *Diaspora* on several occasions, most recently in the winter 1990 issue, in which some of his ideas on the Church are recapitulated.[15]

Gregory Baum

Support for free ministry came from many quarters. Gregory Baum, for many years on the faculty of the theology department at St. Michael's College at the University of Toronto and currently at McGill University in Montreal, was an early ally, arguing in 1970 that free ministers "offer a valid service, a legitimate ministry."[16] The following year he expressed hope that "a sustained conversation with the institutional Church will eventually lead to an acknowledgement of pluriformity in the ministry."[17]

In the introduction to *Searching for Truth* by Peter Kelly, a resigned Jesuit priest, Baum attempted to explain the cultural and theological factors that led to a crisis of faith and calling, not just for Kelly, but for countless others.[18] His analysis helped to locate what was happening in the Church on the larger canvas of the intellectual transformation of the world.

Basically, what was occurring was the painful process of the Catholic Church's reconciliation with modern thought. The science and philosophy of the nineteenth century had presented Christianity with an enormous challenge. Catholicism was slower than Protestantism to adjust because the Roman Church was especially strong in the more traditional parts of Europe—those areas, especially Italy, still tied to the remnants of feudalism.

A revised way of understanding and speaking of God had to be found. For his part, Baum was confident that although the transformation would be stressful and prolonged, the Church was capable of aligning itself with the contemporary world.

However, not every priest agreed with this assessment. The most sensational post–Vatican II book by an American priest was James Kavanaugh's *A Modern Priest Looks at His Outdated Church.*[19] Kavanaugh's tone was one of anger: "I am a priest, and to be such is to be well guarded from the complexity that is truth. . . . My education narrowed my mind into little cubes which reject or distort any information that is new. . . . "[20] The book was a bestseller and catapulted the unrest in the clergy to national consciousness. On the dust jacket of Kavanaugh's autobiographical polemic was a testimonial from none other than Baum who, as he did with Kelly's book, cloaked the author in the mantle of prophet, comparing Kavanaugh's impassioned attack on Catholicism with the evangelists' indictment of first-century Judaism.

After decades of attempting to reconcile the celibate life-style with openness to contemporary thought, Baum left the canonical priesthood and married. Although he has not participated recently in free ministry activities, he continues through his writings to be a voice for reform and is an honorary member of FCM.

Sexual Love and Human Development

One root of free ministry already referred to requires fuller attention. It might well be called "the heart" of the movement. It is the powerful experience of love that entered the lives of many priests. Certainly, many of the thousands of priests who resigned experienced a crisis of faith or dissatisfaction with authority. But it is undeniable that there existed as well a more down-to-earth explanation: There was a sexual awakening of monumental proportions. All over the country and throughout the world priests fell in love. What was going on?

A letter from a seminarian in the *Review for Religious* in July of 1966 addressed the issue that had been gaining increased attention and creating confusion as well as joy in the lives of many vowed religious and priests. It was the issue frequently called "love in the religious life." The seminarian wrote:

> In religious life today there are many problem areas. . . .
> One area where the amount of published, "authoritative"

material is way behind the lived experience of many religious is that of love and what it should mean for a man or woman with vows to love a person of the opposite sex, be they a priest or nun or lay person. . . .

Where can a religious go to find sound, relevant guidelines when faced with questions like: Is a person who has a vow of chastity being unfaithful to Christ and his vow if he loves a person of the opposite sex deeply? What is the place of any kind of external expression of such a love? Is it possible to separate external sexual expression of love from a different external expression that is not basically sexual?

A reply to the challenge from the seminarian appeared in the form of an explanation of the ideas of Pierre Teilhard de Chardin.[21] Teilhard, the Jesuit scientist-theologian initially misunderstood and condemned for his innovative insights, had been vindicated and now was celebrated as a prophet. So, on the question of heterosexual love, he was quoted as saying:

The more perfect man and woman become, the more they will experience a need for each other, a need for each other's complementarity, the need, in other words, of drawing nearer to each other.

Teilhard had a great love for matter. His mystical style of expression led some to accuse him of pantheism, of worshiping the world. But for young people groping for a fuller Christian life, the revered paleontologist spoke words that called them to life. In a "secret of happiness" formulated in Peking, Teilhard envisioned a three-step progression to full human development. He wrote:

No longer simply to develop oneself, nor even simply to give oneself to another who is one's equal; but further, to submit one's life and bring it to one greater than oneself. In other words, first be, then love, and at last adore. Such are the natural phases of our personalization: happiness of growing, happiness of loving, happiness of adoration.[22]

Priests and religious read these words and wondered whether or not their full spiritual development required that they "join themselves in intimate love to an individual person" as Charles Davis had done. They read in Teilhard's *The Divine Milieu*, "By virtue of the Creation and, still more, of the Incarnation, *nothing* here below is *profane* for those who know how to see."[23] They reassessed celibacy as perhaps an incomplete understanding of Christianity. There seemed but two options if one were to grow: Either find a way to love within the blurring borders of celibacy or leave the ministry and marry.

Romanticized Medieval Lovers

A model of the former possibility was offered by an extraordinary pair of religious from the thirteenth century, Jordan of Saxony and Diana d'Andalo. Their letters were published by a Dominican priest, Gerald Vann, just as Vatican II concluded and were read and discussed by many priests and religious.[24] Jordan was a Dominican priest, elected Master General of the Order on the death of St. Dominic. Diana was a Dominican sister. Her letters have been lost, but Jordan's more than fifty letters attest to the deep love they had for each other. Excerpts from the letters communicate the tenderness of the love:

> I saw you recently in a dream: it seemed to me that you were speaking to me and in a manner so sincere and wise that still when I think of it I am filled with joy; and you told me: The Lord spoke these words to me: I, Diana, I, Diana, I, Diana; and then added the same number of times: Am good, am good, am good. I want you to know how consoling I found this.
>
> The longer we are separated from one another, the greater becomes our desire to see one another again. Beloved, since I cannot see you with my bodily eyes nor be consoled with your presence as often as you would wish and I would wish, it is at least some refreshment to me, some appeasement of my heart's longing, when I can visit you by means of my letters. . . .[25]

In his commentary on the letters, Vann made a number of remarks that tended to idealize heterosexual love, reinforcing a message converging from many directions, namely, that human love is essential to human growth. For example, Vann wrote:

> Nature abhors a vacuum: terrible things can happen to a man with an empty heart. That is one reason why it can be

more difficult for a priest or a religious to be a good Christian, living a really vital Christian life, than for happily married lay people. These can without too much difficulty integrate their love of each other into their shared love of God. . . . [26]

Eugene C. Kennedy

To the medieval example of Jordan and Diana were soon added the insights of contemporary psychology. In what would become the classic essay on love in the religious life, Eugene Kennedy, a Maryknoll priest-psychologist, brought to the light of day and affirmed in no uncertain terms the experience and yearnings of many. He said:

> The fact is that many priests and religious have of late found great human love in their lives. It has come unsought and unexplained, as real love often does, and it has borne all the signs of the action of the Holy Spirit. . . .
>
> The Spirit is obviously at work, seeding the world with rich relationships that can never be yielded to the pale but approved calligraphy of the past. Something wonderfully human has entered the Church. . . .
>
> This kind of love, which seems to be a gift of the Spirit, cannot be demanded or actively sought. . . . Nobody will ever believe again that his offering of self for the redemption of the world entails a suicidal destruction of that self at the same time.[27]

Kennedy continued his campaign on behalf of love and his insistence that what was happening was the work of the Holy Spirit. In 1969 he chastised "conservative and authoritarian" Church leaders for not seeing the work of the Spirit in the outbreak of love. Such leaders, he chided, "seem awkward in dealing with this phenomenon, almost embarrassed that Christians should be tempted to love one another."[28] Paradoxically, the man who could say such things was asked by the U.S. bishops to construct a sociopsychological profile of the American priest.[29]

In 1973, *Newsweek* published an article that claimed that "thousands of U.S. Catholic priests are experimenting with what they call 'the third way'—a priestly life-style that includes close personal relationships with women leading sometimes to sex but seldom to marriage."[30] The article cited Kennedy as saying that "the Roman Catholic Church is allowing its latent heterosexuality to come out." The Jesuit sociologist Eugene Schallert, an adviser to the free ministry movement, added that priests "suffer from heterosexual immaturity and don't like themselves for that. Priests feel that they should not exclude one-half of the human race from their experience."[31]

Many priests may have started with "the third way," but thousands found the tensions of a double life unacceptable. They resigned and married. Kennedy himself did so. Currently, he is on the faculty of Loyola University in Chicago, has published books on various aspects of American Catholic life, and is called upon regularly by the media to comment on Church issues.

Most of the priests who resigned and married went on to establish new careers and to shed, as much as it is possible, their clerical identity. However, something new and unanticipated was occurring. A determined segment did not wish to abandon that identity. They wanted to be married priests. Not only that, they were convinced that they were trailblazers for the Holy Spirit, with a vocation to participate in the updating of the Church.

The prerequisites for a social movement were now in place: a set of ideas that offered an alternative to the status quo as well as a strong expectation that change was imminent. But where could those whose hopes had been awakened turn for leadership? How could they organize their resources? Conditions were ripe for the emergence of the free ministry movement.

2

Organizational Beginnings: The National Association for Pastoral Renewal

A more radical cause (of resignations from the priesthood) than the desire to marry lies in the mounting awareness on the part of Roman Catholic clergy that the option to chose one's own life style must be open to all Christians if the church is to foster genuine freedom. . . . The heart of the priesthood is not celibacy, but service to people.

Msgr. Henry G.J. Beck, NAPR adviser, 1968

The initial organization for a freer priesthood had a very clear and modest objective: the right of priests to marry while continuing their conventional priestly ministry. With this approach, a toe was dipped into the icy waters of ecclesiastical tradition. Within a short time other more daring clerics would plunge headfirst into what they were sure would be a successful, if bracing, swim for much more extensive personal and professional autonomy.

In some social movements it is difficult to identify one person as the "founder" or person who made the first phone calls, planned the first meeting, and convinced the group that met to commit themselves to the cause. Such is not the case with free ministry. Carl Hemmer, who had been ordained a priest in 1962 for the Buffalo

Province of the Society of Jesus, took those steps and inaugurated what he prefers to call the *pre*free ministry optional celibacy movement.

In 1966, while studying economics at Columbia University in New York, Hemmer proposed the idea of a meeting to Robert Francoeur, a married priest and professor of biology at Fairleigh Dickinson University in New Jersey. In turn, Francoeur contacted the Rev. Frank Matthews, director of the Office of Radio and Television of the St. Louis archdiocese. The three decided to call a meeting of people they knew who might be interested in the cause of a married priesthood. Matthews suggested St. Louis as a central site and handled the arrangements. On Thanksgiving weekend, 1966, twenty men met at the Sheraton Airport Inn, St. Louis, Missouri. They formed the National Association for Pastoral Renewal (NAPR), and the movement to change the Latin Rite's requirement of clerical celibacy was underway.

Long before the meeting, Hemmer had decided that he wanted to marry and remain a priest. He reached this conclusion after extensive consultation and several conventional Jesuit retreats. However, once he made up his mind, he never wavered in his resolve. While this reshaping of his self-understanding was occurring, Hemmer fell in love with Patricia Harris, a member of the Long Island parish where he said Mass on Sundays.

In attempting to navigate his way through uncharted waters in quest of the dream of becoming a married priest, Hemmer consulted Catholic University moral theologian, Rev. Charles E. Curran.[1] Hemmer asked Curran not so much whether or not he should proceed but rather he sought advice on the best steps to take.

In May 1966, Curran responded. While stating that he agreed "that celibacy should be a matter of freedom of choice for the individual," he cautioned against a "naive personalism" that believed that marriage would easily and quickly bring about self-fulfillment. He warned that there was a danger of using a woman in an effort to fulfill oneself.

Curran went on to review his experience with priests who wanted to marry and the Church's response. At the time, the Church required that a priest first marry civilly and then apply for a dispensation from celibacy *post factum* in order to be freed from the state of sin created by the religiously invalid marriage. Curran advocated *ante factum* dispensations, arguing that it was morally wrong for the Church to require that a man do evil in order to be dispensed.

Responding directly to Hemmer's question, Curran cited a similar case brought to Cardinal Sheehan of Baltimore by a priest who wanted to marry and continue his priesthood. The cardinal told the priest that "the Church would never permit that" and that as far as he knew the Church would never release him from his vow of celibacy ante factum.

Despite this discouraging report, Curran urged Hemmer to present his case in order "to make authorities in the Church more aware of the problem."

Approaching Individual Bishops

Even before receiving Curran's reply, Hemmer had written to Archbishop Paul B. Hallinan of Atlanta expressing a desire to be a married priest. Hallinan, who had a reputation as a liberal bishop, said that he was in poor health and referred Hemmer to Joseph Cardinal Ritter of St. Louis. In a lengthy letter to Ritter, Hemmer argued that he was convinced that he had "the vocation to be a married priest-professor." His vision for his life was that he would be an economics professor at a non-Catholic campus who worked part time in priestly ministry to the campus community.

In his reply, Cardinal Ritter referred Hemmer to his own religious superior as having better access to authorities in Rome and that Hemmer, as a Jesuit, in any case, would have to apply for a dispensation through his superior.

One sentence in Cardinal Ritter's reply was likely to give hope to Hemmer and others yearning for a change in the law of celibacy. Ritter said, "Our Holy Father [Pope Paul VI] is fully aware of the problem and I think like his predecessor wishes to do something about it."

November 1966: Establishment of NAPR

Armed with rejections but still hopeful, Hemmer flew to St. Louis, convinced that organized action would succeed where individual initiatives had failed. He and his collaborators were confident that many people would join them if assured by respected priests that it was appropriate to speak out collectively, if the program of action did not create an unacceptable confrontation with the bishops, and if practical ways to make their views public were provided.

The St. Louis group was comprised exclusively of priests, most of them still celibate, including two prominent scholars, Rev. Alfred McBride of Catholic University and Rev. Eugene J. Schallert, S.J., of the University of San Francisco. Hemmer's notes from the meeting make clear that the group saw itself as loyal to the Church, indeed as helping the Church in its task of post–Vatican II reform.

A Married Priests' Ordinariate

What they proposed, specifically, was an experimental structure, similar to the military ordinariate. Just as chaplains from a wide range of dioceses and religious congregations served under a bishop assigned to the military, married priests would be under the supervision of a special bishop. The group saw the proposal as a five-year experiment, aimed eventually at a more permanent restructuring of the clergy.

The ordinariate idea was suggested in order that the utilization of married priests might begin immediately, using an existing institutional form, and avoiding the problem of some bishops not willing to accept married priests in their dioceses. The ordinariate would be a model that could be observed and evaluated while other changes were worked on, such as the revision of seminary life and the introduction of married clergy to parishes.

Initial Actions of NAPR

After the summit meeting at the airport (so that, as Hemmer quipped, "the group could make a fast getaway"), the process began of mailing out the NAPR statement and a survey questionnaire. By February 1967, the information had been sent to over ten thousand priests and lay people all over the United States.

The mailing focused on the single issue of clerical celibacy. The statement reviewed recent problems such as the decreasing number of seminarians and the increasing number of requests for laicization. It said that Vatican II "has encouraged Catholics everywhere to take responsibility for the welfare of the Church" and urged that allowing a married priesthood would be a concrete way to help reform the Church. The statement reviewed Scripture, canon law, theology, and magisterial teaching on celibacy and then presented the proposal for an ordinariate, suggesting that the American bishops request such a structure at the September 1967 Bishops Synod in Rome.

The paper concluded with a brief questionnaire seeking "yes" or "no" responses to three statements:

1. I endorse a formal study of optional celibacy by the National Conference of American Bishops.
2. I believe the association's proposal deserves serious consideration by the National Conference of American Bishops.
3. I would appreciate information on membership in the association.

Respondents were also asked to supply the names of priests and lay people who might be willing to endorse the initiative. Matthews already had a mailing list of key figures from around the country, but the hope was to generate an avalanche of names so as to strengthen NAPR's claim to widespread support. To be successful, a social movement needs either the backing of a few powerful people or of a large number of ordinary people. The few powerful people were the pope and bishops, and they showed no tendency to take the lead in the proposed change. Therefore, it was considered necessary to enlist so many supporters that, hopefully, the powerful few would be moved to accede to their demands.

The focus of NAPR was exclusively to influence the Catholic bishops. The hope was that evidence of a groundswell of support for optional celibacy, as well as the availability of an appropriate mechanism for implementation, would lead to episcopal action—*immediate* action. The NAPR organizers naively believed that a Church noted for taking centuries to make changes would end the thousand-year-old requirement for priestly celibacy in less than a year.

Movement Spreads Rapidly

The organizers of NAPR did not work alone. Ad hoc groups sympathetic to the cause sprang up around the country. In fact, seven thousand of the ten thousand statements were distributed by others. Robert Francoeur's home diocese of Steubenville, Ohio, mailed the statement with a covering letter from the local ordinary. A group of priests printed copies in the basement of the residence of the bishop of Wilmington, Delaware. The unofficial Chicago priests' association, which would eventually become the Association of Chicago Priests, took the initiative to poll priests in Midwestern dioceses. Others did the same in Florida and on the West Coast.

By March 1967 over eleven hundred endorsements of NAPR's proposals had been received. Rejections of the proposals did not exceed 1 percent of the total responses. Two seminaries polled their students and showed majorities of three to one and nine to one in favor of optional celibacy.

Not everyone was supportive of the specific proposal for an ordinariate. For example, the theologian Frederick R. McManus in a January 30, 1967, letter to Archbishop John F. Dearden of Detroit, head of the American bishops, argued that the concept of an ordinariate was "based upon the distinctive needs or characteristics of the people to be served, rather than on the status of those exercising the ministry." Nevertheless, McManus urged very strongly that a full-scale scientific study of celibacy be undertaken by the bishops.

Actually, studies were already being conducted. One of the members of the advisory board of NAPR, Rev. Joseph Fichter, S.J., then a visiting professor of sociology at Harvard University, had, in September 1966, mailed a questionnaire to a large national sample of diocesan priests. He found that the question of the married clergy in the Roman Rite was a major topic of conversation among priests. In fact, only one in seven said that during the past year he had "seldom" or "never" discussed this matter with his fellow priests. More than six out of ten (62 percent) said that they were in favor of the diocesan priest's freedom of choice to marry. One-third of the respondents said that if a married priesthood were allowed they probably would marry.[2]

A Louis Harris poll conducted about the same time reported that 48 percent of *lay* Catholic respondents approved of freedom for priests to marry. Subsequent surveys have shown that support by lay Catholics has increased steadily, rising to 53 percent in 1971, to 58 percent in 1983, and to 63 percent in 1986.[3]

However, what Fichter, McManus, and the NAPR leaders wanted was for the bishops themselves to commission a study. The constant stress by NAPR on surveys, both the ones they conducted themselves and the one they urged the bishops to conduct, reveals a fascination with scientific research and the belief that whatever was sociologically true would become ecclesiastically accepted.

Also, Hemmer's group thought that they shared common goals with the bishops, who would find a way to support NAPR's position despite Vatican misgivings. It was hoped that if the bishops conducted their own survey it would provide a strong basis for initiating an "experiment" with an ordinariate or a similar structure that would place the first group of married priests under a sympathetic bishop, perhaps Ernest J. Primeau of Manchester, New Hampshire, with whom Hemmer had corresponded early in 1967.

The belief that the bishops were indeed open to a married priesthood was reinforced by the decision made at their April 1967 meeting to initiate a study of priestly life, including the issue of celibacy. By that time over two thousand people had responded to the NAPR mailing, urging that the bishops study the issue.

Flushed with a sense of impending success, Hemmer and his associates had slipped their survey results under the doors of the hotel rooms of the American bishops, assembled in Washington, D.C., for their semiannual meeting. Also, they issued press releases, gaining substantial media attention and stimulating a national debate.

With great self-assurance, NAPR announced in May 1967 a new phase in its activities, namely, "to support and promote the Bishops' study of this problem." Leaders were in correspondence with bishops, meeting with them, and for a time picturing themselves as collaborators in the task of reform.

One of these collaborative activities was a poll of diocesan priests in selected areas of the country. This second questionnaire omitted mention of a special ordinariate, using a broader, more daring proposal, namely, that the American Roman Catholic Church "be empowered to introduce optional celibacy in the United States." There was confidence that the American bishops could *and would* request a national exemption from the universal law of celibacy.

NAPR proceeded to survey priests and by August 1967 was in a position to issue a progress report to members. Already diocesan priests in the fourteen dioceses extending from Connecticut to the District of Columbia had been surveyed. More than thirteen hundred eastern seaboard priests supported optional celibacy. NAPR, while cautioning that its survey was not scientific, argued that this region of the country was regarded as "a center of religious conservatism; if strong opposition to optional celibacy exists among the clergy, it should appear in a survey of these dioceses." No such strong opposition emerged.

Just as the momentum for change was mounting, and possibly as a reaction to it, Pope Paul VI issued an encyclical *Sacerdotalis Celibatus* reaffirming the requirement of priestly celibacy. If hopes were not dashed, at least they were cooled. It now would be impossible for the

American bishops to go to Rome with a request for a married priesthood.

Notre Dame Symposium: 1967

The other major activity of NAPR in 1967 was the sponsorship of a Symposium on Pastoral Problems at the University of Notre Dame, September 6–8. Eight scholars were invited to present papers on aspects of priestly celibacy. All were active priests or prominent laymen with impressive credentials. Besides such Americans as Joseph Fichter, S.J., Alfred McBride, O. Praem, Ignatius Hunt, O.S.B., and John T. Noonan, they included Rev. R.J. Bunnik of Holland, whose writings had provided one of the earliest models for a renewed priesthood.[4] NAPR announced that the conference papers would be sent to the American bishops and the delegates to the Roman synod scheduled for September "to assist them" in studying the issue.

One of the several hundred participants at Notre Dame who also attended the NAPR symposium in St. Louis the following year recalled that whereas at Notre Dame most of the audience wore Roman collars and religious habits, in St. Louis almost everyone was in lay attire. He interpreted this dramatic change in clothing as symbolic of the rapid rate at which clerics and religious were freeing themselves from institutional conformity and expressing their individuality.

A month after the Notre Dame symposium, Catholic syndicated columnist John Cogley reported on the meeting.[5] In particular, he cited the presentation of Rev. John A. O'Brien, professor of theology at the University of Notre Dame. O'Brien said that "nothing can stop an idea whose time has come." The arguments supporting celibacy offered by Pope Paul in his recent encyclical were judged to be unconvincing. In fact, O'Brien quoted the pope against himself by referring to the encyclical *The Development of Peoples* in which the pontiff had declared that marriage was a basic human right grounded in the nature of man. O'Brien argued that if the right to marry was inviolable then the Church could not make celibacy mandatory for those called to priesthood.

Cogley concluded his column with words that certainly captured the mood of those who attended the NAPR symposium:

> The age-old tradition enforcing clerical celibacy will go the way of Friday abstinence, Latin in the liturgy, and the

meaningless routines now being dropped by religious orders—and we will all wonder why it was ferociously defended for so long.[6]

For his part, Fr. O'Brien did not simply speak at the symposium. He also was a member of the NAPR advisory board and edited a book, *Why Priests Leave*, containing the stories of twelve priests, including Hemmer, who had married but wished to continue a ministry.[7] In 1971, O'Brien mailed free copies of the book to National Federation of Priests Councils (NFPC) and SPFM members. In the letter explaining the gift, O'Brien referred to the recently released bishops' study of the priesthood, which, he said:

> . . . disclosed that the great majority of U.S. priests believe that the present requirement of a commitment to lifelong bachelorhood is without any basis in Scripture, apostolic tradition or theology. Hence it should be replaced by optional celibacy. Devoid of such freedom, celibacy becomes for many not a gift but an odious compulsion.[8]

Hemmer's Dealings with His Superiors

Even as he was organizing NAPR, Hemmer was engaged in a struggle with his superiors over the young Jesuit's participation in NAPR. Although the main force behind the group and the organizer of the ongoing national survey of priests on celibacy, Hemmer was not a member of the board of directors. In August of 1967, his provincial made "a final and definite decision" denying Hemmer's request to join the board and to attend the Notre Dame symposium. The provincial asked that Hemmer accept the decision "in the spirit of Ignatian obedience, a spirit to which we both have pledged ourselves in living our religious lives."

Hemmer did not accept the decision. He continued to write lengthy letters, convinced that the provincial didn't really understand his position. At the time there was increasing Jesuit participation in social issues of the day. However, Hemmer was to discover that unlike the Vietnam War and other social issues, celibacy was the line in the sand that Jesuit superiors in the U.S. and in Rome did not want members to cross, because it touched too closely on internal Church discipline.

In 1968 Hemmer left the priesthood and married. On principle he did not seek laicization. Many other priests would follow the same approach. Some would walk away, wanting nothing further to do with the Church and unwilling to submit to what they considered the degrading process of "being reduced to the lay state." Others, like Hemmer, would not resign officially, because they wanted to continue to be priests. For them it would be a lie to ask to be laicized.

1968: A Year of Ferment

Hemmer's resignation from the priesthood was a personal decision, of course, but it was symptomatic of the barrage of events in the world at large and within the Church that pummeled American society in 1968 with a relentless fury. The Vietnam War was increasingly unpopular. Political events included President Lyndon Johnson's stunning announcement that he would not run for another term, the assassination of Robert F. Kennedy, the rioting at the Chicago Democratic Convention, and the election of Richard Nixon. To read through the newspapers for 1968 is to encounter a catalog of unrest and ferment.

Priests, already wrestling with their identity, were shocked out of any remaining complacency by events within the Catholic world itself. Altars were being turned around to face the people, and the sixty thousand priests of the country had to face the fact that the world as they knew it in the fifties had exploded like a rocket headed to the moon and that all their old certainties and securities were gone forever. What follows without specific attribution are some of the developments of 1968 that impacted on priests.

Death of Thomas Merton
Perhaps the most bizarre and yet symbolic occurrence was the death of Thomas Merton in far-off Asia. This convert Trappist monk was searching for a spirituality that would draw from all religious traditions and make Roman Catholicism a more vital force in the modern world. His accidental death by electrocution stunned many who looked to him for guidance, including NAPR leaders. Merton had agreed to serve on the NAPR board. His name, along with the names of ten other prominent churchmen, all with Catholic institutional affiliation, appeared on the early literature of the organization.[9]

Humanae Vitae: The Birth Control Encyclical

A more powerful jolt came from the issuance of the long-waited encyclical on birth control. Pope Paul VI's *Humanae Vitae* precipitated an immediate and deep crisis of authority. Hans Küng would say that the ban on birth control showed that the pope could fall into error. Scores of American priests, including prominent theologians, signed a statement opposing the encyclical. For his public opposition, Charles Curran was dismissed from Catholic University of America, although student demonstrations led to his reinstatement.

Patrick Cardinal O'Boyle of Washington, D.C., who took disciplinary action against dozens of priests who opposed the encyclical, was quoted as saying that the Church could do without those who refused to uphold Church traditions. His censures contributed to the mounting discussion of due process for priests. It became clear that if bishops decided to suspend or otherwise discipline priests, there was no mechanism for appeal.

National Federation of Priests Councils and Due Process

Coincidentally, in February 1968, three hundred priests had met in Rosemont, Illinois, to form the National Federation of Priests Councils (NFPC). In May, delegates representing 114 senates of priests and unofficial associations from 104 dioceses held the first NFPC convention. One of the leaders, Rev. W. F. Graney, called this organization of rank-and-file priests "a manifestation of democracy entering into the life of the Church." He said that the federation would give priests a common voice in national issues.

As the conflict between Cardinal O'Boyle and the dissident Washington priests intensified, NFPC had its first opportunity to speak out on behalf of its constituents and presented a resolution to Cardinal Dearden, president of the National Conference of Catholic Bishops, to establish due process guarantees. Dearden said that the conference would study the resolution. For the Washington priests, however, time was running out. Their leaders expressed strong dissatisfaction with the failure of the bishops to establish procedures for arbitrating such disputes. Eventually, many of them gave up the struggle and left the priesthood, unwilling to bow to the conscience-shattering demand that they recant their position on birth control.

Roman officials, of course, were interested observers of what was happening in the United States. Cardinal Felici in *Osservatore Romano* insisted that Catholics must obey their religious superiors *even if they were wrong* in order to avoid undermining authority.

Demand for a Voice in Church Governance

Yet another aspect of the "priests' rights" issue emerged to center stage, namely, that of a voice in Church governance and in the selection of bishops. In January, 563 priests of the archdiocese of New York petitioned the pope for a role in choosing a successor to the late Francis Cardinal Spellman and in reorganizing the archdiocese. However, in March, Terence Cooke was appointed archbishop without consultation with priests or laity. Some of the priests who had petitioned the pope had warned that the archdiocese would not survive in the secular modern world unless major reforms were made and the principles of continual change and flexibility of mission adopted. There were no signs that the pope accepted their view. Quite the contrary, the pope would weep and call priests who resigned "Judases" and "traitors."

Eugene Kennedy: "Celibacy Is Unhealthy"

In September 1968, the issue of priestly celibacy reached a crescendo. Rev. Eugene Kennedy gathered sixty Catholic psychologists at the American Psychological Association Convention and staged a symposium on celibacy. He said that clerical celibacy was intended for the service of the institution rather than the pastoral needs of the people and that it was collapsing. He argued further that mandatory celibacy was psychologically unhealthy.

Bishops Raise False Hopes

Some bishops unwittingly added fuel to the demand for optional celibacy that was racing like a forest fire across the land. The newly appointed bishop of Brooklyn, Francis J. Mugavero, said in a television interview that there were no theological barriers to a married priesthood or women as priests. He added that he would accept any decision to change the celibacy rule. Priests heard such words and were confident that change was imminent.

NAPR Symposium: St. Louis

It was in the caldron of such events that NAPR held its second (and last) annual symposium in September 1968 in St. Louis, Missouri. A sharp debate took place over whether or not to issue a resolution opposing *Humanae Vitae*. The vote was close, but the majority opposed any direct challenge to the pope's authority. They believed that their cause—optional celibacy—would be better served if they were perceived as loyal to Church teaching, be it ever so unpopular.

Others felt that such a position was cowardly and that it marked the end of the effectiveness of NAPR as a voice for reform in the Church.

It was at this juncture and in the context of rising frustration with the papal documents reaffirming celibacy and condemning birth control that a group of married priests caucused at the symposium and decided to take a step beyond what they perceived as the overly conservative approach of NAPR. They wanted to organize around the issue of *freedom* in the priesthood. The idea contained revolutionary implications. The movement was evolving to a new, more militant stage. The men who caucused would form the Society of Priests for a Free Ministry (SPFM), which immediately superseded NAPR as the organizational voice of married priests.

The process of organizing SPFM is the subject of the following chapter. It remains here to complete the story of NAPR and of Hemmer.

Staffing and Financial Problems

The working leadership of NAPR never comprised more than a dozen men, many assisted by their wives. They held board meetings, published a newsletter, issued press releases, communicated with bishops, organized the two symposia, and conducted a national survey on celibacy.

Thomas M. Pucelik, a married priest and assistant professor of ecumenical theology at Bradley University, Peoria, Illinois, was named president of NAPR once it took firm organizational form. In November 1967, Pucelik wrote a letter inviting people "to join the nearly one thousand five hundred priests and laymen who are already members" of NAPR. He said that funds were being raised to open a national office and appoint a full-time coordinator.

Hemmer was the logical choice for national coordinator and did in fact serve in the position for a few months. However, since he was in the process of leaving the priesthood, getting married, and embarking on a secular career, he decided that he could not devote sufficient time to NAPR. He recommended his friend, Robert M. Duggan, for the post. Duggan, a former priest of the New York archdiocese, was paid a modest salary for a time, but shortage of funds never permitted the establishment of the envisioned full-time national office.

Illustrated here are two problems that would handicap the free ministry movement throughout its course. First, its primary constituency was men who were in the process of making a major, multifaceted change in their lives. Typically, they needed to devote most of their energies to this transition. Compounding the problem was the fact that frequently their priestly experience did not translate easily into marketable secular skills. Those who were educators or who possessed graduate degrees had it easiest and in fact dominated the leadership positions in the early years of the movement. On the other hand, former parish priests often required a lengthy process of career exploration and experimentation in order to establish themselves in the work world.

The second problem, flowing from the first, was that of finances. Most men left the priesthood with little or no money. Often they married women who had been sisters, had taken a vow of poverty, and had left the convent penniless. As interested as they might have been in the issue of optional celibacy, most married priests had neither the time nor the money to contribute to the cause.

NAPR Meeting with Catholic Bishops

One of Duggan's first projects during his brief tenure as national coordinator, and perhaps the most significant action taken by NAPR, was to arrange a meeting in March 1968 in Detroit between Archbishop Dearden and his aide Bishop Zaleski on the one side and NAPR leaders on the other. Representing NAPR, besides Duggan, were Hemmer, Pucelik, Allen Carter, Robert Francoeur, and advisers Joseph Fichter and Daniel Maguire. The topic, of course, was optional celibacy.

Duggan prepared a memorandum that read like a script, indicating the points that each NAPR participant might make in an effort to communicate his position effectively to the bishops. Basically, they asked for assurance that the Bishops' Committee on the Ministry and Life of the Priest be allowed to conduct its study of celibacy "with the highest standards of honesty and professional scholarship." Since the bishops had reaffirmed the rule of celibacy the previous November, there was concern that the research might lack objectivity.

Dearden gave the assurances requested, welcomed the help of NAPR, and invited the participants to remain in contact with Bishop Zaleski. Although the major objective of NAPR would not be attained, meetings with the hierarchy heartened the would-be reformers. The following year the fledgling SPFM, likewise, would meet with representatives of the hierarchy. Eventually, the free ministry advocates realized that the bishops, while listening politely, did nothing. Hemmer's retrospective analysis was that the bishops were saying, in effect, "Get on with your lives. We're not going to let you back."

NAPR Goes into Decline

Despite the split that had occurred at the 1968 symposium in St. Louis, producing two organizations working for optional celibacy, NAPR continued to appear strong. For example, the January 1969 newsletter said that forty five hundred copies were being mailed. Duggan strove to recapture momentum in an upbeat front page letter that began with the words "A bishop sent NAPR $200 last week! What a change from a year ago!!!"

However, NAPR never held a national meeting after the 1968 symposium. Media and popular attention shifted to SPFM, which was attracting vigorous new leadership and espousing a more dramatic program.

As late as October 1970, a few NAPR leaders continued to attempt to define a place for the organization. A status report outlined what were perceived to be the three principal achievements of NAPR during its "first phase" and three objectives for a "new phase." The new phase never materialized but contained strategies that would be adopted by SPFM, including the idea of getting national and local pastoral councils to include celibacy on their agendas and the suggestion that support for a married priesthood be sought from Protestant churches.

However, a look at the achievements of the "first phase" underscores just how much was accomplished by the small band of men who formed NAPR. They had:

1. Established the legitimacy of public discussion of the celibacy issue;
2. Encouraged priests to face the issue squarely in their personal lives and, if necessary, to resign from the ministry to underline their convictions;
3. Initiated discussions with the Church's hierarchy to find a viable way to restore optional celibacy to the Latin Rite.

A Cardinal's Gentle Rebuff

The last official action under the NAPR banner was correspondence between Carl Hemmer, once again with the title national coordinator, and Cardinal Dearden. It is late 1970. The two had last met more than two-and-a-half years earlier at which time the NAPR representatives had requested assurances that the survey on celibacy, which an episcopal committee had commissioned, be conducted with full scientific objectivity. The report still had not been issued. However, Hemmer is not complaining about the snail's pace with which the bishops have been moving, but wonders once again about the purity of the scientific process and whether or not the report's conclusions will be ignored "if they recommend that priests be allowed to marry." Dearden in a press conference had said that although he foresaw the day when a married priesthood would once again be part of the Latin rite, he could not foresee the return of priests who married after ordination. Hemmer laments the prospect that he and other resigned priests would see married "laymen" called to priestly service while they remained excluded. He once again calls for a meeting between bishops and married priests.

In a kindly, diplomatic reply, dated December 3, 1970, the cardinal reminds Hemmer that, with reference to the as yet unissued report, "the whole study must be seen as one. The sociological and psychological findings will need to be measured against the theological and pastoral dimensions of the priesthood that are also a part of the study." In other words, Hemmer's and NAPR's long-standing idea that, in effect, priests could vote for optional celibacy has been a misunderstanding of ecclesiastical reality. As the birth control issue had shown, the majority does not necessarily prevail. The American cultural value of "democracy" does not hold for the Catholic Church.

On the matter of a committee such as Hemmer recommends, the cardinal responds, "In all candor, I must confess that I do not see the purpose of a committee such as you have proposed." He is telling Hemmer that just as Catholics can't vote on Church policies, so also the American bishops have no authority to deal with the issue of clerical celibacy. Two or three years earlier perhaps there was room for discussion, but Rome had made it clear that the issue was closed. The letter suggests that the hierarchy has clarified its position with reference to married priests. The cardinal knows what Hemmer has failed to see, namely, that the time for meetings has passed.

Continuous Commitment to the Cause

When the Hemmers married in 1968, they relocated to the Washington, D.C., area where Carl obtained a position as an economist in the U.S. Agency for International Development (A.I.D.), and then moved over to A.I.D.'s population assistance program where he has worked for more than twenty years. Hemmer quips that his years in family planning work probably represent "appropriate penance for my bad advice on birth control" in earlier years.

Hemmer has been active in his community and served as a city council member for three terms in Fairfax, Virginia. The Hemmers' personal religious practice has been centered in small informal liturgy groups that meet in the homes of members. The current group, the Sunday Bunch, began in 1973. Most participants are married priests who have not found their spiritual needs met by local parishes. Hemmer has baptized and confirmed his two children within this small community and officiates at marriages for Catholics, who because of divorce or some other impediment do not find a welcome in the official Church.

As a principal spokesman for the movement in the late sixties and early seventies, Hemmer was referred to in newspaper articles and appeared on television shows, including "The David Susskind Show." In 1979, he wrote to Phil Donahue, proposing a married priesthood as an appropriate topic for a television program. Pope John Paul had just reaffirmed the law of celibacy, and Hemmer argued that the pope was "at odds with the mainstream of the American Catholic Church on this topic." Hemmer suggested to Donahue that leaders of CORPUS and FCM would be appropriate panelists for such a program.

Nothing came of the suggestion. However, ten years later, in the wake of scandals about the sexual behavior of priests, there was a Donahue program on the priesthood, with the founder of CORPUS, Frank Bonnike, as one of the panelists.

Today, Hemmer reflects that he has considered writing his autobiography. Its title would be *Beyond the Holy City*. His image is that while he was a canonical priest, he lived within the walls of the Holy City. When he left the priesthood, he was thrown outside the walls. Lo and behold, he found that there were numerous other people out there, many of whom called on him for priestly service.

In terms of the present-day free ministry organizations, Hemmer belongs to both CORPUS and FCM. He is a CORPUS area representative and is certified by FCM. Although he is not comfortable with FCM's broad definition of ministry, he, like many other resigned priests, needs the certification for legal reasons in officiating at marriages. While some jurisdictions will accept his status as a "retired clergyman," others want current credentials. Chapter 10 gives a full explanation of the FCM certification program.

When asked to summarize his view of ministry, Hemmer said that worshiping communities need "a qualified enabler who helps people to pray, who guards and transmits the word of God, who presides over the celebration of the sacraments—a priest."

Carl Hemmer today is a man approaching age sixty. He remains in a warm relationship with his wife. They are financially secure. Their children have been raised. Yet the deepest reality for Hemmer remains the conviction that he is a priest. Throughout all these years and despite all the disappointments, his desire to be a married priest shines as brightly in his heart as it did twenty-five years ago when, as a young Jesuit, he founded NAPR.

3

Organizing the Society of Priests for a Free Ministry

All along I felt that there were others who shared my dreams. But where were they? How could I find them? Would they ever discover me?

When I made the trip to St. Louis, I had no idea that I would help form SPFM during my stay there. It happened so suddenly and with such thoroughness that I, for one, have never doubted the outstanding role the Holy Spirit played during those fabulous hours.

When I registered for the Symposium on the afternoon of September 4, 1968 I had the rather moderate expectations of simply picking up a bit of moral support from those whom I suspected would, at the very best, be sympathetic to my efforts as a "free priest."

That naive understanding vanished within hours. Without any direct intention, I found myself meeting one person after another with startling similarities to my particular relationship with the Master. It was amazing how in such a short time so many priests with this unique posture found each other.

By the evening of the 5th of September, this widespread mutual awareness had led us to call a special meeting of those interested at the Travelodge Motel. The room was packed. Over

*forty individuals, mostly priests, crowded into the room, short
staccato remarks from each quarter reinforced our wonderment.
Something was being created. The terribly swift movements of
the Spirit breathed in us all. I can still see Harry Houle, standing
on the toilet seat (every square foot of the room was used),
shouting encouraging remarks to the rest of the group. It was
quite a scene.*

Vincent Eckholm's 1972 Recollections

This Pentecost-like event was how the Society of Priests for a Free
Ministry began. While Carl Hemmer and the other organizers of
NAPR were lobbying for a married priesthood, Eckholm was dreaming of something more, what would be termed a *free priesthood*. He
was amazed to find that many shared his vision.[1]

Eckholm had just been ordained for the archdiocese of Chicago in
that tumultuous 1968, and before the year was over he was married.
Few had experienced such a short celibate priesthood, yet few have
remained so committed to a priestly ministry. After providing
leadership for SPFM and later for CORPUS in the Chicago area for a
number of years, Eckholm's hunger for priesthood moved him to
turn to the Episcopal Church. Today, he serves as rector of St. Ignatius
Episcopal Church in Lindenhurst, Illinois. Nevertheless, not forget-
ting his Catholic roots or his free ministry aspirations, he remains
affiliated with CORPUS and is listed in its directory, which contains
the names of one thousand married priests interested in resuming
some form of ecclesiastically approved priestly ministry.

Many other Catholic priests followed Eckholm's example and have
become Episcopal priests. Ironically, in recent years dozens of married
Episcopal priests have been admitted to the Catholic priesthood.[2]

John Leahy's March 1968 NCR Letter

While Eckholm traveled south to St. Louis from Chicago, Harry
Houle, mentioned above by Eckholm, journeyed north from Phoenix. Houle's involvement in the movement began when he read a
letter by John W. Leahy in the *National Catholic Reporter*.[3] Leahy was
a former priest of the archdiocese of Atlanta, where he had been
superintendent of Catholic schools. He now was married and held a
position in adult education in San Diego, California. His letter
expressed interest in resuming a priestly ministry and invited men
with similar interest to contact him.

Until that time, the accepted wisdom was that priests who left and married had no further interest in priesthood. Furthermore, at least until after Vatican II, such men were considered "fallen priests," "shepherds in the mist," and "traitors." The institutional Church wanted nothing further to do with them. But a new spirit was emerging.

Leahy's letter produced an avalanche of responses. Eventually, he passed on his mailing list to the organizers of SPFM, and it served as the basis for the national network of priests interested in free ministry.

Houle's reaction to the letter was impulsive. With his wife Lu, he drove to San Diego and visited Leahy. A month later, Leahy telephoned Houle and suggested that they meet in El Centro, California, halfway between their homes, to discuss further the idea of trying to organize something. Houle says, "Lu and I left the dishes in the sink, drove to the airport, and flew to El Centro."

Houle had heard of NAPR from one of that organization's founders, Allen Carter, then assistant pastor in the Catholic Church of Rocky Hill, Connecticut. Houle suggested to Leahy that since NAPR was already organized, the two of them should go to the symposium in St. Louis "and see what happens."

Ironically, although it was Leahy in the *National Catholic Reporter* who planted the seed for SPFM, his car broke down in Amarillo, Texas, as he drove to St. Louis. He did not make the meeting and never became active in the movement.

Priests' Caucus, St. Louis, September 1968

Both active and inactive priests were present at the September 5 caucus. However, as one of those present later wrote, "Many of the inactive men turned out to be very active. Many are saying Mass privately. . . . Next week I will be celebrating a nuptial Mass for my roommate and his fiancee in a Baptist Church." Free ministry had already begun. Men with no faculties to function as priests were doing so on their own, responding to the needs and requests of people. It only remained to organize and to propose to the bishops that a Society of Free Ministers be legitimated as a religious order-like structure.

The forty men who met that evening selected a nine-member steering committee representing a broad geographic distribution. They were: Patrick K. Best and Raymond Dakoske in Detroit; Harry Houle in Phoenix; Vincent Eckholm in Chicago; Thomas Pucelik in

Peoria, Illinois; Robert McMahon in St. Louis, Missouri; Frank Bognano in Council Bluffs, Iowa; James Dagenais in Oxford, Ohio; and Ed Steichen in Madison, Wisconsin. Two of them were assistant pastors. Seven were no longer functioning within the Church structure. Of these seven, two were married.

The following day, the committee called together some of those who had met the night before and anounced that a society had been formed. Houle was chairman of the steering committee and Best, executive secretary. All nine were designated regional coordinators.

The committee prepared a press release that said in part:

> The Society of Priests for a Free Ministry is open to priests ordained in the Roman Catholic Church, especially those who are commonly referred to as ex-priests. The purpose of the society is to bring together the many priests, married and single, who have been ministering and who wish to minister in experimental forms to the needs of the people in this transitional period of Church history.

Thus, with lightning speed the group was initiated. Within weeks, Houle wrote a lengthy position paper, and Best set up in Detroit a national office and began mailing a series of newsletters to about two hundred interested people. Virtually single-handedly, Best coordinated the loose network, and in April 1969 brought together in Detroit a group of twelve that would formally elect officers, adopt a constitution, and plan a convention.

Harry Houle's Position Paper

Since it was the first, if tentative, formulation of what SPFM was all about, Houle's position paper merits close attention.

The first page made clear that SPFM embodied a much more radical vision than did NAPR.

> The society looks forward to the official recognition of its ministry by the Roman Catholic Church. In the meantime, members of the society will continue to serve the Church according to their unique circumstances.

To a Church tightly bound to a strict authority system, this declaration of independence was a revolutionary challenge. Whereas to members of SPFM it said that their ministry was valid, to Church authorities it was an act of rebelliousness bordering on schism. In the months to follow, the more theologically skilled members of SPFM would attempt to reconcile the tension between a profession of loyalty to the Church and a decision to function without episcopal authorization.

For Houle, another purpose of SPFM was to provide a welcoming fellowship for priests departing from the official clergy. He recounted the remark of an assistant pastor at the September 5 meeting. The priest somewhat facetiously said, "When I leave, I'll just tell my mother I'm joining a society of priests. I won't really be leaving the priesthood; I'll simply be going from one form to another."

Houle saw SPFM as a bridge between clerical life and secular life, especially by offering employment assistance. From the beginning, "free ministry" included the expectation that the ministers would provide for their material needs through secular employment. This financial freedom was seen as essential. There was the feeling that economic dependence on the institutional Church was a barrier to maturity and a mechanism for maintaining control over the clergy.

With reference to marriage, Houle argued that SPFM was not a group of married priests, but rather a group that "recognizes a man's right to marry and sees no discrepancy between the sacraments of holy orders and matrimony residing in one and the same person." He reiterated the already popular argument that the Church has no right to demand celibacy as a prerequisite for orders.

To priests unaccustomed to political action, Houle argued that organization is essential "if we hope to produce an effective wedge in the present ecclesiastical structure." A basic dimension of SPFM from the outset was the conviction that it had a mission to reform the Church. This idea was present in NAPR as well but not with the assertiveness that would characterize the new organization. Vatican II had, in the minds of free ministers, legitimated the sort of initiatives in which they planned to be engaged. Although SPFM had just been established, Houle would state confidently that it was "one of the forces for renewal at work in the Church."

But what about obedience? How could the members of SPFM explain their readiness to "disobey" their religious superiors? Houle distinguished between obedience and conformity, insisting that SPFM was obedient to the Gospel but refused to be bound by the demand on the part of the hierarchy for lock-step conformity. Free priests would serve the people better because they were "not hampered by organizational mechanisms." The institutional Church acted too slowly. People couldn't wait. Free ministers acted within the guidelines of "sound theology," not the "archaic theology" of the institution. Houle referred specifically to the "depersonalization" of Catholics who approached ecclesiastical courts with marriage cases. Free ministers would officiate at marriages of divorced people without requiring the time-consuming, cumbersome annulment process.

Houle also argued that one need not obey unjust authority. What might appear to be rebellion was in fact mandated of those committed to fidelity to the Gospel. His enthusiasm led him to proclaim that the fledgling SPFM possessed the truth and that Church leaders had gone astray. He said:

> This Society recognizes authority in the Church. We lament the abuse of authority or that use of authority which is not founded upon love and service.

Carried along on the crest of a wave of rhetoric, Houle predicted that the society would grow to the extent that there might be more SPFM priests than priests under the jurisdiction of bishops, and that, seeing this, the bishops would "come to the realization that it is ridiculous not to use us in the direct service of the people."

With the fervor of a prophet and in the oratorical style of the recently murdered Dr. Martin Luther King, Jr., Houle concluded his position paper. It was with these words ringing in their ears that the pioneering SPFM members went about their organizational tasks:

> There is every reason to believe that the Spirit will inspire the members of this society. There is every reason to believe that prophets will come from this society. There is every reason to believe that charismatic grace will abound in the membership of this society. . . . There is likewise every reason to believe that this society will be first ignored and later cursed by the official church. . . . There is likewise every reason to believe that this society could harm the church just as easily as the officers of the church. But if this society in no way deviates from the Gospel, if this society in no way abuses its charism, if this society remains faithful to the Spirit, there is no reason not to believe that the Spirit will mold the members of this society in the form of the

loving and serving Christ to whom alone conformity is owed.

Houle Works in Israel as a Married Priest

Personal problems soon led Harry Houle on an unusual odyssey. In 1968 he was thirty-nine and had been married for two years after serving for nineteen years with the Carmelites, eleven of them as a priest. He held a J.C.L. from the Lateran University in Rome and had been chancellor and vicar general of a missionary diocese in South America for seven years. This ecclesiastical experience was not directly marketable for employment. However, he also had a masters degree in library science and at the time of his involvement with SPFM was manager of a branch of the Phoenix public library.

However, he was not happy with the position. In November 1968, he wrote to Eugene Bianchi, who had resigned recently from the Jesuits and had attained some prominence through his scholarly publications. Bianchi, now on the faculty in the department of religion at Emory University in Atlanta, had written to John Leahy in response to his *National Catholic Reporter* letter in March. Houle saw Bianchi's name on the mailing list and sought advice from the man who the following April would bring Houle's tenure as leader of SPFM to an end by being elected the organization's first president.

With words that echoed the identity struggle of many resigned priests, Houle wrote: "The only things which interest me are my priesthood and religion." He indicated interest in teaching theology and asked Bianchi for suggestions on the easiest route to obtain a doctorate, without which there was little hope of getting a position.

Nothing worked out. In April 1969, Houle met Bianchi for the first time when both attended the SPFM organizational meeting in Detroit. The following month Houle wrote to Bianchi again, this time to submit his resignation as a member of the executive board of the society. He had accepted a teaching position in Israel.

Due to the need for discretion, Houle did not reveal to Bianchi that he was going to Israel *as a priest* and that he would wear a cassock once again and celebrate Mass within the jurisdiction of the Melchite Rite. Houle had met a Lebanese family in Phoenix who put him in contact with the archbishop of Galilee. The archbishop, not concerned about Houle's marital status, invited him to work in his diocese.

At the time, Houle and his wife had no children and lived in a furnished apartment. They put their few possessions in their car, drove to Lu's family home in Michigan where they left all their belongings, and flew to Tel Aviv.

After three weeks in the archbishop's residence in Haifa, they were sent to Nazareth, where Houle taught religion and English at a high school conducted by the Melchite Church. However, after seven months he came to the conclusion that the cultural differences were too great. Despite being accepted as a married priest, he was not able to establish with the Eastern Rite clergy the camaraderie he had known with American priests. He and Lu returned to Phoenix.

Houle's Life in Phoenix

Houle's experience in the late sixties was unique. He had fashioned a dramatic vision of a new priesthood and then gone off to live what he hoped would be an embodiment of that vision. Chastened by the shock of an alien culture, he resumed his life as a librarian while his wife worked as director of the nuclear medicine department at St. Joseph's Hospital in Phoenix. Together they raised two sons, both of whom attended Catholic schools.

When he returned to the United States, Houle made contact with SPFM, but found that it had moved to a position with which he was not comfortable. He envisioned the society as limited to Catholic priests, not broadening out to accept nonordained men and women as active members. When CORPUS was established in the midseventies, Houle found the new group more consistent with his views and has been affiliated with them ever since.

One of Houle's experiences was not untypical of priests who have left the canonical ministry. He had been ordained for the Chicago Carmelites in 1955, and in 1980 wrote a letter to the *Carmelite Review* suggesting a twenty-fifth anniversary reunion of his class. He discovered that of the fifteen men ordained in 1955, one had died, and of the others, only four were still in the community. Eight or nine classmates got together for a nostalgic weekend. However, the provincial denied them permission to meet at the Carmelite retreat house in Chicago. This rebuff was painful to men who wished to retain modest ties with the community. Eventually, as will be illustrated in the following chapter, dioceses and religious orders did revise their policies and in many cases established cordial relations with their former colleagues.

Today, as he plans his retirement, Houle attends Mass each morning in the local parish church. On Saturday evenings, he and Lu worship at St. Mary's Basilica, a Franciscan church in downtown Phoenix. On Sundays they breakfast with a couple with backgrounds similar to their own. The husband had been a priest in Peru and his wife a Maryknoll sister. Houle, the energetic man who from a toilet seat in a hotel room had shouted encouragement to his brothers on that long ago evening in St. Louis and who had authored the SPFM position paper with its bold challenge to the Church, is not involved in any free ministry groups and does not celebrate Mass at home. To all appearances he is a conservative, aging Catholic, faithful to his prayers. But once there was a fire in that priestly heart.

Pat Best: Organizing the Dream

If Houle provided the initial vision of a free ministry, Patrick Best did the practical nuts-and-bolts organizing. Immediately upon returning from the caucus, he began to publicize the new group. His hometown paper published an article in which Best announced the establishment of "a new kind of Catholic brotherhood of priests that would parallel to a degree historical (religious) communities."[4] Just one month after the St. Louis meeting, Best formed a Detroit chapter of SPFM and said that the purpose of the new society was to let priests function according to their consciences, with freedom in worship and freedom in speaking to issues of the day. "Our bag is to be honest and to love Jesus."

The picture accompanying the newspaper article showed a round-faced, bespectacled man wearing a tie. Beneath the picture were the words, "Father Best." Then thirty-one, Best was a priest of the diocese of Des Moines, Iowa, who was on leave "but had no intention of going back to the traditional priesthood." Best had arrived in Detroit only three months earlier to be a caseworker for the Wayne County vocational rehabilitation office. His credentials for the position included a degree in special education from the University of Omaha and six years' experience as chaplain at a school for the deaf.

The records attest to the enthusiasm and skill with which Best applied himself to the formidable task of getting the new group off to a successful start. With the smallest of budgets, he sent out a series of newsletters, surveyed the regional representatives as to where and when they would want to meet, and eventually made all the arrangements for an April 1969 gathering in Detroit.

In the newspaper interview, Best revealed the combination of zeal and naiveté that made so many free ministers both attractive and vulnerable. When pressed on the implications of his analogous linking of SPFM with groups like the Jesuits and Dominicans, Best replied that SPFM would be different from such religious orders because they "are really part of the system" whereas SPFM would be "free of control by the system."[5]

Counseling Independence for SPFM

In a September 13, 1968 letter to Houle, Best emphasized his belief that the new group should not get itself entangled with the official Church. Although fewer than ten days had passed since the St. Louis meeting, dialogue through letters was well underway. Responding to a point by Houle, Best said:

> I agree that we should emphasize that the Society is for all priests who want to be free ministers of the Good News. I don't think, however, that we should *emphasize right now* that we seek official recognition. I think this is our ultimate goal, but I think we have a lot more important goals in between, namely, experimenting in a free ministry, unencumbered and unworried about official decrees.

On September 17, in a letter to John Leahy, Best tried to clarify what he thought should be the relationship between SPFM, NAPR, and the hierarchy. His main point was that "we should maintain our independence." He stated his rationale for this stance:

> Our advantage as inactive priests is that our concern is primarily for people in real life, and only secondarily for Church structural reform. To do otherwise is to waste a lot of valuable Christian energy on intramural activities.

Each of the stream of letters that Best wrote to interested priests added, as it were, another brick to the new structure that he and the others were designing and constructing without the advantage of a blueprint. So, in an October 1968 letter to Patrick Kelly in Minnesota, Best said:

> The idea of the Society is to operate as priests outside of the structure, and to give each other support and new ideas. There are many guys all over the country, married and

> unmarried, who have junked the system and are searching
> for new ways. We'll search better if we stick together—
> priests inside and outside the system—the common bond
> being ordination and alienation from the old ways.

The degree of "freedom" for which Best called has been too extreme for many advocates of reform of priestly life. In fact, Best encountered the hesitancy of his fellow married priests quite directly when, shortly after the St. Louis meeting, he told a group of Detroit married priests about SPFM. The group, which called itself Contact, had about seventy members and focused on practical needs of men in transition such as finding jobs. On hearing Best's ideas for SPFM, they were "stunned," "confused," and "defensive," as Best reported to Houle. Best was not discouraged, attributing the reaction of his fellow resigned priests to the difficulty they had overcoming their dependency on and fear of the institutional Church.

First SPFM General Mailing

On November 6, Best sent out the first SPFM mailing. A cover letter explained to the two hundred recipients what had happened thus far and said that the steering committee was drawing up a draft of a constitution. Funds were solicited and a pledge made that there would be monthly correspondence.

Included was a chart showing the nine regions into which the society had been divided, together with the notice that the appropriate regional coordinator would contact the reader soon to arrange a meeting. Best added a report of his organizational efforts in Detroit to serve as a model for other areas.

Finally, he enclosed Houle's nine-page position paper and suggested that it be the basis for discussion at the regional meetings.

At the same time that Best sent this bulky package of materials to all who had expressed interest in free ministry, he sent a separate mailing to the nine regional coordinators, providing them with the names of people in their region and step-by-step guidelines for them to follow. For example, they were to hold a regional meeting during November at which the position paper was to be discussed. A summary of that discussion was to be sent to Best by November 30. During December they were to hold a meeting on the draft of a constitution that would be mailed to them shortly. Summaries of the discussion of the constitution were to be sent to Best by December 31.

These details are given to illustrate both the speed and precision that characterized Best's work or at least his initial expectations. The December newsletter acknowledged that the pace was too rapid. Most regional meetings had not been held in November. In a more practical tone replacing his earlier haste, Best wrote: "One thing about a free ministry is that the ministers' time is not free——it is hard earned and has to be spent on other interests equally as important; an example of this is earning a living."

In that December letter, Best listed the date and place for each of the scheduled first regional meetings, a clear indication that he had maintained contact with his far-flung collaborators. However, after three months, five of the original nine coordinators had been replaced. Apparently, it was one thing to volunteer in the excitement of the meeting in St. Louis and quite another to follow through and set up meetings back home.

Philadelphia Report:
Confusion of SPFM's Purpose

Eventually, the regional meetings were held and reports submitted to Best. James J. Dagenais's report, written for the gathering held at Temple University in Philadelphia on December 14, was typical in that it focused on the struggle to understand the meaning of this new organization. What was meant by *free*? What does it mean to be a *priest*? What is *ministry*? What is a *society*? Every word in the name of the group was subjected to close examination. This type of discussion would continue for the life of the organization and throughout the history of the movement.

Definitional tensions were evident in several places in Dagenais's report. In particular, the idea of "priesthood" in the traditional sense of those who had received Holy Orders was debated in the context of the emerging view that the "priestly caste" should be eliminated and the priesthood of the laity highlighted. However, as was true at most SPFM meetings, there were no "lay people" present other than the wives of some of the priests. Of the seventeen men and women who attended the Philadelphia meeting, fifteen were married priests and the other two were the wives of two of them.[6]

After six hours of discussion, the group agreed that they were "priests seeking fuller and freer participation in the life of the Church," and they expressed the hope that the purpose of SPFM would be made more explicit at future meetings. Also, they called on the society "to draw the laity into, or into sympathy with the movement."

This latter insight, that the success of the movement required the recruitment of the laity, would never be fully grasped by SPFM. Despite protestations to the contrary, it would remain a lobbying group for married priests, rather than a response to the needs of the Christian community. As will be seen, numerous experiments were undertaken in an effort to develop new ministries. However, all were initiated by free ministers and with minimal lay collaboration.

Dagenais appended two pages of "Personal Reflections" to the report in which he analyzed the response pattern of the sixty people to whom he had sent an invitation to the meeting. He concluded what every regional organizer would discover, namely, that geographic distance would make it impractical for many interested people to attend meetings. He called for more local organization within each region.

Draft of Constitution Discussed

While the regional coordinators were encountering difficulty attracting people to meetings, Best was having financial problems. In his December 31, 1968 financial report, he indicated that SPFM had taken in $229 and had bills outstanding totaling $631, including payments on a mimeograph machine. In order to keep the national office operating, he had advanced $251 of his own money. He suggested that the regional coordinators be assessed $15 per month until April, at which time he anticipated that a constitution would be approved, including provision for dues.

With the February 1969 newsletter, Best sent to the now over three hundred names on the mailing list a five-page draft of a proposed constitution. As he had done with Houle's position paper, he asked that it be the basis for discussion at regional meetings. The suggestions of all would be taken into account at a "constitutional assembly" in the spring.

In most respects, the draft was standard, with articles on membership, executive board, voting, and amendments. However, the proposed preamble began, "We, ordained Roman Catholic priests, adhering faithfully to the authentic spirit and structures of the Roman Catholic Church. . . ." Indicative of the nonclericalist, ecumenical orientation of the leadership that emerged, these words were changed substantially in the constitution adopted in April. That final version said: "We are priests and people striving to be open to the Spirit of a New Pentecost, and to embody that Spirit in a Church that is Christian."

In a similar vein, while the draft limited membership to "ordained Catholic priests," the final version added an associate membership category for "all who share the ideals and goals of the Society." Even this remnant of a two-class system was soon eliminated.

Adding a personal note to his January letter to the coordinators, Best announced that he was getting married in June. One by one, the organizers of SPFM took this step, which was a crossing of the Rubicon, severing them definitively from their official ministerial status. It had been hoped that the new organization would attract both celibate and married priests, but, in fact, SPFM quickly became almost exclusively an organization of married and therefore noncanonical priests.

April 1969 Organizational Meeting

After surveying the regional representatives, Best announced in March that the coordinators' meeting would be held in Detroit the weekend of April 25–27. Twelve men would assemble and with remarkable efficiency put SPFM on a firm organizational footing. Five of the delegates were carry-overs from the nine named to the steering committee seven months before in St. Louis: Best, Houle, Eckholm, Steichen, and Pucelik. The other seven were more recent additions to the leadership ranks. They were Ken Faiver of Lansing, Michigan, Richard Lipka of Baltimore, Richard Cassidy of Middletown, New Jersey, Gerry Fallon of Los Angeles, Thomas Durkin of Oakland, California, Eugene Bianchi of Atlanta, and Rocco Caporale of New York.

Two of the newcomers—Bianchi and Caporale—stood out from the others. They were university professors, former Jesuits, and published authors. They brought to the group an impressive level of theological and sociological sophistication but also, it would turn out, a position that was too radical for most resigned priests. Bianchi was selected president and Caporale vice president and editor of the SPFM newsletter.

Best had enlisted the assistance of the "underground" community, to which he belonged, to host the meeting. The DeVrees family, part of Best's network of friends, moved out of their Mt. Clemens, Michigan, home for the weekend so that the men could work, pray, eat, and sleep without interruption. Other community members met the delegates at the Detroit airport and prepared their meals.

At 9:00 P.M. on Friday the dozen men celebrated Mass with the theme of *leadership*. Best had prepared the liturgy, although, ironically, the leadership was about to pass from his hands. He would be elected treasurer, but the other three officers would be newcomers: Bianchi and Caporale as already mentioned and Durkin as executive secretary. These three men would be the heart of the movement for the next few years. Chapters 4 and 5 relate their contributions.

Best composed a prayer on leadership for the service, which was held at a dining room table. The prayer reflects the grandiose expectations that the group had for itself. It depicts the twelve men as twentieth-century apostles, self-commissioned to proclaim the Gospel. Best prayed:

> We come from many miles to this city today. We meet as one. Earlier today we were apart, separated, non-communicating. We were as the Church, the Establishment, is on this day in 1969. But we wish to unite in community. We do this for a reason: to clarify our way that we might clarify the way for others. If we wish, we may call ourselves innovators, originators, men strong enough, with Christ, to step away from, ahead of the Church as we see it today. There are people waiting for us. If we wish, we may call ourselves leaders.

Best himself would soon disappear from the free ministry leadership ranks. He attended the 1969 convention in Washington, D.C., where he gave a treasurer's report but within months receded into obscurity. The term *burnout* had not yet been coined, but it is apt for describing the psychic fatigue that overcame so many of the early leaders.

The Revised Position Paper

The notes on Bianchi's copy of Houle's position paper show that Bianchi, who had been an assistant editor of the Jesuit publication, *America*, employed his literary and theological skills to clarify and tighten Houle's impassioned and lengthy document. The final two-and-a-half page statement of purpose was the distillation of the thinking that had been going on during the previous year as filtered through the new president's orderly mind. It would serve for several years as the official self-definition of the group.

Excerpts from the statement are the most effective way to communicate the understanding that SPFM had of itself as it embarked on its crusade:

> The members of the Society understand themselves as living in the historical tradition of Catholicism. They do not separate themselves from this church, but rather they desire to serve humanity through their church tradition in new and creative ways. In a time of intense reform and transition in Catholicism, the Society intends to be a source of fraternal support and inspiration to priests, particularly those who elect to minister outside official structures.
>
> The purpose of the Society is to contribute in a concrete and experimental way to a far-reaching renewal movement of the Church's ministry. Within this total ministry of the Church, the Society sees the priest not as an ecclesiastical functionary, but rather as a free enabler according to the Gospel of Jesus Christ. With the active aid of the Christian fellowship in each place, the priest, through his various ministries, strives to enable God's word to come alive in a community of faith, hope, and active, justicing love. The priest as enabler is a brother among his brothers and sisters; their charisms of wisdom and love complement his own gifts.
>
> While the Society recognizes the necessity of incorporating into its designs continuing self-renewal, its immediate aims are rather concrete. First, there is the task of creating critical awareness of the present situation of Roman Catholic priests. The primary responsibility for this situation belongs to priests themselves. Second, by well-informed and diverse experimentation in styles of worship and witness, the Society hopes to contribute to a healthy pluriformity. . . . To achieve this purpose SPFM intends especially to be educated by other Christian ministers and from dialogue with the members of their communities.
>
> The need for education through practical experimentation, beyond that now permitted within official Catholic structure, is derived from repeated testimony in church history. Biblical, liturgical, and ecumenical reforms in

Catholicism often began on the periphery of the church and only gradually—often despite official opposition—made their way to the center of ecclesiastical approval.

SPFM believes that tension and multiformity within the Christian community are not necessarily divisive but can be positively unitive. For reasons both of conscience and the needs of contemporary communities, some SPFM members choose to operate beyond the limitations of canonical legislation. But they in no way wish to cut themselves off from the body of the faithful. On the contrary, their new ministries are in response to the Spirit speaking through the communities which they serve.

The following chapters will show how SPFM attempted to translate this vision into concrete action. Although many of the initiatives failed, the statement itself possessed an enduring quality. Basically, it said that free ministers felt called to contribute to the process of Church reform. They might, in some sense, be outside the walls, but they detected faults in those walls, faults that only those who were on the outside could see and repair.

A More Radical Minority Report

Although most participants at the April 1969 meeting subscribed to this statement of purpose, Ed Steichen of Madison, Wisconsin, submitted a minority position paper that was included in the report of the weekend. Steichen's main point was that

> our document places too much emphasis on the "priests' ministry," the context implying the "ordained priest." This seems to me to be subtle clericalism. . . . It's the same old usurpation of our own rights and rationalizations as priests.

In other words, Steichen maintained that the statement did not go far enough in its call for a reform of ministry. Eventually, this minority view would lead to a schism within the free ministry movement, with those subscribing to the "clericalist" view gravitating to CORPUS and those sympathetic to Steichen's "populist" view attracted to FCM. In short, the role of the priest in the Christian Church continued to be controverted. Many emphasized the distinctive position of the ordained priest within the community. Others preferred to stress the "priesthood of all the faithful" and a more communitarian approach to ministry.

Toward the First National Convention

A press release, based largely on the statement of purpose, was picked up by the Associated Press and used in articles in newspapers around the country. In general, the press focused on celibacy, a word not even used in the statement. This tendency to oversimplify the issues has plagued the movement throughout its history. A headline such as "Anti-celibacy move grows among priests" obscured for the general public the more sweeping objectives of the new group.

On May 7, 1969, Best sent out his final newsletter. It included the notice that future correspondence be sent to Tom Durkin in California. As he concluded his tenure as first executive secretary, Best quoted Joseph Kerns, a former Jesuit, who said, "If we win we will all be heroes, but if we lose we will all be traitors." It was in the hope of being heroes and with protestations that they were not traitors that the new leadership made plans for a conference in Washington, D.C.

Part II
Shaping a Vision, Issuing a Call

4

The Theology of a Free Ministry

At its first convention in Washington, D.C., in 1969, the Federation of Christian Ministries (then SPFM) used the term "enablement" throughout. A main purpose of this movement in the late Sixties was the "enablement of personal and social wholeness." The men and women who met in Washington, and a year later in Berkeley, were mainly from the Catholic tradition, but their search was an ecumenical one. They were seeking new ways of ministering according to the gospel, ways more appropriate than those they had experienced under the formal structures of clerical ministry.

Eugene C. Bianchi, 1983 FCM convention

The *National Catholic Reporter* letters page had served as a vehicle in March 1968 for John Leahy to present the call for a national organization of ex-priests. Fourteen months later *NCR* printed a letter by Eugene C. Bianchi announcing that he had been elected president of just such an organization, the Society of Priests for a Free Ministry (SPFM).[1] Bianchi's letter included the address and telephone number of SPFM's executive secretary. As Leahy's letter had prompted two hundred replies, so Bianchi's generated scores of inquiries and memberships.

When Bianchi emerged from the Detroit meeting as the first president of SPFM, many people were disposed to listen to this man who had earned a reputation as a scholar with a clear, incisive style. For the next few years he brought to a wide audience the awareness of SPFM as an organization and the vision of a reformed ministry for which it stood.

Bianchi's vice president, Rocco Caporale, was similarly talented and well-prepared for the task of introducing a radically new idea, disseminating it, and organizing people to implement it. The work of these two men would serve as the intellectual and organizational baseline for the free ministry movement.

Eugene C. Bianchi: Shaping A Vision

Although Bianchi is a soft-spoken, gentle person by temperament, his ideas for SPFM were revolutionary. Whereas Carl Hemmer might have been satisfied with the freedom of priests to marry, Bianchi's agenda was a sweeping revamping of ministry and a total overhauling of ecclesiastical structures.

Bianchi's theology of ministry was articulated in *Reconciliation* in which he called for "intelligent experimentation with new forms of church life."[2] He argued that this experimentation was needed to refashion the Church, which, he claimed, had lost sight of its mission to provide in the world "communities of shalom" that would help to heal the alienation that increasingly characterized modern life. To achieve this goal, there was a need for "new forms of church ministry."

Creative Resistance

Paradoxically, according to Bianchi, reconciliation would occur only if people were courageous enough to organize in opposition to the reactionary intransigence of religious officials. All institutions, not excepting ecclesiastical ones, are in need of continuous reform, and "this task of adapting long entrenched institutions to new needs requires the organized pressure of resistance movements."[3]

Although SPFM was in the earliest stage of formation and had not yet held its first convention, Bianchi referred to it in *Commonweal* as a group that might contribute to the "creative resistance in action which must complement the intellectual-theological renewal." His justification for such a position was that "the gospel urges Christians to the kind of revolutionary resistance that Jesus exercised towards the ecclesiastical institutions of his time."[4]

That *Commonweal* article was referred to numerous times in correspondence among the pioneering band of free ministers. Their leader was presenting what for them was a convincing case for their cause. It also gave fair warning to Church leaders that their authority was being challenged.

The social movements of the sixties had considerable impact on Bianchi as well as on many of his contemporary academics and churchmen. References to the civil rights movement, the anti–Vietnam War movement, and other "liberation" efforts of the day punctuated the literature on the need for a freer church.

Interest in revolutionary movements and their religious implications found further expression in Bianchi's book *The Religious Experience of Revolutionaries* in which he argued that "Che" Guevara, Malcolm X, Abbie Hoffman, Frantz Fanon, Daniel Berrigan, and Dr. Martin Luther King, Jr., embodied authentic religious impulses, even if some of them denied such motivation.[5]

Thus, on the one hand, Bianchi was the theorist, formulating revolutionary plans, while, on the other hand, he was an activist, attempting as president of SPFM to implement his ideas. He would live this divided life for a time but eventually grow weary of the activist role and withdraw to the more comfortable world of ideas.

Reconciling Dissent with Loyalty

In the *National Catholic Reporter* letter in which Bianchi introduced himself as president of SPFM and invited other priests to join him in his crusade, he made a number of points that located SPFM theologically, culturally, and pastorally. He wrote:

> A new phenomenon, one hardly conceivable 20 years ago, is that many priests now leaving the traditional clerical structures continue to operate in various ways as priests. This phenomenon can also be observed in France and Holland.
>
> SPFM, a loosely organized national association of about 500 priests (some within present clerical structures), wants to contribute to the renewal of the church's ministry in a concrete way. SPFM hopes to give these priests a national identity. This national presence can encourage their own ministerial self-awareness and also express the value of their ministry for the whole church. While SPFM upholds the right of priests to marry, it focuses mainly on fostering experiments in worship and witness now going on across the land.[6]

In the letter, actually a substantial essay, Bianchi also addressed the sticky question of how SPFM could engage in unauthorized ministries while proclaiming its loyalty to the Church. He argued that the interplay between obedience and dissent was like a Marxist dialectic, interacting to produce a higher level synthesis:

> Obedience and dissent are not mortal enemies, but rather two poles of a creative tension leading to the progress and health of the whole body. Moreover, obedience itself is not to be given blindly to church officials as though they spoke with the mouth of God. Obedient action should be motivated by a much broader sense of God's reconciling mission in the world, as seen in the needs of particular communities.

Bianchi concluded his letter by locating SPFM within "an ever wider movement in contemporary society for maximizing man's development through freer options in human community."

Media Attention, but No Groundswell of Support

The April 1968 meeting at which Bianchi was elected president of SPFM received considerable media attention. "Rebel priests" were a novelty, especially since they began to organize. The publicity generated increased interest to the extent that by the end of 1968 there were one thousand names on the mailing list. However, dues-paying members never exceeded three hundred fifty, contributing to the disappointment of the leaders and to the continuous financial emergencies of the organization.

Bianchi also received personal mail in reaction to the founding of SPFM. A priest active in a Michigan parish wrote, "We need guys like you. Perhaps in your initial days you might need guys like me. Together I hope we'll be able to serve and share." On the other hand, there was some hate mail from Catholics scandalized by what Bianchi and his collaborators were doing. One long, rambling letter from a lay person contained these words:

> We do not need priests who set a bad, bad example for the children and young people they were supposed to teach. What kind of priests were you? So lukewarm, so incompetent, with so little faith that when God needed you most, put you to the test, you failed Him. . . . So get the Hell out NOW.

From the beginning, Bianchi himself was not completely comfortable with the organization he had helped establish. Just days after the Detroit meeting, he wrote a letter to his fellow officers requesting their help in addressing what he called "a critical problem," namely, "What are we all about?"; "What do we have to offer as a national organization?"; "Why should someone who wants to work as a free minister in his own community join this new organization?" Bianchi recalled the answers contained in the statement of purpose but wondered if they would be convincing to priests and interested lay people. How do you present effectively a case for a new structure designed "to cultivate the role of priest as free enabler by fostering educational, political and fraternal actions" on the local level?

This questioning by Bianchi, while appropriate from an intellectual point of view, and, by hindsight, quite prescient, was not likely to generate enthusiastic support. If the leader is hesitant, how can he inspire people to follow him? This Hamlet-like posture of Bianchi would characterize his presidential addresses at the three national conventions held during his term of office. Those addresses reflect the development that occurred in his thinking about free ministry as SPFM floundered in its attempt to implement his ideas. Some details of each convention will be necessary in order to provide the context for Bianchi's presentations.

Call for a Radically New Priesthood

Arranging the first convention was no easy task. The responsibility fell to a small group headed by Richard Lipka of Baltimore. Lipka and his wife, Sue, enlisted the help of Lee and Carol Ann Breyer and Carl and Patricia Hemmer. Besides internal conflicts as to the format and purpose of the meeting, the organizers had to cope with suggestions offered by Bianchi, Durkin, and others.

Although SPFM and its successor, FCM, has held national meetings for twenty-three consecutive years, the accomplishment has entailed an annual crisis over the location and program for the gathering. The organization depends completely on volunteers, many of whom have limited experience in planning meetings and who invest various amounts of time and talent in the demanding task of publicizing the event and attracting people to attend.

Despite the obstacles, fifty-six people assembled in the appropriately named Center for Christian Renewal in Washington, D.C., on November 7, 1969. The agenda for the weekend was simple. Bianchi would give the keynote address on Friday evening. On Saturday, the other officers would report on other aspects of free ministry. On Sunday morning, there would be a business meeting at which a press release would be formulated. The program would conclude at noon with a liturgy.

Bianchi's address began and ended with pointed references to the place of SPFM in the wider context of the social movements that embroiled the nation and the world at the time. He said:

> I understand SPFM as a small and open-ended freedom movement which is part of a much wider freedom move-ment in our society. For if we look around us today, we see the people of color, the oppressed in the third world and radical students striving to achieve manhood and com-munity through revolutionary programs of self-determi-nation in social and political life. It is important to realize that SPFM is intimately associated with the humanizing aims of these wider movements.[7]

The summons to "revolutionary programs of self-determination" went well beyond the call for reform issued by NAPR through Carl Hemmer, who had also attended the weekend conference. Years later, Hemmer would say that he was not comfortable with the radical direction taken by SPFM, and although he had agreed to help organize the national conference and served for a time on the executive board, he distanced himself from SPFM's more revolu-tionary ideas and actions.

Bianchi wasted no time indicating just how quickly he wanted to move. However, the leader was too far out in front of his followers, most of whom needed more time to adjust to the changes that were taking place. For example, Bianchi immediately urged the new group to shed any lingering clericalism by changing its name from the Society of Priests for a Free Ministry to a Fellowship for a Free Ministry, which name would reflect more accurately "the primordial priesthood of all believers which is shared by lay priests and ordained priests." He was telling men who wanted to be priests that ordination was secondary to baptism and that there should be no sharp line between the ordained and the unordained. In effect, Bianchi was aggravating what would become the decades-long identity crisis. If everyone is a priest, then what is the meaning of ordination?

Underlining his position, Bianchi urged his audience to move away from "the paternal and vertical style of priesthood we have known in the past to more fraternal and horizontal styles of Christian community." Ministry could not be understood accurately "unless it is the ministry of the whole community."

Reference to community led Bianchi to insist that the primary task of free ministers was to function experimentally within small communities, engaging in "liberating alternatives in worship, community life, and secular involvements." He predicted that there were many people alienated from the institutional Church and from modern society who would welcome such ministry. The free ministry movement would become "a catalyst for liberation within the church and within the broader civil society."

Bianchi concluded his address with a quotation from Dr. Martin Luther King, Jr. The words were to be prophetic for King and perhaps also for Bianchi.

> Some of us, of course, will die without having achieved the realization of freedom, but we must continue to sail on our charted course. We must accept finite disappointment, but we must never lose infinite hope. Only in this way shall we live without the fatigue of bitterness and the drain of resentment.

The address appeared in edited form in *Commonweal*.[8] If Bianchi's vision was radical at least it was getting a hearing, and if SPFM remained somewhat suspect at least it was obtaining some legitimacy in the Catholic intellectual world.

Second Annual Convention: Berkeley, California, 1970

SPFM had started in the Midwest and then moved to the East. For its 1970 meeting it turned to the West Coast. Tom Durkin, the executive secretary, was the organizer. For Bianchi, it was a coming home to his native state.

Attendance was modestly larger than it had been the previous year—some eighty-four people. However, of the fifty-six participants in Washington, D.C. the year before, only five were at Berkeley: three of the officers—Bianchi, Caporale, and Durkin—in addition to Roméo DiBenedetto and Charles Sullivan, both of whom had already assumed major roles in the organization and will be featured in subsequent chapters. The lack of continuity from one convention to the next would be a serious concern. Besides the obvious explanation of travel costs, it might also indicate that people who attended one convention felt no urgency to attend another. In any case, it soon became clear that despite dreams of large numbers, the movement would be carried forward by a few highly motivated people.

Bianchi's "State of the Society" address in 1970 reviewed the themes of the previous year but developed with greater precision the idea that SPFM was a movement more than an organization. Although the mailing list had grown about 50 percent during the past year to nearly 1500 people, Bianchi insisted:

> More important than numbers is that the movement tries to make concrete and feasible an idea, tries to get an idea abroad. It is not important that SPFM grow enormously, but it is important that we be able to dramatize and express an idea and get other groups and organizations through-out the community interested in that idea. It is not a question of gaining more members for our organization but of creating a new consciousness.

A National Petition
Conscious that the movement had not yet made much of an impact, Bianchi insisted that SPFM must have a specific issue that would rally the support of lay and clerical groups. To this end, he proposed a petition to be circulated nationally in which American Catholics called upon the bishops

> to accept and encourage the ministry of Roman Catholic priests who wish to publicly serve the pastoral needs of our communities, but who are forbidden to do so because of present canonical restrictions. We now wish to call these priests, married or not, back into our service. We need their priestly ministry now.

Bianchi reminded his listeners that SPFM leaders had met with bishops on several occasions but urged that "it is time now to take this to the people." He envisioned as many as a million signatures, "which would show that lay people, contrary to what many people think in the church, are quite ready for new forms of ministry." His timeline for getting the signatures was six months. He felt that the petition would have an educative effect on the Catholic laity and also would be a dramatic message for the Synod of Bishops to be held in Rome in 1971.

A half-page ad headlined "A National Petition" was placed in the *National Catholic Reporter,* asking that lists of subscribers to the petition be sent to Bianchi at Emory University.[9] A *New York Times* article, which covered the convention, highlighted the petition.[10] Further, a diocesan paper said that the petition would be a referendum on what lay Catholics thought of married priests.[11] While the convention was still in session, a California newspaper quoted Durkin as saying that support was sought from laymen who shared with the married priests a "distaste for oppressive regulations and practices."[12]

Despite the fanfare that accompanied the announcement of the petition, the project fizzled. After a few passing references in *Diaspora,* it was not mentioned again. No figures as to the number of signatures obtained were ever published.

Third National Convention: New York, 1971
It was in the context of disappointment and uncertainty that Bianchi prepared what would be his third and last presidential address to a national convention. One hundred and six persons assembled at the New York Theological Seminary in New York on Labor Day weekend, 1971. The numbers attending the meetings were increasing slightly, but factions and uncertainties were rampant. Durkin had written a letter detailing why he was resigning from the board and would not attend the convention. Bianchi, in his address, announced that he would not run again for president. After two-and-a half years, all the original officers were gone.

The title of Bianchi's presentation, "Does SPFM Have a Future?," expressed in dramatic fashion his serious questioning of the free ministry movement in general and SPFM in particular. After devoting a few paragraphs to "Past Gains," the bulk of his paper addressed "Present Problems/Future Directions."

On the positive side, Bianchi said that the most important accomplishment of SPFM had not been as a political force for change in the Church or as a vehicle for experimental forms of ministry but as a fraternal network "of encouragement and fellowship among people who share the same hopes for a renewed church." Through the years, many would echo this sentiment. SPFM, FCM, and CORPUS provided precious friendships for people who had shared similar experiences of Church service and who enjoyed the continuity that such organizations provided.

Should SPFM Disband?
Turning to his more central concern, Bianchi asked if perhaps SPFM had served its purpose and should disband:

> So few organizations ever want to self-destruct; maybe we ought to set a healthy example of meritorious suicide amid church groups for whom survival is all.

Why would Bianchi make such a drastic recommendation? He pointed to the patterns of men leaving the priesthood and said that although many continued to resign from the clergy, relatively few seemed interested in joining SPFM. Why might this be? Bianchi offered possible explanations:

> Can we attribute this to identity traumas in resignees and to their struggles to get a job during the years immediately after leaving? Or can we say that this lack of interest in our movement is due in large part to general negative feelings that the resignees have about fruitful possibilities for change in the church? In such a mood, SPFM would seem as futile as any other renewal group. Or have these departing priests transcended the institutional church and gone directly with gospel values to humanistic endeavors? Whatever the reasons for this phenomenon, we must ask ourselves if we are the right movement at the right time.

From what follows in his paper, it is clear that Bianchi did not actually expect SPFM to disband. But his own disillusionment was painfully evident. He had invested two-and-a half years in a frustrating task. Whereas earlier addresses had envisioned SPFM as generating a national groundswell for ministerial reform, he now spoke of the organization as "a prophetic gadfly" that must "learn to live happily with a low profile image." Free ministry had been rejected by the official Church. At best, SPFM could hope to be "a modest movement that preserves and reveals a great idea whose time will come."

Continuity and Failure in Bianchi's Personal Life
Bianchi's formulation of the theology of a free ministry was critical to the development of the movement, and his doubts about it were symptomatic of widespread uneasiness with its direction. After

relinquishing the presidency of SPFM, Bianchi continued to write and speak and never abandoned his initial conviction that the reformation of the Church was far from complete.

The anchor of stability in Bianchi's life has been his career at Emory University, an institution that has emerged in recent years as a foremost educational center. Bianchi was a junior faculty member in 1968 when he first heard of SPFM. Today he is a senior member of the department of religion, and his numerous publications have earned him a full professorship.

In his personal life, however, there has not been the same continuity. On July 4, 1969, Bianchi married Cathryn Cummings, a twenty-eight-year old former nun whom he met in one of his courses. The wedding took place in California while Bianchi was teaching a summer session at Stanford University. Cathryn collaborated for a time with her husband in his free ministry work. At the 1970 convention, for example, she chaired the nominating committee.

However, just as the initial high hopes of SPFM were not to be realized, so also the marital hopes of Bianchi met with disappointment. He and Cathryn were divorced after a few years. Since then Bianchi has been married and divorced twice more. There have been no children from any of the unions.

It might be said that while Bianchi led one social movement, he was a casualty of another, namely, the women's movement. After leaving the SPFM presidency, he wrote a monthly column for *National Catholic Reporter*. In one article, titled "Man to Man on Women's Liberation,"[13] he referred to his ambiguous feelings when placing his wife's maiden name on their mailbox. Cathryn had gone through the legal process of getting her family name restored as a symbol of "new levels of consciousness of man-woman relationships." Before long, the marriage having dissolved, he took her name off the mailbox.[14]

When asked to reflect on the fact that the man who led the battle for a married Catholic priesthood had himself not experienced a stable married life, Bianchi responded that life has its failures, that one tries to learn from them and move on. He said that now when he dates he looks more closely at the values of a woman. He said that in the past he was not as attuned to whether or not a woman was interested in religion, adding that he had entered too quickly into a couple of his marriages.

Obviously, the marital experience of Bianchi or any other individual is no argument either for or against clerical celibacy. Still, most free ministers interviewed for this book stated that their marriages were strong and that their wives were supportive of their ministries and often were close collaborators.[15]

1983 Convention Keynoter: A Plea for Deeper Spirituality

After several years in the background of the movement, Bianchi emerged to conduct a workshop at the 1976 FCM convention in Washington, D.C. His topic, "Spiritual and Personal Growth," reflected his growing interest in spirituality as an essential condition for effective ministry. That interest was even more pronounced when, in 1983, he gave the keynote address at the convention in Berkeley, scene of the 1970 gathering. Much had happened to the organization, to the Church, and to Bianchi himself in the intervening years. Not the least significant development was the simple fact of aging. Bianchi and most of the free ministry stalwarts were no longer headstrong young Turks, but men well into midlife.

His talk was titled "Empowerment of the People,"[16] which was not a ringing call for a more aggressive approach by an organization growing less and less confrontational but rather an exploration of the paradox that true power emerges from human weakness. Bianchi had just published a book on this theme, *Aging as a Spiritual Journey*.[17] A reviewer wrote:

> Bianchi is at his best in his analysis of the midlife crisis. Key to any spirituality here is one's experience of brokenness, of finitude, of mortality. Midlife calls one to confront the threat of decline and to accept the reality of contingency. . . . The tendency to view one's relation to the world in terms of control and domination, which may be very helpful in building a youthful self-image becomes counterproductive in midlife. . . . For the one who accepts mortality, power as domination will yield to power as service.[18]

In the convention address, Bianchi echoed this theme, in effect offering a formula for the future to a movement undergoing a midlife crisis of its own. The man who in his youth had summoned priests to revolutionary action now assumed the role of spiritual director, urging his middle-aged audience to pray and to reflect on the fact that, in God's plan, growth is the product of suffering and faith.[19]

Rocco Caporale: Structuring the Future Church

Catholic bishop: "Rocco, someday this free ministry thing
                  will be nothing more than a footnote in
                  the history books."
Rocco Caporale: "Perhaps, Bishop, but we love that foot-
                  note!"

The life of the first SPFM vice president, Rocco Caporale, has
unfolded very differently from that of Eugene Bianchi. However,
there were some basic similarities that contributed to an intellectual
and organizational collaboration that got SPFM off to an auspicious
start in 1969. Nevertheless, as creative and productive as these men
were, by the fall of 1971 both had become discouraged and suggested
that the movement was dead. But they had planted the seed too
deeply in the hearts of others for that to happen. The movement
continued although not on the scale initially anticipated.

The two men share an ethnic heritage that may have contributed
to the apparent ease with which they challenged Church authority.
Bianchi, an Italian-American, wrote of the impact that his cultural
background has had on his personality and values, and, in particular,
on his attitude toward women.[20] Caporale, born in Italy in 1927,
exuded a "European" perspective on the Church that, while challenging, was too anticlerical and antiauthority for rank-and-file free
ministers to accept. Caporale's vision contrasted sharply with the
traditional Church, formed, as it was, in the "Irish" mentality, with
its deep respect for the clergy and awe of the hierarchy.

Another dimension of similarity between the two men is their
Jesuit formation, with its emphasis on intellectual rigor and what
might be called *clerical virtuosi*; that is, men who fashion a specialized
expertise and who, while remaining loyal to the group, nevertheless
develop rather individualistic life-styles. This is in contrast to the
formation of diocesan priests, which stresses the pastoral and whose
rectory life-style is rather standardized.

Both men possess doctorates and were well-established in careers
as university professors (in non-Jesuit institutions) when they embarked on their free ministry adventures. But whereas Bianchi's
major field is theology, Caporale is a sociologist, much of whose
work is in the sociology of religion. At St. John's University in New
York, with which he has been affiliated for over twenty years, he has

taught courses in the sociological analysis of church organization, including the Catholic parish.

Even before assuming a role in SPFM, Caporale was conducting research on "underground church" groups, which, he said, were spreading rapidly and which provided alienated Catholics with an alternative to traditional parishes.[21] He had been invited by lay people to participate in such a group near St. John's and saw this extra-legal phenomenon as an appropriate structure for the services of free ministers.

Whereas Bianchi is low-keyed, almost self-effacing, Caporale is dynamic and self-assured. The two men complemented each other not only in terms of personality but also in their linkages within the Church. Bianchi had connections with bishops and theologians throughout the United States, while Caporale enjoyed contacts in Europe, especially in Rome. Interestingly enough, there is little evidence of correspondence between the two men themselves. They had not met prior to the April 1968 meeting in Detroit, and for geographic reasons, if for no other, had little opportunity to work together directly thereafter. To a large extent then each man formulated his ideas independently. There was nevertheless congruence between their positions and a complementarity of approach that provided not only theological rationales for the movement but concrete models for its practice.

An Enigmatic Figure

Some element of mystery always surrounded Caporale. Little was known of his past. The general belief was that he had left the Jesuits—he ceased using the initials S.J.—and had been adopted by an Italian bishop who left him free to roam, both geographically and intellectually. While most free ministry priests were narrowly American in their travels and outlook, Caporale was an almost exotic cosmopolitan figure. Although his English was flawless and highly advanced, his accent and animated gestures, not to mention his incisive mind and depth of learning, made him an impressive, if enigmatic, figure at meetings.

Part of the puzzlement was that although he was deeply committed to free ministry, he remained celibate and in some sort of vague good standing in the Church. It was only years after his association with SPFM that he married and, for a time in the eighties, functioned as a married priest in the FCM-affiliated St. Sebastian's Church in New York City. This will be discussed in chapter 14.

Whatever his ecclesiastical status, Caporale was the embodiment of a free minister during the sixties and seventies: a tenured professor with considerable leeway to write, speak, travel, and attempt to influence the Church. He gave the impression that his contacts in Rome included those close to the center of power. For example, at the 1970 convention in Berkeley he said of himself:

> I minister to the ministers. My ministry is one of reflection and service ranging from computers and organizing a symposium in Rome, to advising some of the Vatican ministries.

Contributions to the Movement
Caporale made three major contributions to the free ministry movement:

1. He linked American free ministers with their European counterparts;
2. He wrote several papers that were key documents in the formation of the movement's self-understanding;
3. He founded the newsletter *Diaspora* and edited it for two years.

International Communication
Through the pages of *Diaspora* and his own travels and speaking engagements, Caporale made American priests aware that the movement was a worldwide phenomenon. He was convinced that pressure applied from many directions was sure to influence the Vatican.

However, his initial effort at international organization proved disappointing. At the 1969 SPFM convention, Caporale reported on the First European Assembly of Priests that had just been held in Rome and that he had attended as an observer. He said that the two hundred European priests had failed to reach any consensus and that their meeting had been a failure because they had been

> sidetracked into a preposterous parody of the past Council (inclusive of schemata, amendments, deliberations, etc.) instead of clearly focusing on concrete objectives.

Also, Caporale was disturbed by the raucous, confrontational tone of the assembly. The members denounced the decision of Pope

Paul VI to grant an audience to the American Apollo astronauts who had just walked on the moon while refusing to meet with the radical priests. However, Caporale did alert the liberal European priests of the value of collaboration with their counterparts in the United States and elsewhere. Due in part to his efforts, the first international meeting of priests for a free ministry was held in Holland in 1970. Nevertheless, it would be many years before significant international assemblies of married priests would be held, including one in Holland, once again, in 1990. The involvement of American free ministers in these meetings will be discussed in chapter 14.

In 1970, *Diaspora* reported that Caporale's paper, "Blueprint for a Liberating Structure," to be discussed shortly, had been published in five languages by the International Documentation on the Contemporary Church (IDOC). Further, it was announced that the free ministry group in Holland, Septuagint, would place married priests in communities willing to accept them, without waiting for a ruling from the Dutch episcopate. At the time there was speculation that a breakthrough might occur in Holland, where a liberal episcopate was considering acceptance of a married clergy as well as other reforms. Eventually, strong pressure from Rome brought the Dutch bishops back into line with Vatican policies.[22]

References in *Diaspora* to free ministry activities in Italy, France, New Zealand, Ceylon, and elsewhere served to remind Americans that even if direct collaboration was not yet possible, they had compatriots all over the globe.

Plan for a Renewed Church

While Caporale was flying back and forth between the United States and Europe and editing *Diaspora*, he was also formulating a plan for a renewed Church. Three documents in particular encapsulate his sociotheological plan:

1. The first, "A Blueprint for a Liberating Structure," was issued in a twelve-page booklet and also was published in the *Proceedings* of the 1969 SPFM convention.
2. The following year Caporale gave an address at the convention titled "Parallel Forms of Christian Vitality in the Local Church" that once again appeared in the *Proceedings* for the 1970 meeting.
3. Several years later, having distanced himself somewhat from the movement, Caporale presented a paper, "We've

Moved from a Temple Religion to the People of God," that further developed his thinking.[23]

"A Blueprint for a Liberating Structure"

The "Blueprint," in circulation within months of the founding of SPFM, attempted to provide a model or "structure" for free ministry. Caporale wanted the paper to be a minitextbook that might be studied by free ministers in their efforts to build the "renewed Church." Whereas Bianchi articulated the theory of free ministry, Caporale attempted to answer the question, What will the church communities of the future be like?

The term *structures* had become a dirty word for those who considered them oppressive. Caporale argued that structures were necessary but that they need not be oppressive. Free ministry would offer "an alternate formulation of the Christian experience, within the mainstream of the church's own historical diversity." The new structure would be "liberating," that is,

> freeing man from the limitations of a narrow concept which restricts the Christian experience to one style of life, one parish community, one form of ministry based on clerical life-style, caste interests, monopoly of control, celibacy, and uniformity.

Like Bianchi, Caporale found the sociological concept/social movement appropriate for describing what was happening in the Church and argued that his blueprint would "give concrete form and visibility to the widespread grassroot movement that had fermented in the church." Pointing to new forms of worship that had at first been proscribed by Church authorities but eventually incorporated into the Church's institutional life, Caporale predicted that "there is not the smallest doubt that, after a time of resistance, opposition and resentment the church will absorb and live by the principles and forms of the Free Ministry." He added confidently: "Our mission is to minister to the church until that day comes about."

"The Shape of Things to Come"

The heart of the blueprint was the section titled "The Shape of Things to Come." To a large extent, Caporale's vision embodied what was already happening in the "underground churches" or "floating parishes" of the late sixties. Although "the things to come" may seem unimpressive now, at the time they were daring innovations for a Church encrusted with hundreds of years of structural rigidity. The blueprint projected:

1. *Small Christian communities.*
   More or less enduring without fixed territory, coordinated with existing parishes but distinct from them. The communities might represent friendship groups, action groups, professional groups, or age groups.
2. *A variety of ministries and ministers.*
   Celibate priests in conventional parishes, married priests within or without parishes, part-time priests with secular occupations, weekend priests, priests for a term of years, and heads-of-family priests. Each of these categories would have distinct competences and functions.
3. *Coexistence of these new forms and existing structures.*
   Ministerial innovation supplements not replaces traditional parishes, ecclesiastical organizations, and lay associations.

Caporale added that his plan for a new configuration of worship communities implied that

> priests who have left the formal priesthood (whether they have married or remained single) are entitled to continue in the exercise of their ministry for the benefit of the community of which they are part.

Bishops Must Be "Prophetic Ministers"
Although Caporale insisted that free ministers were not divisive or schismatic, his analysis of the role and function of the hierarchy struck a blow at the very heart of the institutional Church. In syllogistic form, he argued that *prophetic ministry* is the essential component of Christian ministry. The bishops had abdicated their prophetic function. Therefore, they had lost their authority to exercise power in the Church.

Caporale did not define prophetic ministry nor did he prove that the bishops had failed in this ministry or, if they had, that they thereby forfeited their power. He said that an episcopacy was necessary but insisted that only those priests "who minister to the community and world" could aspire to the "plenitude of priesthood." He came close to saying that only free ministers were appropriate candidates for Church governance.

Parallel Forms of Christian Vitality

In Caporale's 1970 address to the SPFM convention, "Parallel Forms of Christian Vitality in the Local Church," the word *individualism* replaced *freedom* as the central concept. If his "Blueprint" envisioned "new structures," now he was forecasting what sounded like a formless religious free-for-all. Using an evolutionary model of history, he argued that perhaps a church had been needed in former ages but that in the present social order people had arrived at the level of development that enabled—and entitled—them to live and worship without being hindered by a Church. Caporale argued that the Church was "a transitional institution" and that now Christianity was entering "the post-ecclesiological stage."

Christ was presented as the champion of individualism who came not to erect a Church but to move beyond such structures. A few statements from the talk illustrate how sweepingly Caporale dismissed the Church.

> The very last thing that Christ wanted his disciples to do was to establish another synagogue, another tribe of Levi, another holy temple, or to put it bluntly, another Church as we know it today.
>
> If the Church of today embodies the will of Christ, one is at a loss to make sense of the Gospel.
>
> The tragedy of today's institutional Church is its utter irrelevance where it purports to be indispensable.

If then the Church was irrelevant, what was the need for ministers? Although Caporale argued that ministry must be freed "from the monopoly of clerical control and collectivized normativeness," he admitted that he did not have a clear picture of what came next. He was confident that a free minister was "a man who has matured to the degree to which he could develop a functional vocation of deep relevance to himself and society." The inability to give a clearer picture of new ministry derived from what Caporale forecast were near-apocalyptic changes about to take place. He warned:

> We are approaching a major breaking point in the structure of our social organization. How this breaking point

will happen, I don't know. A revolution, a catastrophe, possibly! We do not have adequate models and mechanisms to help us through this period of transition.

Caporale must have experienced frustration with the reaction to his presentation. The report of the "open discussion" at the conclusion of his talk recorded that the convention audience reaffirmed their love for the Church, which Caporale had excoriated as oppressive and obsolete.

From "Temple Religion" to "The People of God"

Whether the free ministers did not agree with Caporale's analysis or just didn't understand it, he realized that he was too extreme for men who, in general, did not want revolution, but legitimacy. For all her faults, the Church was mother and the children loved that mother and were aching for her embrace.

One symbol of that long-withheld embrace was the convocation of resigned priests that was sponsored by the Priests' Senate of the Diocese of Brooklyn in April 1977. Brooklyn was one of the largest dioceses in the country, and scores of clerics had resigned during the previous decade. They felt rejected by the diocese. Now they were invited to the college seminary for a celebration of reconciliation.

Over two hundred of them filled the meeting room and were moved by the words of Msgr. Anthony Bevilacqua, chancellor of the diocese and later the Cardinal Archbishop of Philadelphia. Speaking on behalf of the bishop of Brooklyn, Bevilacqua said that the Church was sorry for any pain that might have been inflicted on brothers who had left the ministry. He thanked them for their years of service and asked for understanding and forgiveness.

Then Rocco Caporale was introduced to give a presentation on the modern priesthood. Caporale was still "active" as a priest and enjoyed a reputation as articulate and challenging. Seven years after his address at the SPFM convention, he remained convinced that a drastic transformation of religious organization was needed and imminent.

Arguing that Christ had rejected the priest-centered religion of the Jews and established a nonpriestly form of religion, Caporale went on to point to Confucianism and Hindu-Buddhism as examples of priestless or quasi-priestless religions that had endured for thousands of years. He insisted that Christianity had begun as a nonpriestly religion and that it was only under the influence of the Roman

Empire that a rigid hierarchically arranged Church structure emerged. After tracing the history of priesthood, he concluded that contemporary trends were moving inexorably in the direction of a Church in which "the dichotomous notion of *lay* and *cleric*" would be replaced with "the notion of *minister*," and the "total ministerial function of the Church would be rethought."

Resorting as he had years before to a sweeping forecast and, in effect, once again articulating the more radical free ministry dream, Caporale made the following statement, which later appeared in the May–June 1977 issue of *Diaspora*:

> No amount of reactionary intervention can stop the movement from a male-dominated hierocratic (priest-centered) structure to a participatory community of charismatic members, each endowed with particular gifts institutionally recognized.

Although the specifics had been forgotten and the hopes not realized, years later men who were present recalled Caporale's passion and eloquence. His vision might have been reckless, even foolhardy, but it was a vision nonetheless, so rare in the experience of most. He looked the bishop's representative in the eye, smiled broadly, stretched his hands toward the crowd of would-be pastors and said:

> Like the exodus of the Hebrew people from Egypt, the exodus of thousands of priests from the clerical structure is not a tragedy. It is just one more stage of the ongoing process through which a "highly mobile" God keeps his people moving towards new promised lands. There was no need for a temple and its priestly attendants while the Hebrews journeyed toward the promised land.

Diaspora: Voice of the Movement

Caporale understood that communication was the key to activating what he was certain were the latent energies for transformation of Christian ministry. At the organizing meeting in Detroit in April 1969 he volunteered to take over the editing of the SPFM newsletter from Pat Best. The eleven issues that he edited between August 1969 and July 1971 reflect his crisp literary style, his ability to synthesize and highlight what was happening, and, perhaps also, a tendency to exaggerate the successes of the group in the hope of generating wider support. In any case, he set on a firm basis a publication that continues to appear up to the present without interruption.

Under Caporale's editorial direction, *Diaspora* was a true newsletter, filled with names of people, places, and events. There was a tone of excitement, of issuing bulletins, of not having enough space for all the news coming across Caporale's desk. There was no room for extended articles. In fact, in two years, only one essay appeared, a paper titled "Creative Ministries," which Eugene Bianchi delivered at the National Federation of Priests Councils' convention in Baltimore in March 1971. By contrast, in recent years, *Diaspora* has become more a journal than a newsletter, with "idea pieces" replacing news. The editor frequently pleads with readers to submit material.

Dark Clouds Roll In

With unanticipated suddenness, the facade of success eventually collapsed. The tone of Caporale's final issue of *Diaspora* (May–July 1971) was a sharp departure from the optimism that had characterized his earlier writing. He played taps for a movement that, until then, he had trumpeted so confidently. Gone were upbeat claims. Now he asserted that the movement had not taken hold. Growth had ceased. Finances were low. Divisions were rife. What was to be done?

His answer, in an article titled "Two Images of the Future," suggested converging with other church reform groups. He pointed to the 1971 convention in New York as the opportunity to forge an alliance with a wide spectrum of kindred, but equally frail, organizations, and thereby rescue SPFM from imminent demise. Reviewing what had happened and what was needed, he concluded:

> Over the past few years, it has become compellingly evident that the forces for change are faced with two precise alternatives: a guerrilla-type little campaign around magnified occasional issues, that appeals to one or another group; or a massive and coordinated movement of renewal along a well-formulated set of goals of long range import and ordered into priorities.
>
> One can understand why, until now, the first alternative has been followed. But conditions have changed and this strategy is no longer tenable; the alternatives are no longer open and the only choice now left is between coordinated mobilization and gradual, but sure, extinction.

Thus, Caporale posed in *Diaspora* the same radical challenge that Bianchi would present in his convention address, "Does SPFM Have a Future?," and Tom Durkin would echo in his letter of resignation. Men so articulate and so committed to free ministry had become discouraged. They had presented the dream of a new order of Christian service to the thousands of priests who had left the active ministry. Few had subscribed to their vision, joined their ranks, or provided financial support. The wonder is that the movement survived at all. But it did. New leaders emerged, men who while not as brilliant, were much more patient.

5

Free Ministry Moves West

I hereby submit my resignation from the position of Vice-President of SPFM and decline any further nominations to serve on the Executive Board.

Tom Durkin, August 1971

I am submitting my resignation from the Executive Board and from the Society itself; the struggle to preserve my priestly ministry has deepened to be a struggle to live the Christian life. The decision to leave SPFM is, in effect, my decision to leave the Roman Catholic priesthood—even an updated, married version of it.

Tom Durkin, June 1973

For me, the priesthood as I have known it is over; the Roman Catholic Church as I see it is over too and with it the Christian West with Pope, Cardinal, Bishop, and Priest—all are over. The Patriarchal Age is doomed . . . This letter is my final signature in Diaspora.

Tom Durkin, January 1990

Free ministers are men who are passionately in love with their priesthood but unable to live it within the parameters determined by the hierarchy. They have more of a need to express their convictions than to conform to Church policies. They want to play ball, but they refuse to accept the rules of the coach. They try to play alone or to put together their own team but find that their field of dreams is deserted. Fans who cheered them while they challenged the institution from within turn away when they move outside. The bishops may not have the best game or the best players, but for most Catholics theirs is the only game in town.

However, this is said by way of hindsight. Early free ministers believed that they could rally enough support to change the game to conform to their sense of how it should be played. In the late sixties and early seventies they worked energetically to transform the Church. Two such men were Thomas J. Durkin and Roméo R. DiBenedetto. They had been ordained from large eastern archdioceses within a year of each other in the midsixties. Almost immediately they got into serious trouble with their bishops because of their views and behavior. Both moved West, seeking new lives in a young, growing section of the country. They occupied key roles within the free ministry movement and invested themselves generously on its behalf. Who they were, what they did, and how their lives have unfolded are central to an understanding of the movement.

Thomas Durkin: No Escape from Priesthood

Despite a series of dramatic resignations from SPFM and FCM, Durkin has remained in a symbiotic relationship with the free ministry movement. His most recent resignation was in January 1990, yet later that same year he attended both the CORPUS and FCM conventions in San Jose and the international meeting of married priests in Holland.

The son of working-class Irish immigrants, Durkin had been ordained a priest of the archdiocese of Philadelphia in 1964 by Cardinal John Krol. Notwithstanding an uninterrupted history of rebelliousness, Durkin retained a lifelong relationship with the man who had anointed his hands with holy oils and who had prayed over the kneeling youth words that made him a "priest forever." Durkin is a classic example of the Prodigal Son, wandering far from home yet tied inexorably to his father. The relationship with Krol is symbolic of Durkin's love/hate relationship with the Catholic Church and its priesthood. He had been seized by God, and try as he might, Durkin could never escape the pull of that divine power. He would run to California, to Hawaii, to India, to Australia, seeking a new way to understand his existence. Always the God of his childhood would hound him, and Durkin would return to those with whom he had shared his young manhood.

To an extreme degree, for sure, Tom Durkin represents the attachment that all free ministers have with their past. Some men who left the priesthood could establish new identities, shedding the old like skins that had been outgrown. Probably, as Bianchi discovered, most priests are like that. They can walk away and not turn back. Not so with Durkin or with the hundreds of others who remain haunted by the conviction that they are priests and should be allowed to serve.

In 1968 Durkin left the ministry in Philadelphia over what he called a "conflict of conscience" after he was forbidden to preach on race and war. This was the last straw. As early as 1966, he had been suspended for celebrating an underground Mass. In September 1968, Durkin married Gail Ewing in Philadelphia. The couple moved to Oakland, California, where a son was born the following year.

Although Durkin was certified as a marriage counselor, most of his time was devoted to a continuation of his priestly work. He met other resigned priests in the Bay Area, volunteered to be regional coordinator of the fledgling SPFM, went to the April 1969 organizational meeting in Detroit, and there was chosen its first executive secretary.

For the next two-and-a half years a flood of letters emanated from his home as he strove to transform the idea of SPFM into a significant organization. More than any other early leader, he labored to be a free minister, proposing and then living a series of what proved to be abortive models of ministry disconnected from the official Church.

Priesthood as Social Activism

If Durkin had caused problems with the Church in Philadelphia over his opposition to the American involvement in Vietnam, he caused similar problems with the government in California. In October 1969, he and three other "rebel priests" were arrested for sitting in at the U.S. marshall's office in San Francisco. Durkin used the ensuing media attention to promote SPFM. The *San Francisco Examiner* described the thirty-one year old Durkin as "an intense, articulate young man" who claimed that SPFM was "a general renewal movement within the church."[1]

While Bianchi and Caporale were writing articles and making speeches on free ministry, Durkin was leading fifty or so Bay area SPFM members and sympathizers in what would later be called "peace and justice issues." They set up an office near the Oakland army base to counsel servicemen with, in the words of the *Examiner* article, "problems of conscience relating to the Vietnam war." They also supported a group that was raising money for those arrested for expressing their political convictions. For Durkin, priesthood had to include what Caporale had called "prophetic ministry" and not be limited to liturgical and other strictly religious functions.

It was in this context that Durkin had conflict with the organizers of the first SPFM convention. He took it upon himself to invite Paul Mayer, a resigned priest and antiwar activist, to present a paper. Carl Hemmer protested that this would detract from the central purpose of the meeting and of SPFM. Durkin's reply to Hemmer expresses one of the tensions that would divide free ministers as they groped toward a renewed understanding of priesthood. Durkin said:

> If all we deal with in Washington, D.C., is ministry as it relates to celibacy, the sacraments, and the traditional priestly duties, I feel we will be neglecting the prophetic mission of the priest to challenge the consciences of the People of God.

Despite his political activity, Durkin did not neglect his role as executive secretary of SPFM. Immediately after returning to California from Detroit, he had stationery and brochures printed and began mailing regular reports to the executive board as his predecessor Pat Best had done. Even more time-consuming was the task of sending out literature and personal replies to the hundreds of letters that came to his home, especially in response to Bianchi's letter in the *National Catholic Reporter*.

Durkin was a tireless traveler. In July 1969, for example, he and Gail drove to Mexico where they spoke about SPFM to a number of priests at Cuernavaca. Ivan Illich, director of the language school there, could not comprehend a nonecclesiastical or noncanonical ministry. Durkin attributed this to the fact that Illich had been trained as a canon lawyer. Illich was himself a maverick who eventually would resign from the priesthood and gain a reputation not just for the language school that he continued to direct but for his controversial books on education and health care. Although Illich was perhaps an outstanding example of a free minister, he never affiliated with the organized efforts to bring about change. In 1971, Joseph Burns, who succeeded Durkin as executive secretary of SPFM, invited Illich to write an article for *Diaspora*. Illich sent a two-line reply: "I am not interested in free ministry."[2]

Paul Mayer's Call for a Radical New Priestly Life-Style

Most of the 1969 convention weekend concerned itself with the issue of SPFM's purpose and organizational structure. Only the talk by Paul Mayer, titled "Reflections on New Styles of Ministry," attempted to propel the attendees into the broader world of ferment and change. Durkin himself did not make a presentation. It would seem that Mayer was his surrogate, insisting that a radical break with the life-styles of the past was needed and that organizations like SPFM must lead the way. Taken with a sixties fascination with youth, Mayer said:

> Unlike the majority of Christians, many of today's young people engaged in this revolution are determined to live now as if the kingdom were already among them. They have rejected the plastic values of the American way of death by their very life style. Their long hair, rock music, beads, sexual freedom and mind-expanding drugs are simply expressions of their desire to experience their life and world in a new way.

This image of the youthful, life-affirming individual made a deep impression on Durkin, who as the years progressed became a stereotypical hippie. Pictures would show him with long hair, beads, and exotic forms of clothing. He divorced Gail in 1975, lived in a tent commune in the Northwest, fathered a daughter, went to India and sat at the feet of a guru, never held a regular job, appeared on television with a woman who worked as a surrogate partner for men undergoing sex therapy, and along the way advocated a long shopping list of Eastern formulas for happiness. He never found it himself.

All that would be in the future. In 1969 his energies were committed to transformation of the priesthood. In the seminary he had been molded in a pattern that was hundreds of years old. He had broken the mold and was attempting to fashion a new one. What would it be like? Paul Mayer, at the same 1969 convention, gave him the answer:

> To move from the wall-to-wall rectory into the Brooks Brothers swinger-set of suburbia is just a new way of becoming a buttoned-down monsignor. The gospel man

needs to identify himself with those causes and life styles
that represent a search for human decency and justice
wherever he is. "The proclamation of the Lord's death
until he comes" surely means more than celebrating an
occasional underground liturgy in someone's living room.
It must mean living on the edge of security, financial and
psychological. . . . The willingness to live with risk is a
decision presupposed by the Beatitudes with their call to
poverty, gentleness, and the daily expectation of persecution and imprisonment in the cause of justice.

This excerpt from Mayer's impassioned talk sounds like the
spiritual biography of Tom Durkin. It may be that he needed someone
to give him a plan for his life. The one that Cardinal Krol had given
him years before was no longer workable. Mayer's plan, which
sounded consistent both with the Gospel and the spirit of the sixties,
might be the alternative.

Coordinating the 1970 Convention
Durkin returned to California not only energized by this challenge
but equipped with a mandate. SPFM had launched a campaign to
raise $9,000 so that Durkin could be paid $500 a month plus expenses
to serve as full-time executive secretary. At the time, there was $114
in the society's treasury. A year later the financial report would show
that a total of $3,156 had been raised during the year. Durkin had
been paid nothing. Despite this lack of financial support, he worked
as if he were a paid staff member, continuing his prodigious output
of letters and organizing efforts.

The major project for the year was planning and hosting the 1970
convention at the Center for Human Interaction in Berkeley, California. Unlike the first convention that had only general sessions, the
second included eight workshops grouped under the headings
"Examples of Freer Forms of Ministry in California" and "Sharing
the Experience of the Free Ministry Movement." Durkin was determined that SPFM would move from theorizing about free ministry
to learning about and developing lived examples of what it meant.

Team Ministry Project
One of the workshops was titled "Team Ministry." Durkin and Mike
Mooney, a former Franciscan priest from Chicago, presented their
proposal that they be authorized by SPFM to "concretize the idea of

married priests actually ministering to communities in an organized way on the local level."

Durkin argued that up until then the focus of SPFM had been on the national front, creating a national presence. It was time to put more effort into the experimental side of the society, namely, "building the new Christian communities which will be able to carry the Gospel in new forms for the future."

The experience of the failure of SPFM the previous year to raise $9,000 for his position as executive secretary did not deter Durkin from proposing a new fund-raising plan. He believed that as an outgrowth of the personal contacts developed through the proposed team ministry, he and Mooney could raise $36,000 to support themselves and the SPFM national office that would be moving from Durkin's Oakland apartment to New York City.

The team ministry proposal was discussed at length at the convention. Aware of the difficulty of raising money, and perhaps not completely comfortable with Durkin's vision of free ministry, the society approved a compromise. It would commit $1,815 to Durkin, collected from the people present at the convention, on a three-month experimental basis. Mooney would join the ministry if and when funds became available.

Durkin had left the 1969 convention with the expectation that he would be supported in his role as executive secretary. Now, having moved from being secretary to national vice president, he left the 1970 convention with seed money for what he was certain would be a vigorous ministry and a focal point for substantial fund-raising.

The team ministry project was terminated after four months. Durkin reported that it had been impossible to organize married priests. "What appears to be difficult is for them to act in a concerted way apart from the institutional church." Such men supported SPFM as a catalyst to transform the Church, not as itself a counter-church.

This was a key insight into the position of the majority of married priests. They would not participate in something that they felt was schismatic or was, in any way, a rival of the official Church. It would be this cautious attitude that would lead to the increasing difficulty of SPFM to recruit new members and to the popularity of CORPUS when it was founded several years later.

Durkin Appeals to Rome
In May 1969, through Bishop Floyd L. Begin of Oakland, Durkin had sent a petition to the Sacred Congregation for the Doctrine of the

Faith, or Holy Office, requesting that he be allowed to serve as a priest
in the context of a "free ministry." More than a year later, Bishop
Begin forwarded to Durkin a response from the Holy Office. Durkin
publicized the correspondence, suggesting that since Rome had
mentioned SPFM and "free ministry" while denying his petition it
somehow had granted recognition to the movement.

The correspondence reflects the thinking of free ministers in the
late sixties as well as the official Vatican reaction to such thinking.

In his petition, witnessed by the Officialis of the Oakland Diocese,
Durkin said:

> I have chosen to petition the Holy See for a release from the
> obligations of clerical life including the oath of celibacy. I
> do so because in my personal life I have exercised a prior
> inalienable human right—that of marriage. I accepted the
> oath of celibacy because canonical legislation at the time
> required this oath as a necessary condition for the ordina-
> tion to priesthood. That such an oath is freely taken is open
> to question. I no longer believe the two styles of life—that
> of celibate and priest—are inseparable. Therefore I have
> chosen to marry and at the same time to continue my
> ministry as a priest in the historical tradition of Catholi-
> cism. . . . It is my intention to continue to serve the needs of
> Christians in so far as my situation as a priest in the world
> permits. I cannot refuse to Christians what the Church has
> ordained me to offer—the Word and its Celebration. As a
> member of the Society of Priests for a Free Ministry, I, with
> others, shall continue to minister beyond official ecclesi-
> astical structures in the hope my ministry will hasten the
> renewal of the ministry of the whole Church.

The response from the Holy Office, signed by a subsecretary, was
dated July 30, 1970. A copy of the Latin original and an English
translation were given to Durkin in late August. The response said
that the petition had been denied unanimously by a special commission of the Holy Office. Usually such decisions were transmitted
without explanation. What made this case unique was that the Holy
Office decided to add a few paragraphs that, for the first time,
directly addressed the idea of a free ministry. The response said:

> Permit me to clarify this decision with a few words for a
> better understanding of the mind of this Holy Office. The

petitioner belongs to a group of priests, who, imbued with entirely false ideas, presume that they are called to reform the Church, not indeed with sanctity of life, but through so called "prophetic gestures," namely by attempting civil marriage and by exercising a priestly "free ministry." This man in his own words says that he does not wish to return to the lay state, but to remain in a married priesthood. But this manner of acting is based on a false theology of the priesthood and of the Church, which is common to the promoters of the afore-mentioned society of priests for a "free ministry" (Society of Priests for Free Ministry.) [The name of the organization was given in English in the Latin text.]

Since . . . the petitioner has placed himself through his civil marriage and through his entirely false ideas against the spirit and the letter of the Code of Canon Law, your Excellency by reason of your pastoral office and to protect the common good of the Church might wish to proceed according to the norm of Canon 2388 #1 by inflicting the punishment of degradation on the lapsed priest. But if in the meantime the petitioner should come around to more gentle counsels and should change his mind at least in so far as the acceptance of a reduction totally to the lay state and renunciation of any "free ministry," then your Excellency might refer the matter here again.

Durkin did not yield to "gentle counsels" by the bishop who, for his part, did not "degrade" the "lapsed priest" but did tell him that he had no right to continue to perform priestly functions.[3]

Other Efforts at Dialogue with the Official Church

First as executive secretary, then as national vice president, and finally as regional vice president, Durkin presented SPFM to the Church authorities as a bona fide organization with which they should engage in dialogue and even negotiate.

Hundreds of copies of the *Proceedings* of the 1969 SPFM convention were still on hand as the 1970 meeting approached. Durkin sent copies to the priests' personnel boards of all the dioceses of the country with a cover letter that offered SPFM as a

referral for your priests who have already or are planning to leave the active ministry. Not that we are encouraging them to do so, but if in conscience, they have made up their minds about this decision already, their many useful talents should not be permanently lost to the service of the Church. Canon law can, in time, change.

In September 1970, Durkin wrote to the National Federation of Priests Councils (NFPC), requesting permission to present at their provincial meeting in Santa Cruz, California, several resolutions that called on the association of active priests to support the goals of the inactive priests. Durkin addressed the group. As will be seen, other free ministers likewise pursued the strategy of attempting to forge an alliance with canonical priests.

SPFM Officers Meet with Bishops

Closer to the center of Church power was the National Conference of Catholic Bishops (NCCB), which met twice a year to discuss issues of interest to the American Catholic Church. The NCCB had a liaison committee for priests before which SPFM representatives appeared on several occasions, beginning in October 1969, a month before the first SPFM convention. Durkin continued the effort to get a hearing from the bishops. In the spring of 1970, there was an exchange of carefully worded correspondence between Durkin and Bishop, later Cardinal, Joseph L. Bernardin, general secretary of the NCCB, and also between Durkin and Bishop Thomas McDonough, chairman of the liaison committee. As a result of Durkin's efforts, the liaison committee met on March 23 with SPFM officers Eugene Bianchi, Patrick Best, and Charles Sullivan.

At first Durkin was elated that the bishops were giving SPFM a hearing. Soon he realized that listening did not mean acceptance of the free ministry message. Eventually, even the listening stopped.

Letter to All U.S. Priests Proposed

Durkin, who had been a major force in the planning and execution of both the 1969 and 1970 conventions, did not attend the meeting held in New York in 1971. Instead, he wrote an impassioned letter of resignation from the board, a sentence from which appears at the beginning of this chapter. Like the canary taken into a coal mine whose death signaled the buildup of toxic fumes, Durkin's resignation was a powerful clue that all was not well within the movement.

Paradoxically, neither his creativity nor his energy subsided. When it became clear that the October 1971 Synod of Bishops in

Rome would not provide the hoped-for breakthrough, he proposed to the board that a letter be sent to all sixty thousand priests of the country, inviting them to join SPFM. Durkin argued that the time was ripe for such a move; that many priests, disappointed by the synod, would decide to leave the ministry and join the SPFM.

Durkin estimated that the mailing would cost $4,800. He proposed that each SPFM board member put up $500, which hopefully would be repaid from contributions that would be generated by the letter. The board discussed the idea but took no action. The organizational crisis was too pressing. Furthermore, the conviction was deepening that any dealings with the institutional Church were futile.

Durkin's Spiritual Wanderings

As hopes for reforming the Catholic priesthood faded, Durkin undertook a search for a new identity in a wide range of experiences. On January 6, 1973, he sent a belated Christmas letter to his friends. Referring to the Feast of the Epiphany on which he was writing, he said that he could identify with the searching of the Wise Men. "Five years ago at Christmas time I began my own search with a decision to leave the clerical Catholic priesthood and follow the 'star' of a new grouping of the Christian community," he wrote.

In the letter, Durkin was frank in his assessment of his life. His relationship with Gail had undergone changes. Both had participated in "consciousness-raising groups" in an effort to "confront the oppressive sex-roles which society had laid on us from childhood." Next, Tom and Gail decided that "the traditional nuclear family was destructive as an environment for us to grow and open our relationship to others, and for Michael, our only child."

Accordingly, the Durkins moved into a large house with four other adults and a two-year old girl. The dream of a utopian communal life soon led to disillusionment. Durkin said:

> The experience of living with strangers and trying to make a family with them has been the most difficult of my life to date. . . . All the little resentments, annoyances, petty injuries since we moved in seemed to converge on me Christmas day and I became so depressed no one could reach me—until last Thursday when I moved out.

Durkin went on to say that he prayed with some Christians and was "healed." He moved back into the little commune and committed himself to work within what he called "a sort of transcendental community linked beyond space and time."

Recommends Change of Name and Direction for SPFM

In the midst of this personal turmoil, Durkin once again dramatically resigned from SPFM. The letter of resignation was published by *National Catholic Reporter* and reproduced on the front page of *Diaspora*, together with a response by the SPFM president, Bernard McGoldrick.[4] The editor of *Diaspora* said that the correspondence was printed just prior to the 1973 convention in order to assist in the discussions that would take place as to the future direction of the group. Durkin's letter was given the bold headline "To Exit or Disperse?," which was reminiscent of Bianchi's 1971 address, "Does SPFM Have a Future?"

The group that gathered in Staten Island, New York, on Labor Day weekend did indeed change the name and direction of the organization. In January 1974, his suggestions having been heeded, Durkin renewed his membership in the organization, now known as FCM. The group attempted to cut itself off from the vestiges of a male clerical priesthood and embrace a more ecumenical, nonsexist style of ministry. In the minds of many, what it actually did was sever itself from the Catholic Church and begin its long wandering in the desert of confusion. It was to this desert that Durkin had prodded his colleagues, and it was in this markerless place that Durkin himself would wander, perhaps for the rest of his life.

A Little Boy's Shopping Bag

Just once in twenty-three years has *Diaspora* printed a poem on its front page. It was the Spring 1982 issue, and the poem was Tom Durkin's "Turtle Talk." Perhaps better than any documents or deeds, it summarizes his life and can serve as a spiritual autobiography. It begins with the words:

> When boy is little he collect many things:
> old tears, bandaids and scabs, childhood sweetheart,
> mother father sister brother
> heartache, joy, fear, toys, half eaten bologna
> sandwich, stale package Hostess Twinkies,
> first lover, vomit bag from airplane.
> he put in shopping bag
> and carry around.
> boy grow up; he feel lousy,

all weighed down.
he feel dragged down by shopping bag
but will not let go.
he think shopping bag contain power and life.

Roméo DiBenedetto: Seeking a Rainbow

When Eugene Bianchi's letter announcing the establishment of SPFM appeared in the *National Catholic Reporter* in May 1969, one of the first to respond was Roméo DiBenedetto, a young priest in Albuquerque, New Mexico. The executive secretary, Tom Durkin, replied by naming DiBenedetto the New Mexico state coordinator. In the next few years, in partnership with his wife, Vicki, DiBenedetto would serve as national vice president, executive secretary, publisher of *Diaspora*, and one of its most active local organizers.

What follows is based on an interview conducted in February 1990 and DiBenedetto's lengthy unpublished autobiography titled *Meditations for a Rainbow Odyssey*, started many years ago and updated in 1990. This latter document offers a rare opportunity to examine elements of a man's private life and provides insight into his character and the direction that his life has taken. Certainly, each individual is unique, but just as Homer's *Odyssey* can be applied to the journey of us all, so can many free ministers see themselves in DiBenedetto's "odyssey."

Becoming Priests in a Time of Transition

Ordained in 1965 for the archdiocese of Newark, New Jersey, DiBenedetto saw his classmates as similar to the Roman god Janus—with two faces, one looking back and one looking forward. When he entered the major seminary in 1959, he spent a year with deacons who would be ordained in 1960. Those men entered the priesthood before Vatican II began and before the "spirit" of the council had a chance to permeate the texts used in the seminary. The men ordained in 1960 joined the "old Church," with its stress on obedience and a deep suspicion of Protestantism and change.

On the other end of his six-year seminary training, DiBenedetto spent a year with the young men who would be ordained in 1970. He saw them as being very different from their colleagues of a decade earlier. Gone was the narrowness and fear. Imbued with the new individualism and a sense of human rights, they were less hesitant to "express their views and disobey anyone or any law which they considered foolish or detrimental to people's lives."

He and his classmates of 1965 were right in the middle, neither the old nor the new, but

> an inconsistent co-mixture of these two mentalities. We vacillated a lot between these two philosophic priorities of obedience or conscience. My perception was that the class of 1960, as a whole, felt in conscience that they had no choice but to obey external authority, whereas the class of 1970 saw their conscience as inviolable and primary.

The class of 1965 was transitional, between the "old breed" and the "new breed." Some members would join those older men who resisted change; others would enlist in the ranks of those promoting change, but the predominant mood was one of ambivalence.

Stormy Priesthood from the Start

DiBenedetto was assigned to a New Jersey parish. Almost immediately he experienced antagonism from the pastor who said he was "too far out" and had crazy ideas. Without success, DiBenedetto attempted to assure the older man that he and his classmates "were harbingers of deeper changes in attitude that were coming." DiBenedetto soon was transferred because of "an inappropriate relationship in which I had become involved."

After a brief period in another parish, DiBenedetto's odyssey took him to Via Coeli monastery in New Mexico for an extended retreat. He had been a priest in his home diocese of Newark for scarcely two years. The retreat was intended to motivate the young rebel to change his ways: to accept authority and uphold Church teaching.

It did not have that effect. Through the kindness of Archbishop James Davis of Santa Fe, DiBenedetto was assigned to a parish in San Juan Indian pueblo and then sent to a largely Hispanic parish in Albuquerque. Almost immediately his problems with superiors resumed.

In a Mass for young Hispanics, he used tortillas for the eucharistic bread. The pastor was furious. When *Humanae Vitae* was issued in 1968, DiBenedetto read the text in *The New York Times* and then from the pulpit summarized and critiqued the encyclical. He said that there was room for an alternative interpretation of the teaching on birth control. When he returned to the sacristy, one of his fellow priests was there in tears and asked, "Why are you destroying the Church?"

The incident did not die there. It was brought to a deanery meeting where DiBenedetto's colleagues censured him for criticizing the pope. Indicative of DiBenedetto's mentality was his defense that those who voted against him had not read the encyclical themselves, so did not know what the pope had said. Furthermore, they had only hearsay knowledge of what *he* had said. DiBenedetto was unable to accept that public support for papal pronouncements was considered essential. The priesthood was like the army. The frontline troops were not to question their superior officers but to obey them without question.

This incident was a crisis point. Although he had faculties to work in the archdiocese, DiBenedetto was not incardinated there. When the pastor would no longer allow him to work in his parish, the only employment he could find was as occasional retreat master at the Dominican retreat house. However, even this did not last. When priests heard that he was conducting retreats, they would not advertise them, so fewer people attended, seriously hurting the income of the retreat house.

Living in a mobile home and with no money, DiBenedetto realized that something had to be done. He could leave Santa Fe and go to another diocese or "shut my mouth and stop thinking my own thoughts." He decided that he could not violate his conscience and that wherever he went the same sort of problems would arise. After two years in Newark and two years in Santa Fe, his priesthood seemed to have fallen apart.

Early Doubts about Celibacy

Uncertainty about his life's calling went back a long way. DiBenedetto places great importance on his family of origin. His parents were Italian immigrants—he was the youngest of five children and the only boy. His mother died when he was young, intensifying his attachment to his father, a simple, hardworking man whose dream was to see his son marry and have children. In fact, the father built a house that he planned to give to Roméo as a wedding present. As to the father's reaction when the son revealed his desire to become a priest, Roméo wrote: "I could see his dreams and plans collapse. He did not understand; but he did not interfere."

In the major seminary, one professor stood out, Anthony Padovano, who had studied theology in Rome during Vatican II and came to the classroom eager to share his vision of the Church. The young students adored him, referring to Padovano as "the Fourth Person of the

Blessed Trinity." DiBenedetto chose him for his confessor. In time, Padovano would become one of the principal figures in the free ministry movement and is the central subject of chapter 14.

As ordination to subdiaconate approached, with its requirement of celibacy, DiBenedetto wavered. He was not certain that he wanted to forego marriage and considered dropping out of the seminary. In fact, he was not ordained a subdeacon with his class, requesting a year to think it over. Seminary authorities gave him three months. Under this pressure, he decided to go ahead and caught up with his less hesitant classmates.

Like many free ministers, DiBenedetto has never sought to be laicized, since he wished to be a "free priest" and not a layman. However, the serious doubts that he expressed as a seminarian might serve as evidence that he did not accept celibacy with complete freedom, providing grounds for granting him release from the promise of celibacy.

When in 1969 DiBenedetto announced that he was leaving the priesthood to get married, his father's response was, "It's about time!" A son was belatedly making his loving father happy. The father lived until 1986 and was proud to see his son married, a father, and well-established in the respected career of college professor.

One indication of the importance of pleasing his father was DiBenedetto's determination to obtain a doctorate. Long ago, while still a priest in Albuquerque, he had obtained a master of arts degree in sociology from the University of New Mexico. This proved providential, equipping him with credentials to teach at the community college level. Still, his father urged him to obtain the doctorate, the true symbol of a college professor. Even as he was dying, his father made him promise to continue his studies. After a number of setbacks that would have discouraged most people, DiBenedetto was awarded a doctorate of education in educational management and development by New Mexico State University in 1989. He was fifty years old.

Organizing for SPFM

During his final, trying days as a priest in Albuquerque, DiBenedetto became associated with Victoria Kingston, a Dominican sister and director of the retreat house where the beleaguered priest gave retreats. When DiBenedetto was appointed SPFM coordinator, Sister Victoria helped him locate married priests as well as active priests sympathetic to the goals of the new organization. They began to hold public meetings and discovered that they had as many names of married priests living in the greater Albuquerque area as there were priests working in the parishes of the city—about fifty-five.

After joining SPFM, DiBenedetto went to see Archbishop Davis, who said that the unassigned priest could continue to have faculties as long as he was not married and didn't break any Church laws. As it turned out, Roméo and Vicki had fallen in love and decided that they would marry. It was only a matter of time before DiBenedetto would have to relinquish his tenuous hold on priestly legitimacy.

Shortly thereafter, Eugene Bianchi stopped in Albuquerque on his way from California to Georgia. DiBenedetto arranged for a press conference and the two appeared together on a local television show. Bianchi was in a suit and tie, DiBenedetto in a Roman collar. The television host asked, "Well, Father DiBenedetto, how does it feel to be excommunicated?" DiBenedetto replied, conscious that he was splitting hairs, "I'm not excommunicated. There's a Church law against getting married. At this point, I'm only engaged, and there's no law against that."

Vicki left the Dominicans in August 1969 and moved to Virginia to spend several months with her uncle and aunt. In November, enthusiastic about the prospects for a free ministry, DiBenedetto flew to Washington, D.C., where he and Vicki attended the first SPFM convention and where Roméo was named to the executive board and volunteered to be publisher for the organization. His first charge was to publish the proceedings of the convention.

Legal Incorporation of SPFM

Back in Albuquerque, Roméo obtained a position with a drug rehabilitation program. He and Vicki were married in August 1970, and, as he says, "attended the second annual SPFM conference in Berkeley on our honeymoon." As publisher, Roméo gave a report, which included the news that he had arranged for the legal incorporation of SPFM through Fred McCarthy, an attorney. McCarthy was one of the men present at the 1968 NAPR caucus in St. Louis when SPFM was established. Now he was present at the group's legal birth. And, as DiBenedetto remarked in his report:

> It is interesting to note that SPFM was legally born in the Archdiocese of Santa Fe (Holy Faith) within the little town of Belen [where McCarthy lived], which is the Spanish form of the name, Bethlehem.

Fred McCarthy was one of the married priests whom DiBenedetto located in New Mexico. McCarthy had served as an Air Force pilot in World War II and then became a priest, having been ordained in 1953 for the Springfield, Illinois, diocese. Later, he joined the Missionary Society of St. James the Apostle and worked in Peru until 1968. Early in life, he had obtained a law degree from Georgetown University Law School and at the time of his association with DiBenedetto was director of the Navajo Legal Aid Society. He has since retired.

A Move to El Paso and Away from Free Ministry
Two crises intersected in the lives of the DiBenedettos early in 1973. Roméo lost his job, and he and Vicki became disillusioned with free ministry. These developments marked the end of one major period in their lives and the start of another. They moved to El Paso, Texas, where Roméo had obtained a position as instructor of sociology at the community college and where he has worked ever since. He and Vicki have raised two daughters. Spiritually, they began an odyssey that would take them far afield from their traditional Catholic heritage. Among other things, they consulted psychics, explored the meaning of dreams, and investigated New Age mysticism.

The move to El Paso coincided with the turmoil occurring within SPFM that resulted in the organization changing its name and its direction. For four years DiBenedetto had been publisher of *Diaspora*, using the services of an Albuquerque printer. However, when he moved to El Paso, he relinquished that position and effectively closed the door on his involvement with the organization.

DiBenedetto recalls that even before they moved, he and Vicki had decided to discontinue their free ministry efforts. They felt that they were doing more harm than good. What was being achieved seemed to be outweighed by the negativity generated. One member of their group in Albuquerque, for example, was told to quit SPFM or take his children out of the parochial school. Others were afraid that their involvement would endanger their employment. Most Catholics rejected their ministry. From the perspective of more than seventeen years, Roméo reflected:

> We felt that it was immoral of us to attempt to force people to change. Most Catholics didn't feel it was right to change from the bottom up. They wanted change from the top. That wasn't happening. So we stopped organizing meetings and began to pay more attention to our own lives.

A Life in Retrospect

Roméo DiBenedetto's intellectual interests today include research on community colleges and dialogue with Eastern European scholars on the concept of "character." He has sponsored international speaker exchanges and hopes to contribute to greater world harmony. When asked to summarize what free ministry had meant to him and how he felt about the Church today, he said:

> SPFM was an outlet for me to continue in some way a meaningful ministry. I was not quitting because I hated the Church. SPFM was a magnificent opportunity to get involved with other priests across the country. I was optimistic. Vatican II was not that far behind us. I felt the Church would change in the direction Pope John XXIII had wanted. In 1965, right after ordination, I went to Rome and said Mass over his tomb. I thought that the changes I was trying to make were a manifestation of Pope John's principles. I felt an obligation to move the church closer to the model I felt he had presented. I felt like Martin Luther when he said, "Here I stand. I can do no other."
>
> Although I still feel like a Catholic, and my daughters have attended Catholic schools, I have looked for a more meaningful spirituality in other directions. I am interested in mysticism and have read and been impressed with some New Age writings. I'm still interested in what happens in the Catholic Church, but don't need it anymore and have little confidence that it will be reformed.

6

Extending the National Presence and Striving for Convergence

*Challenge the resigned priests and religious and their lay col-
leagues to work with the institutional church. . . . Put a hold on
some of the more esoteric ministries recommended by FCM and
on CORPUS's single focus request for the immediate reinstatement of priests to preside at the Eucharist. Let the Bishops
see that there are many men and women who don't wish to
embarrass or harass them, but who just wish to serve the Church
publicly and lovingly.*

Joseph J. Burns, Diaspora Fall 1990

A social movement needs three types of leaders. Initially, there must
be those who can articulate a vision, a blueprint for a better society.
There must also be people willing to go out into the field and spread
the ideas, people who know how to get attention and "sell" the
vision. Finally, there must be others who staff the home base,
answering mail, writing reports, coordinating activities, and sched-
uling meetings.

Obviously, there is overlap. Besides providing ideological leadership, Bianchi and Caporale also traveled extensively, and Durkin
and DiBenedetto provided ideas and traveled as well as serving in
"home office" positions. However, some people did provide more
specialized skills to the free ministry movement in its earliest years.

Charles Sullivan and his wife, Pauline Fox Sullivan, became "representatives-at-large" for SPFM and spent more than a year traveling the country spreading the message of free ministry.

In the meanwhile, Joseph Burns, from his home in New York City, provided a somewhat fixed base of operations, kept the society's records, and, most importantly, organized the 1971 convention, one that would be a watershed for the movement.

The spiritual roads that the leaders of the free ministry movement have taken present striking diversity. Durkin and DiBenedetto are examples of those who have wandered away from the Church, perhaps yearning for a missing part of themselves, but not ready for reconciliation and compromise. Sullivan and Burns, on the other hand, represent those who move beyond the pain of rejection and the need to have it all to a willingness to work within the limits acceptable to the institution. They are men who say to the hierarchy, "Utilize my services on *your* terms, not mine." Their love for the Church is greater than their need to change it.

Charles Sullivan: Ambassador of Freedom

There are some similarities between the early years of Tom Durkin and Charles Sullivan. Both were major seminarians during Vatican II and were catapulted, as it were, into the maelstrom of change and uncertainty that ensued. Both very quickly antagonized their bishops and some parishioners for controversial stands on social issues. Durkin used the pulpit to preach against American involvement in Vietnam. Sullivan used the same forum to challenge the Church's policies on race relations. Both disconnected themselves within a short time from the institutional priesthood, avoiding thereby the deep imprinting of what might be called the "clerical culture." Their life-style and perception of ministry were different from that of men who had spent many years in service to the Church and who were most comfortable when near the altar. Durkin and Sullivan are men fully at home in the larger society, "worldly priests" as contrasted with "churchy priests."

Models of Prophetic Priesthood
Both men moved far away from their place of origin, traveled extensively, and never were attracted to what might be called a "secular career." Perhaps more than anyone else from the early days of the free ministry movement, they lived, without interruption, the

spirit of the sixties and invested themselves with the "prophetic priesthood" of which Rocco Caporale wrote and to which Paul Mayer summoned them at the first SPFM convention. Both men engaged in "civil disobedience" and had the experience of being arrested. Both rejected the excesses of capitalism and hungered and thirsted after justice. Although they favored a married priesthood and other ecclesiastical reforms, their energies were concentrated on chiding both Church and government for complacency with injustice and complicity with the values and interests of the privileged.

A Radical Voice from the Deep South

However, whereas Durkin was ordained for Philadelphia, a quintessential northern Catholic city, Sullivan was ordained for Mobile-Birmingham, Alabama, at a time when the South was undergoing the cataclysmic transformation of desegregation. As fate would have it, Sullivan's first assignment, in 1966, was to a small black congregation not far from Selma, scene of one of the most significant racial confrontations of the civil rights era. Six blocks away from Sullivan's church was an all-white church that blacks were not permitted to attend. Sullivan concluded that he had been sent to maintain segregation. After two years, he refused to continue what he considered a hypocritical ministry, publicly criticizing Archbishop Thomas J. Toolan for his policies on race relations and calling on him to retire.

In September 1968, Sullivan left Alabama and traveled north, uncertain as to what direction his life should take. For six weeks he stayed at various religious institutions, including Fordham University and New York Theological Seminary in New York City. Eventually, he went to Minnesota, where previously he had taken courses at St. John's University, Collegeville. Still not having officially left the priesthood, he worked part time as Catholic chaplain at the University of Minnesota Newman Center.

Sullivan says that his exposure to the more liberal ideas of the North had a profound impact on him. Sen. Eugene McCarthy, a former professor at St. John's and in 1968 running for the presidency on an anti-Vietnam War platform, spent five days in the Twin Cities while Sullivan was there. Also, Rosemary Radford Ruether, who was a guest speaker at the university, introduced Sullivan to the idea of a free ministry, and, in particular, to the possibility of a "parallel structure" as a vehicle for implementing experimental new ministries.

In the summer of 1969 Sullivan returned to his family home in Birmingham. On the way, he stopped at Memphis, stood at the place where Dr. Martin Luther King, Jr., had been killed, and realized that he, like King, was a Southern clergyman called to devote his life to the cause of justice. He spent two months painting his parent's house and wrestling with the question of what to do next. His family was staunchly Irish Catholic; his grandfather was Archbishop Toolan's lawyer. Sullivan considered returning to the service of the diocese, but in the end he realized that he had traveled too far along the road to a new life.

Joining the Movement
Like many others, Sullivan had heard about SPFM through Eugene Bianchi's article in *Commonweal* and decided to attend the first convention in November. On the way north, he visited Bianchi in Atlanta and was further converted to the prospect of continuing his priesthood in a more liberated context. His enthusiasm was transformed into action when, at the convention, he offered himself to work full time for the new group. He was appointed director of development and ambassador-at-large. The understanding was that he would be given as a salary 30 percent of the money he raised. Local coordinators would be informed of his plan to visit their area and asked to provide him with accommodations as he traveled. For the next two years, until the 1971 convention in New York, Sullivan crisscrossed the country in the first concerted effort to organize local chapters.

Sit-in at Bishops' Meeting
Sullivan's tenure as SPFM activist got off to a dramatic start. The semiannual closed door meeting of the National Conference of Catholic Bishops was held in Washington, D.C., the week after the SPFM convention. Sullivan conducted a one-man, five-hour sit-in. He was quoted in the newspaper as saying that his protest was "a sign of concern of those who are alienated by the bishops but are still looking for a sign of hope from them." He expected to be ejected from the meeting but was allowed to stay. A kindly bishop even brought him a sandwich.[1]

Although gratified that the bishops permitted him to remain, he was critical of them for not being more concerned about the issues of race, war, and poverty.

Sullivan knew personally a number of the bishops, some of whom were to move on to leading positions in the American hierarchy. In 1990, Cardinal Bernard Law of Boston came up to Sullivan at a meeting in Washington, D.C., and said, "Charlie, great to see you.

Just the other day, Archbishop May [of St. Louis] and I were talking and I said, 'Remember the old days when Sullivan did the sit-in?' We had a great laugh."

Attempt to Establish a "Parallel Structure"
Since he was free to travel, Sullivan became a regular SPFM representative at a variety of meetings. In January 1970, with Vince Eckholm, he attended in Chicago the executive board meeting of the Major Religious Superiors of Men at which Eugene Bianchi delivered an address. In February, with Mike Byrne, the SPFM treasurer, he represented the organization at a meeting of the short-lived coalition of American Priests Associations. In March, with Bianchi and Pat Best, he met with the liaison committee of the American bishops, and in May, he was in Cleveland for the SPFM executive board meeting. Since he was having little success raising money, he proposed that each SPFM affiliate group be asked to raise $250 in hopes of accumulating $6,000 by the August convention in Berkeley. It sounded like a reasonable proposal, but it never was implemented.

All along the way he received media attention, especially since his ecclesiastical status was ambiguous. He had taken a leave but never resigned officially. Early in 1970, the newspaper of his home diocese in Mobile-Birmingham published a lengthy letter from "Rev. Charles Sullivan, Director of Development, Society of Priests for a Free Ministry" that explained the purpose of SPFM. With the exaggeration common at the time, Sullivan claimed that SPFM was

> a national organization of close to 1,000 priests who feel that the traditional style of priestly ministry is inadequate in today's world. Some are functioning as priests in new modes of bringing Christ to people. By broadening the concept of ministry through experimentation, these priests are not saying the traditional parish structure is wrong or should be abolished immediately, but that the parish for many, especially the young, is not fulfilling their spiritual needs, and that a priest should have the freedom to decide his own style of life and the best possible avenue in ministering to these alienated-from-the-parish Christians.[2]

Sullivan himself was one of those who was attempting to develop "new modes of bringing Christ to people." With Minneapolis as his home base, he tried to form a "parallel structure." Although a number of people expressed interest, this free ministry venture did not succeed. It did, however, yield something of lasting value for Sullivan. Through it he met his future wife.

Sullivan was living with Joseph Selvaggio, who recently had resigned from the Dominicans and was getting started in a program to develop housing for the poor that has since become a national model for low-income housing. Today, Selvaggio is executive director of the multimillion dollar Minneapolis-based program "Project for Pride in Living." In 1970, he invited Pauline Fox, who had just left the Sisters of St. Joseph, to a gathering of the little community and introduced her to Sullivan. The pair soon commenced what has turned out to be a personal and ministerial partnership that has spanned the decades.

Promoting and Organizing SPFM
In March 1970, in one of the numerous newspaper articles that recounted his ventures and ideas, Sullivan once again inflated the number of priests for whom SPFM spoke, saying that a place should be found in the Church for the estimated ten thousand men who had left the priesthood to marry in the previous two years. He suggested that the ideal leader for these priests would be James P. Shannon, who had resigned recently as auxiliary bishop of St.Paul-Minneapolis in order to marry. Bishop Shannon was contacted by SPFM but never expressed interest in assuming leadership in what certainly would have been a schismatic Church.[3]

Diaspora also included a series of reports from Sullivan. In the January–February 1970 issue, the peripatetic "representative-at-large," in the first flush of zeal, was quoted as saying, "The more people I meet, the more I read, the more I think, the more I become convinced that the free ministry is the direction we must pursue if organized Christianity is to survive." Sullivan's campaign strategy was to make two-week "tours of our centers" from his Minneapolis home. Some of those centers had already lost momentum and could have used an injection of enthusiasm. The following issue of the SPFM newsletter reported Sullivan's visits to Chicago and to New York. In Chicago, meetings had been suspended for four months but were revived again by Vince Eckholm, the local coordinator. Sullivan's appearance on Chicago television and radio helped to reawaken lagging spirits. However, Eckholm was to complain later that, although resigned priests wanted to be linked with home liturgy groups, few were willing to give time or money to the larger cause of SPFM.

In New York it was the same story. Sullivan was able to get people to meet again "after several months of relative slow activity." And this was in early 1970, less than two years into SPFM's existence. Caporale was to complain that the work of the organization had fallen on the shoulders of four or five people and that a broader base of active support was needed. It never materialized.

Sliding into Marriage

On a personal level, Sullivan and Pauline Fox had been companions for several months, when in the summer of 1970, just before the convention in Berkeley, he revealed that they had "slid" into marriage. That is, they began living together, deciding not to acquire a license for two reasons. First, Sullivan argued, a license was "static" but love was a "process." He wrote, "We both feel at peace knowing that love is the only reason we are together."

The second reason was to maintain as long as possible his canonical status as a priest. DiBenedetto had quipped that he was not excommunicated because he was only engaged. Sullivan insisted that he not be barred from priesthood because he was not married to a woman, only living with her. In fact, he contemplated asking for due process if his bishop excommunicated him, arguing that he had not attempted marriage. In the same vein, he wrote, "I may continue to wear my collar. In other words, I will try to pursue their legal system and hopefully force it up a dead-end alley."

These were exhilarating and frightening days. Charlie, then twenty-nine, and Pauline, thirty-one, had no idea where it all would lead them, but they were savoring the adventure of a lifetime. For over a year they lived in their van, traveling in slow stages to California to New Mexico to Texas and then up to Washington, D.C., and, finally, to New York. Charles reminisces with obvious delight on the experiences they had such as picking grapes in the Salinas valley, driving into Mexico, discussing their ideas with Dorothy Day, and being jailed in the nation's capital for protesting the war.

The Sullivans eventually did marry legally but have not had children. Charlie wonders if they would have been able to live the type of life they have lived had they been parents.

Political Radicalization

While attempting to shape for himself a new priesthood, Sullivan's life was also undergoing a major metamorphosis on another level. He was being radicalized, vis-à-vis the government and the economy, in the same way that he had already been radicalized regarding the bishops of the Church. For a time he worked in a gas station "being exploited at $1.75 an hour." Somehow this pedestrian experience of pumping gas and changing tires led him to state in a letter to a free ministry colleague: "You can feel the evils of capitalism and this has radicalized us to the extent that we may try to visit Cuba in the future."

In fact, a trip to Cuba almost materialized. During their year of traveling, Charlie and Pauline had camped outside Rosemary Ruether's house and so got to know her quite well. On a later occasion during a demonstration in Washington, D.C., she searched in vain for them. A group going to Cuba, at a time when it was forbidden by the U.S. government, wanted several religious people to join them, and Ruether thought Pauline and Charlie would be ideal.

A New Year's Letter

On January 1, 1971, Sullivan wrote a lengthy "what we've been doing during the past year" letter to friends. It recounted not just their wanderings but the essential shape that their new ministry was about to take. Although they would fantasize about spending two years traveling through Europe, Asia, and Africa before settling down, they soon would put down roots in Texas. Ironically, they who wanted to be free were to dedicate their lives to liberating those who were literally imprisoned, lobbying for prison reform, first in Texas and then in the entire country.

After leaving the SPFM convention, the letter relates, they did some honeymoon-like sightseeing, including hiking to the bottom of the Grand Canyon. Their ministry was always foremost on their minds, however. In Phoenix, they had an opportunity to publicize SPFM on television as well as to explain free ministry to "conservative Christians."

They then spent two months in Albuquerque with the DiBenedettos, preparing the convention *Proceedings* while sleeping in their van, parked in the DiBenedettos' driveway.

Introduction to Prison Ministry

Finally, nearing the end of their travels, Charlie and Pauline drove the five hundred miles across the Texas desert to San Antonio. Here they met Tom Flowers, an antiwar activist founder of Hennesey House, which was intended as "a community of politically-oriented individuals living together." Flowers became Sullivan's mentor and role model. Together they ran out on the football field during the Texas-Arkansas game with a banner "telling the 66,000 fans and millions watching on television not to pay their telephone war tax."

Sullivan and Flowers were not arrested during this civil disobedience, but Flowers was arrested subsequently for distributing antiwar leaflets on a military base. He was sentenced to six months in jail. Sullivan wrote: "I visit Tom every day through my collar and even had a Mass for the cell block. So far, I imagine the Chancery has not found out."

With Flowers in jail, the Sullivans felt obligated to remain and keep Hennesey House in operation. On Christmas Day their soup kitchen fed one hundred twenty people. The house itself, rather than a community of "politically-oriented individuals," had become a refuge for "winos" and homeless women and children. Despite his idealism, Sullivan confessed that the life was stressful. For her part, Pauline was tasting the underside of life in America as a substitute teacher in an inner-city school. However, rather than becoming disheartened by these experiences, they felt that at last they had found a place where they might exercise a ministry.

Being arrested was a badge of prestige and a sort of rite of initiation for activists. Sullivan had his opportunity to join the club when he and Pauline engaged in a civil disobedience in a campaign to reform the Bexar County, San Antonio jail, "one of the worst prisons in the United States."[4] Sullivan reported that being in the jail gave him the opportunity to experience personally "the horrible conditions and injustices to which the inmates are subjected." As part of the effort to bring about reform, he and Pauline went on a hunger strike. The experience of working for prison reform would soon provide them with a long-term direction in their lives.

May Day Mass Arrests, 1971

In the meanwhile, they were to have another prison experience, and for a different cause. The Vietnam War continued to poison the American soul and drive thousands of idealists to engage in protest actions. At the beginning of May 1971, the Sullivans were in Washington, D.C., joining thousands of others who wanted to pressure President Nixon and the Congress to end what they considered an immoral conflict. Both Charlie and Pauline were arrested. During that first week of May, a total of fifteen thousand people were hauled off to jail or to temporary detention centers, the largest mass arrest in the history of the U.S. Charlie says that the experience of spending several days in jail was like a retreat with a lot of deeply spiritual people.

The American Civil Liberties Union filed a lawsuit, claiming that the arrests were illegal. Twenty years later, in 1991, the court ruled that indeed the rights of citizen had been violated. As indemnification for being arrested, the Sullivans were awarded $2,300.

From SPFM to CURE

As well as prison reform and opposition to the war, there was, of course, SPFM, to which the Sullivans were still committed. In a letter to Bianchi in the summer of 1971, Sullivan said that SPFM was his community but that more efficient communication was essential, noting that the mechanics of a national organization required that mailing lists be kept up-to-date, new area coordinators named, and dues payment systematized.

The Sullivans attended the September convention in New York, to be discussed shortly, and in 1972 were in Los Angeles for the fourth national gathering. But that would be their last. By then, free ministry had been replaced by prison reform as the passion of their lives.

Although Sullivan had little success either as fund-raiser or organizer for SPFM, he and Pauline would successfully organize Citizens United for the Rehabilitation of Errants, or CURE, first as a lobbying group for convicts' rights in Texas and, since 1985, as a national organization based in Washington, D.C.

Sullivan's final link with FCM was through a 1974 *Diaspora* article, where he described the prison ministry in which he and Pauline were then fully absorbed.[5] No reference was made to priesthood, ministry, or Christ. Sullivan permitted their work to speak for itself. At the time, FCM had a mailing list of three hundred. CURE already had three thousand.

The present-day FCM and CORPUS leaders do not know Charlie and Pauline Sullivan nor do they know many of the others who were trailblazers for the movement. Collective memory can be short. Nevertheless, the landscape of American ministry is enriched by the contributions of those who decided that even if the institutional Church did not acknowledge them, they would continue to serve.

The Hierarchy as Supporters

Over the years, Sullivan, who once criticized bishops, has learned diplomacy. He has disassociated himself from free ministry in order not to endanger the solid working relationship he has with the Catholic Church. He says that the bishops are most supportive of the prison reform cause and that some CURE chapters receive funds from the Church's Campaign for Human Development. He relates that an official in the Texas Catholic Conference said to him, "Charlie, if you performed marriages or said illicit Masses, you would be burning every bridge you have built over the years."

Sullivan has learned that if you don't threaten them "on their own turf," bishops are most cooperative. One of his dreams is for them to issue a pastoral letter on prison reform.[6]

Reflecting on his life, Sullivan says that he does not want to be a priest anymore. He has no need to celebrate Mass or preach. He is happy, totally absorbed in a ministry to help others obtain the freedom he himself has found. He and Pauline do not promote free ministry as they did when they traveled the roads of America in their van, but they have not stopped living by its spirit.

Joseph J. Burns: Keeping Communication Lines Open

A profile of Joe Burns in the Spring 1980 *Diaspora* begins with the words, "Before there was FCM there was Joe Burns." While still active in the diocese of Brooklyn, Burns had organized the Association of Brooklyn Clergy (ABC), which in the late sixties drew hundreds of priests to meetings designed to promote solidarity among rank-and-file clergy and to plan for the anticipated greater democratization in the post-Vatican II Church. The ABC was one of the largest of the voluntary, union-like organizations that sprang up for a few years and then faded away. Many of the leaders, such as Burns, left the priesthood in frustration at the slow pace of change. The ABC was both a ray of sunlight and a futile effort to liberalize the Church. For Joe Burns, it was a continuation of his lifelong love affair with the priesthood in general and with the diocese of Brooklyn in particular.

Iona College Pastoral Counseling Program
Burns had prepared himself for a new career and a new consciousness even while serving as assistant pastor. He obtained a masters degree in pastoral counseling at Iona College in New Rochelle, New York. Many priests in the New York area had found the Iona program in the sixties a refreshingly freeing perspective on human life and a dramatically new approach to education after the

restrictive seminary formation of the fifties. New friendships were made, with women as well as men. Emerging theological ideas were shared over coffee. The long drives home were times to ask serious questions in the painful expectancy of stirred up hearts.

On his days off in the parish, Burns worked part time as a counselor in Harlem Hospital, giving him a foot in the door to what would become his new career as a hospital administrator. When he resigned from the priesthood in 1968 he took a position at Harlem, then in the turbulent process of becoming an institution more responsive to the needs of a poor, minority community.

A Career in Hospital Administration
Returning to school once again, this time for a degree in hospital administration, Burns began to move into increasingly more responsible posts in several New York area hospitals, eventually becoming vice president of St. Francis Hospital, Roslyn, New York.

In the mideighties, feeling the need for a change, Burns resigned his hospital position and attempted to start his own marketing and consulting business. When this failed, he returned to administration, this time with the Home Nursing Agency in Westchester, New York. Ever the vivacious, personable salesman, Burns, now sixty, his curly hair gray and his smiling Irish eyes framed in wrinkles, shows up regularly at gatherings of resigned priests in the New York area, making brief, impassioned speeches on his love for the priesthood and his confidence in Christ's abiding presence in a troubled Church and world.

Burns has been married for over twenty years. He and his wife, Audrey, have two sons, the older of whom attended Cathedral Prep High School, his father's alma mater. Initially, Audrey attended free ministry activities with her husband. Soon, however, she admitted that she was not interested in the issue and devoted herself to providing a home for her family.

Recruited by SPFM Leadership
By the spring of 1970, Durkin had decided that he did not want to serve a second year as SPFM executive secretary and approached Burns about assuming the post. Burns had been New York coordinator for several months, having taken over from former Maryknoller Joe Buko, who found himself too busy to continue. In that position, Burns had held several meetings, including a spring day of renewal at the New York Theological Seminary at which forty people heard

a presentation by resigned Vincentian James Megivern, former head of New York's St. John's University theology department.

In July, having received no reply, Durkin wrote a letter that convinced Burns to accept. Durkin challenged Burns with these words:

> It is very important to the future of the free ministry movement in the U.S.A. that SPFM have a committed executive secretary in a major city. The other priests in SPFM in your area have highly recommended you as the best man in N.Y.C. for the job. I hope you will accept—for the good of the Church.

In August, Burns attended the convention in Berkeley and met for the first time with the national leaders of the movement. In his response to Eugene Bianchi's presidential address, Burns underscored Bianchi's stress on ministry, rather than celibacy, and the determination not to criticize the Church but "to get in there and build something that is going to be of service to the people whom we love."

Preoccupied by his responsibilities back in New York, Burns told the convention delegates:

> At the hospital in Harlem where I work there are at this minute three hundred and forty young addicts who are sitting in the hospital taking it over because the city officials have talked about the drug problem for so long and have done nothing. The kids are tired of words and promises. . . . They want action.

Burns went on to say that he found the idea of free ministry creative, forward-looking, and positive. It was evident that his dream was to continue his work at the hospital but to do so as a priest in good standing.

Risk, Reconciliation, and Redemption

Central to that first recorded statement by the new SPFM national officer was the caution that the group must resist the temptation to go it alone, to turn its back on the institutional Church. The unwavering hallmark of Burns' ministry has been to work to change the Church, not to abandon it. Although he has remained a member of SPFM/FCM, he has opposed the separatist direction that the organization would take when spurned by the hierarchy.

In a report on the 1970 convention, Burns said that just as school was about to reopen and the children's work on the three "R's" resumed, so there were three "R's" that he had learned at the convention, namely, risk, reconciliation, and redemption. He said that risk was evident in "the national campaign for lay support for the married ministry and the place of women in every level of church structure." Risk was involved also in the team ministry proposal of Durkin and the concomitant fund-raising.

Reconciliation was evident in the tone of the convention, which was to avoid bitterness and regret and, according to Burns, "to struggle along lovingly with the brothers and sisters, whatever their outlook."

Finally, there was redemption. Burns drew attention to the ultimate purpose of all ministerial activity, namely, "the continuing Incarnation, the Word always being made flesh around us and hopefully, in small ways, because of us."

A Stressful Position

Despite his enthusiasm and pride with being on a team with people like Bianchi, Caporale, the DiBenedettos, and the Sullivans, the day-to-day tasks of secretary soon proved overwhelming to Burns. Whereas Durkin was a skilled and disciplined letter writer, Burns's correspondence was disjointed and filled with apologies for delay in responding.

Already by November, Durkin and DiBenedetto had complained to Bianchi about Burns's failure to forward any new names or address changes to the printer in Albuquerque. Bianchi wrote a tactful "Dear Joe" letter, urging the importance of an up-to-date mailing list and wondering if any clerical assistance might be offered.

Burns may have been negligent about correspondence, but he was a competent spokesman for SPFM at several important meetings. In November 1970, he attended the final day of the bishops' conference in Washington, D.C., distributing a press release and attending the press briefing. When it was announced that there was time for only one more question, Burns rose and inquired, "In view of the recent SPFM press release on the favorable returns of the American lay Catholics to the notion of the married ministry, are the bishops giving further consideration to this question, especially in view of the continuing exodus of priests from the structure?"

Cardinal Dearden responded that "this matter was going to be on the agenda for the April meeting, in preparation for the 1971 synod.

I don't think the priests who have married shall return to the active role as priests so much as married men will be ordained wherever there is need. At least this is the way it looks to me."[7]

1971 Convention: Convergence or Impotence?

Burns's major contribution to SPFM was coordinating the 1971 convention. As Durkin had organized the 1970 convention near his home in California, so his successor assumed the responsibility of planning a meeting in New York. Burns selected Union Theological Seminary as the site, scene of his most successful previous gathering, and went about the task of developing an agenda. However, whereas Burns hoped to attract participants by enlisting well-known speakers, the other officers were concerned with the more critical issue of the organization's future.

For example, just a few days before the Labor Day convention, Burns received a lengthy letter from Durkin that contained an ominous message, one which presaged what would be the stressful tone of the convention. Durkin wrote:

> Yesterday (August 21), at the West Coast SPFM pre-convention workshop, sixteen of us came together to ask some hard questions. Like why should SPFM continue to exist? What evidence is there our priestly ministry is being called for or even used? Why are we broke financially, attracting few members to our movement, especially from among those recently leaving the clergy, and ignored for all intents and purposes by most priests and all the bishops? Will any bishops or local priests attend our NYC convention (count them!)? Are we fooling ourselves by continuing SPFM?

Durkin's gloomy reflections seemed well founded, judging by the attendance at and the results of the convention. Despite Burns's substantial preconvention publicity, including ads in *National Catholic Reporter* and *Commonweal* and a mention in the Brooklyn *Tablet*, only 106 people assembled for what had been heralded as a major assembly on convergence.

Echoing Durkin's concerns, outgoing SPFM president Bianchi delivered his "Does SPFM Have a Future?" address. Rosemary Radford Ruether's paper was titled "Organizing for Survival," but it might have been called "Does the Catholic Church Have a Future?" Her words were heavy with pessimism about the prospects for reform and presented what must have seemed like an impossible challenge to struggling groups like SPFM.[8]

The SPFM leadership had identified five other groups as likely collaborators in a reform coalition: NAPR, NFPC, National Association of the Laity (NAL), National Assembly of Women Religious (NAWR), and Seminarians for Ministerial Renewal (SMR). All had been invited to send representatives, and several did. Among those who heard Bianchi and Ruether issue the summons for convergence, or at least closer cooperation, were Sister Ursula Reid, representing NAWR, Rev. Joseph Stewart of NFPC, and Richard Kissner of NAL. Also present were influential figures who might lend their weight to the cause, including William Birmingham, editor of *Cross Currents*, and the theologians Gregory Baum, James Megivern, and Steven Kelleher.

Post-convention Follow-up

Burns attracted media attention to the convention. A picture of Burns listening to future FCM president William Manseau appeared in *The New York Times*, together with a brief article that stated that all six organizations "favor self-determination for priests and nuns on the question of marriage, experiments in styles of worship and freedom of choice for religious in dress, employment and residence."[9]

Although Burns's term as executive secretary ended, he once again succeeded the mercurial Durkin, this time as national vice president and assumed responsibility for attempting to follow up on the convention's call for convergence. It soon became clear that three of the six organizations were virtually defunct and in no position to participate.

SMR had never been more than a few liberal-minded candidates for the priesthood attempting with little success to fashion an SPFM-like organization. Not only were they not represented at the 1971 convention, they did not respond to any subsequent correspondence.[10]

NAPR, out of which SPFM had emerged, had ceased to hold meetings and when approached about convergence, its president, Robert Francoeur, suggested a merger of the two groups. Responding for SPFM, Roméo DiBenedetto countered that since NAPR was virtually defunct, it should just turn over its mailing list to SPFM.

NAL had become little more than a paper organization, comprised of a few reform-minded people who had generated some initial attention to their conventions but had soon lost momentum. Correspondence with William Caldwell, NAL president, revealed scant organizational energy for survival, let alone for joining forces with others for what Rosemary Ruether envisioned as a parliamentary structure to represent the Catholic Church in America.[11]

A fourth group, NAWR, through its coordinator, Sister Ethne Kennedy, had expressed some interest in the idea of convergence. In May of 1971, Sister Kennedy had replied to an invitation from Eugene Bianchi to the SPFM September convention by indicating that the idea of convergence was "in the air" but that perhaps more time was needed before a serious project might be undertaken. She referred to a letter from Rosemary Ruether that stressed the need for the convergence of renewal movements, since the bishops were "paddling backwards as fast as possible." However, Ruether gave Kennedy a convenient excuse for avoiding immediate action by adding:

> I would think that in about 18 months perhaps the various renewal movements might have matured to the point where they might be interested in undertaking a really high level, well planned and financed conference with the best people in the country to bring together our thinking on what the shape of ministry and community should be becoming.[12]

After several abortive attempts at convening a meeting, Burns made one last effort early in 1972. In a memo to the SPFM executive board he reported:

> On our efforts to get the renewal groups together this month, I only heard from E. Kennedy—and she could not make the February 19th date.... I have the strong suspicion that the other groups are either not too strong, or are not interested in converging.

NFPC: Final Hope for Convergence
The final group to which SPFM turned in its initiative on convergence was NFPC. That group's president, Frank Bonnike, was highly supportive of SPFM and, as will be seen in chapter 9, worked hard to obtain admission of the married priests' group to NFPC, which represented the active priests of the country. However, the effort to forge some kind of alliance with NFPC also would fail.

The March–April 1972 issue of *Diaspora* summarized the arduous process of negotiation with NFPC in words that indicate that the road to convergence with active priests had proven to be a dead end as had the hope of establishing a working relationship with the hierarchy. Roméo DiBenedetto's report said, with a tone of resignation:

> We believe this verifies that we in SPFM must head in a new direction, since NFPC is quickly retreating from [its more welcoming position of last year.] NFPC is losing its young and liberal members who try to update the church and whose hearts are with us. The more conservative membership is rapidly growing in strength.

Retreating to the Local Level

Hope for convergence having faded and SPFM still floundering in its search for a viable strategy, Burns resigned from national responsibilities and turned his attention once again to local needs. He sent a letter to resigned priests in the New York metropolitan area asking if there would be interest in attending "what might become a monthly affair at the Bavarian Inn [a Manhattan restaurant]." The letter explained that the purpose was to provide a setting, "Rotary Club style," for resigned priests to meet and exchange information on such matters as job prospects, suggestions for necessary additional schooling, and where the nearest "alive liturgy" might be found.

Burns said that he was a member of SPFM and had invited Rocco Caporale and SPFM New York representative Jerry Grudzen to attend and to "outline what has been happening around the country." However, Burns was very careful to insist that the lunch was not a "plot to enroll formers in any organization." He had learned that SPFM tended to frighten away as many people as it attracted.

Shepherded by Burns, the Bavarian Inn meetings were held monthly for several years, providing a valuable service to men, especially while in the process of transition.

However, the national demographic shift to the suburbs had an impact even on married priests. The Bavarian Inn location was convenient only for people working in the city. As resigned priests moved to outlying areas, the Manhattan group was discontinued and a similar one inaugurated at Hofstra University on Long Island. It has continued as a monthly social event for about ten years.

Brooklyn Convocations

Burns lived within the confines of the Brooklyn diocese most of his life, maintaining warm relationships with many active priests. One of those priests, John Fagan, was on the Brooklyn Priests Senate and with Burns established a subcommittee of its personnel committee called "Fratres in Unum," which was authorized by Bishop Francis J. Mugavero to develop a program aimed at healing the wounds suffered by many in the process of leaving the active ministry. To this end a series of convocations was initiated at the college seminary in 1977. It was at the first such gathering that Rocco Caporale delivered his address "From Temple Priesthood to People of God." Although attendance has dwindled, meetings continue to be held twice a year, serving as occasions for a retreat-like experience for former colleagues and their wives. At times, it has been suggested that the group take a more activist direction, but the suggestion has been met with polite silence.

Burns also worked with Fagan to develop guidelines for the utilization of married priests in local parishes. Many pastors were not comfortable having married priests in their congregations and were hesitant to allow any participation without a clear signal from the bishop. In order to resolve this problem, a letter was drawn up and about to be issued by Bishop Mugavero, when the newly elected Pope John Paul II severely restricted the process of dispensation from the priesthood and signaled to the bishops that being too cozy with resigned priests was not appropriate. Bishop Mugavero never sent the letter.

Burns's attendance at the Brooklyn convocations is witness to his affection for the priestly fellowship. The name of the sponsoring committee, "Fratres in Unum," recalls the song that was sung decades ago by the younger seminarians as a serenade to those who were about to be ordained from the Seminary of the Immaculate Conception in Huntington, Long Island, New York. Burns was one of those who sang that song for five years as he watched his brothers go off to their lives as priests. On the sixth year, in 1954, as his own class embarked on the deceptively tranquil waters of the priesthood, he heard for a final time:

> "Behold how good and joyful it is for brothers to dwell together in unity."

In his heart, Joe Burns still sings that song.

Part III

Transformation of SPFM into FCM and the Founding of CORPUS

7

From Theology to Politics

When official leadership abdicates its creative responsibilities in times of both Christian and worldwide crises, then the resultant power vacuum is a direct and awesome vocation to groups such as SPFM to provide transitional leadership out of which a new official leadership will emerge. We can no longer shirk this responsibility by continuing in a purely reactive posture. Converged, we can turn this church of ours around and still preserve the best of our traditions and of our faith. Separately, we are rather easily and summarily dealt with.

This is the creative moment.

Bernard McGoldrick, SPFM president, 1971

Movements and organizations are like relay teams. One leader runs a lap as fast as he or she can and then, at the point of exhaustion, passes the baton to a fresh teammate. When Eugene Bianchi reached the end of his term, Bernard McGoldrick was there on the dusty track, his hand outstretched, to accept the presidency from his enervated predecessor. McGoldrick was relatively new to the movement and not yet been touched by the sense of defeat that infected some of the pioneers. However, within the two years of his term, he also would stumble and fall several times. What he accomplished, though, was of critical significance. When the initial goals seemed unattainable and initial strategies futile, McGoldrick reconceptualized the movement, offering a fresh direction to a disoriented constituency and infusing, for a time, renewed momentum into a cause on the brink of dissolution.

As a counterpoint to McGoldrick's effort to mobilize a national coalition and an international power base, Robert Duryea offered an appealing example of local pastoral leadership. A man with no pretensions to scholarship, he was one of the most witty and lovable of those priests who had been seized by the dream of a free ministry.

Bernard McGoldrick: The Church as a Political Institution

In October 1990, the rape of a high school student in a Paris suburb precipitated a student protest movement that, within three weeks, put more than one hundred thousand demonstrators on the streets of Paris. At the same time, about one hundred fifty thousand students marched in dozens of other French cities. The students demanded better security and other improvements in the country's forty-seven hundred senior high schools.

The movement was coordinated by three ad hoc student committees and quickly won support across France from teachers' unions, major political parties, and parents' associations. In mid-November, President François Mitterrand met with the student leaders and promised that many of their demands would be met.[1]

Two decades before, Bernard McGoldrick, a professor of political science at California State College at Fresno, had hoped to generate a similar denouement to the free ministry movement. If an alliance could be forged with other reform groups, then the authorities would be forced to negotiate. The game was politics and the weapon was power.

McGoldrick articulated his strategy in a front page article in the November–December 1971 *Diaspora.* He wrote:

> Sufficient time has elapsed since our New York Convention (September 3–5) to permit an assessment of some new directions in which SPFM is headed. These new paths are implicit in SPFM's commitment to leading the way toward "convergence" of all renewal groups in the U.S.A. Convergence is a political program. What is new about it is that it is recognized explicitly for the first time that new theologies of Christian ministry must be partially

theologies of power. Political power and charism are clearly not contradictory.

When the French high school students initiated their protest movement in mid-October of 1990, they could not have dreamed that by early November they would be backed by hundreds of thousands of students, allied with powerful elements of French society, and sitting down with a president very concerned about the implications of the protest for his government. Bernard McGoldrick did dream of something along those lines for the free ministry movement. *His* dream, however, did not come true.

Lessons in Political Science

In his writings and addresses, McGoldrick used his training in political science to teach free ministers lessons in power politics. He said that SPFM had been weak because it was reactive rather than active. He argued that waiting for a spontaneous grass roots renewal of Christian ministry was futile and actually aided the "reactionary power-holders" of the Church to "freeze us out of our Christian inheritance." What was needed was for SPFM to accept the opportunity for leadership: "Latent pressure groups and interest groups become actualized only through leadership."

For McGoldrick, "the politics of convergence" was the key to renewal. Under SPFM leadership, the champions of reform could rescue the Church in America from stagnation. His analysis of the situation echoed the Marxist political ideology then so attractive to many academics and revealed a firm confidence that he hoped would spark a revolution within the Church. He wrote:

(The American bishops) now seem relatively helpless. We must neither abandon nor scorn them. We must help them by affording, on a temporary and transitional basis, the hope and encouragement that thousands of priests and millions of Catholics need. They need to know that potential unofficial leadership will not stand idly by while actual official leadership reneges on the promises of Vatican II. . . . The dreary fact is that most of the hierarchy, under Pope Paul's direction, has effectively retired. The future official leadership will be drawn from among those men and women who now find themselves in the position of loyal opposition.

Advice from Cardinal Suenens and Hans Küng

In 1990, having just retired from Fresno State and reflecting back over the nearly two decades that had elapsed since his leadership position in free ministry, McGoldrick told two stories to illustrate how he felt then and how he feels now.

In March 1971, Cardinal Leo Suenens of Belgium visited the United States. Suenens was a reform-minded prelate, open to giving the free ministry idea a fair hearing. Suenens met with Bianchi in New York and with McGoldrick in California. McGoldrick brought his wife to the meeting and was told that she could not be included. McGoldrick bristled and said, "No. It doesn't work that way. This is what it is all about. No wife; no talk." The cardinal's aide agreed on the condition that the press not be told of the meeting.

The conversation was pleasant, with Suenens indicating that he was being criticized by conservatives for his overtures to reform. As the meeting ended, McGoldrick asked the cardinal if he had any suggestions. Suenens answered, "Seek and find Jesus in your own life."

McGoldrick rejected this advice, convinced that the issue was power. He recalled that his reaction had been "Talk of spirituality is bullshit." The struggle was about who was going to run the organization. However, as the years passed, McGoldrick became less of a radical firebrand and more reflective. "I'm over sixty now, and I think I've grown a little wiser. It's a massive thing we have here. It's like trying to move the rock of Gibraltar."

On another occasion, several SPFMers had dinner in Los Angeles with Hans Küng. The eminent theologian counseled patience and prayer. Once again McGoldrick was disturbed. "These guys are useless. They don't realize that what we are involved with is a brass-knuckles type of old-fashioned political battle. It has nothing to do with God, Jesus Christ, faith, or anything else. It's pure politics." Once again, as time passed, McGoldrick came to appreciate the wisdom of Küng's words, commenting: "I think I was half right, but I had lost sight of the other half."

Congruence Between Free Ministry and the Jesuit Tradition

McGoldrick was a native of Philadelphia. In 1949, halfway through college, he joined the Maryland Province of the Society of Jesus. Equipped with a Ph.D. in political science from Georgetown University, he undertook a predictable career in Jesuit schools. However, in 1969 he met his future wife, Catherine ("Cappy"), who had been a member of the religious of the Sacred Heart order. He resigned from the Jesuits, married, moved to California, and undertook what would be a twenty-year tenure at Fresno State. The McGoldricks have two children, now in their late teens. They live in a small town near the southern entrance to Yosemite National Park. Cappy teaches part time in their local high school.

Like Hemmer, Bianchi, and Caporale, McGoldrick brought a Jesuit theological perspective to the formative period of the free ministry movement. That perspective, according to McGoldrick, included a distinction between Church and kingdom, between the ecclesiastical organization and the Kingdom of God.

Furthermore, the Jesuit tradition allowed for more freedom in ministry than did that of secular priests. There was no sense of being locked into a diocesan structure. Superiors were viewed more as peers than bishop-like authority figures. In this regard, Jesuits were well suited to provide leadership to the movement for fuller ministerial self-determination.

McGoldrick contends that the modern world demands a new priesthood. There is such strong emphasis on the integrity of the individual, on the need to affirm one's own self, that the model of ministry inherited from the past is totally inadequate. He says:

> I didn't go through all that training to be an altar boy. I'm a grown and mature man, on the same footing as a bishop. Priests have been reduced to the level of altar boys. It shouldn't be that way. Each is called to ministry by God. The foundation of priesthood is not based on a bishop. It's personal.

It was this sense of his innate right to self-determination in ministry that animated McGoldrick in the early seventies and remains with him today.

Hopeful Early Experiences in Free Ministry

McGoldrick's initial experience of the potential for a free ministry occurred in the very setting in which Hemmer several years earlier had envisioned exercising his own ministry—on the campus of a secular college. McGoldrick found the Newman chaplain at Fresno State open to collaboration with a married priest. Meetings were held, liturgies celebrated, and free ministry speakers invited to address the collegiate community.

McGoldrick found the climate of the late sixties and early seventies favorable for discussions of a married priesthood. He was even invited to address the bishop and priests of the diocese of Stockton, California. However, after a few years of such openness, he found that the official Church closed down and wanted to hear no more from what was felt to be a discredited band of dissidents.

Assuming the Mantle of Leadership

McGoldrick first met the SPFM leaders at the 1970 convention and went to New York the following year excited about the cause and armed with his political strategy. What he encountered there was a movement on the verge of disintegration. Bianchi, Caporale, and Durkin were unwilling to continue in office. Since there was no one else with a plan of action or the heart for leadership, McGoldrick accepted the position of president.

In a series of articles in *Diaspora* during the following year, he wrote glowing reports of the strides being made toward achieving the goals of the movement. In fact, in the July–August 1972 issue, just before the convention in Los Angeles, McGoldrick asserted:

> This has been a year of genuine and measurable progress for SPFM and for the Free Ministry in general. For example, our "Convergence" theme, worked out in N.Y. last year and aimed at bringing U.S. Catholic renewal groups together for certain projects, has now been adopted as a program for the National Association of Laity and has been taken over as an editorial policy of the *National Catholic Reporter*.

Actually, as has been indicated, NAL was nearly defunct, and the reference to a *National Catholic Reporter* "editorial policy" is puzzling at best. McGoldrick did, however, have a lengthy article published in *NCR* in which he analyzed the Church as "an underdeveloped political system" and "a threatened authoritarian regime." He argued that "oppression in the church, especially of the priests' liberation movements, is not only scientifically inevitable but also healing and creative" in terms of the process of institutional development.[2]

Probing International Linkages

Another arrow in McGoldrick's quiver was the prospect of an alliance with free ministry groups in other countries. In words that would lead the casual reader to imagine that SPFM must indeed be a powerful group, McGoldrick wrote:

> The new hope consists in unmistakable signs that the Free Ministry mission, both here and abroad, is beginning to take hold. . . . We are in contact now with free ministers on four other continents.[3]

In line with this global perspective, the 1972 convention called for the convening of an International Congress on Ministry and Social Change to be held in Geneva, Switzerland, in two years.[4] Attending the convention, along with about one hundred others, was Carlos Rodriguez, president of the International Association of Married Priests, based in Bogotá, Colombia. Together, McGoldrick and Rodriguez conceived the idea of an international meeting to which NFPC, the Canadian Conference of Priests, and the European Association of Priests would be invited. The expectation of cooperation from NFPC would be puzzling in the light of the rebuff SPFM received in March to its request for affiliation were it not for the fact that the NFPC president, Frank Bonnike, attended the SPFM convention and continued to be supportive of its goals.

McGoldrick's vision was more grandiose than an assembly of priests. He proposed that the meeting be ecumenical. He wrote:

> Although the initiative for such a congress comes from a movement (SPFM) with ties to and peculiar interest in Roman Catholic Ministries, we intend this suggestion to be a seriously ecumenical one since the crisis of ministry is not confined to any one communion. Our urgent suggestion is, moreover, what appears to us to be only a logical development of what has been taking place along national lines for some time both in the USA and elsewhere, that is, the gradual realization of the need for concerted efforts of various in-structure and out-of-structure renewal groups to replace words and ideological posturing with concrete, practical action and organization of new christian ministries.[5]

To implement the proposed international congress, an SPFM international communications committee was established in Chicago. Vincent Eckholm, one of the founding members of SPFM as

well as Chicago area coordinator, served with Ben Giovanne and
Frank Netzel. Sparse evidence suggests that groups contacted expressed some interest but offered no active participation in the
planning process. That was left squarely in the hands of SPFM, which
proved incapable of marshaling the substantial commitment of
resources required.

IDOC: International Documentation on the Contemporary Church

In conjunction with the planned international congress, McGoldrick
himself wrote to International Documentation on the Contemporary
Church (IDOC), headquartered in Rome, requesting their participation. They replied that they wanted to be kept informed on the
progress for implementing the meeting. Potentially, IDOC could
play a valuable role in the process of internationalizing ministerial
reform. Although not a priest's group, it had plans for a special
project called "Exchange and Documentation among Priests." That
project, however, was canceled. In one of several letters to SPFM
officers, the IDOC director, William Jerman, said that the IDOC debt
was "at least 40,000 times as large as that of the SPFM." This reference
to debt was in the context of thanking SPFM for sending IDOC a free
subscription to *Diaspora*.

Supportive of the belief that the time was ripe for the interna-
tionalization of the movement was a document published by IDOC
that summarized developments in the priesthood in countries around
the world. The report concluded:

> Symptomatic of the unrest is the post-Vatican II burgeon-
> ing of priests' organizations—official and unofficial—in
> many countries. Among or despite their differences, the
> outstanding feature common to all of them is a sense of
> independence, surely without parallel in the history of the
> Church, and itself a characteristic of contemporary church
> life.[6]

Misreading the Spirit of the Times

In light of this unrest and the worldwide urgency for change, why
did so many free ministry plans in the early seventies fail? Year after
year, impressive projects were announced, only to die aborning. It
was as if words were spoken in a dream, only to be forgotten upon
awakening.

The basic problem was a gross misreading of the spirit of the times. McGoldrick had said in his call for the meeting in Geneva:

> Masses of believing but bewildered peoples around the globe await action that is clear, decisive and creative in the tremendously important area of ministerial leadership. The time is ripe for a total revamping. . . .

To be successful a social movement must appeal to "the masses," as the movement of French students referred to earlier rallied thousands of people to action. However, since 1966, when NAPR began the effort to generate enthusiasm for a married priesthood, the widespread support never materialized. Although surveys consistently showed that a majority of Catholics would accept married priests, such support could never be transformed into action. When it came to the more radical agenda that was emerging in SPFM, even people sympathetic to a married priesthood became uncomfortable. The free ministers beat the drum to summon the crowd, but few responded.

There were three reasons for this apathy on the part of Catholics: 1) American Catholics did not sense that there was a crisis. Most had not yet experienced any shortage of priests. 2) Even if there was a shortage and even if the "working conditions" of priests were unsatisfactory, the importance of the priest had declined in the lives of most Catholics. It was not the same as if there had been a shortage of doctors or teachers or hairdressers. In a postimmigrant-generation, highly educated Church, the traditional role of priest had become less essential to the community; and 3) most importantly, as free ministers were to find over and over again, while many Catholics might criticize the Church and even walk away from it in disgust, very few would engage in active rebellion against it.

Is Mandatory Celibacy Unconstitutional?
Yet another political initiative made by McGoldrick was an attempt to have mandatory celibacy declared unconstitutional. His argument was developed in a letter sent in March 1972 to a Washington, D.C. lawyer and also to the American Civil Liberties Union.

The lawyer had been recommended by Daniel Maguire of the Marquette University theology department. Some five years before, Maguire had contemplated taking Catholic University in Washington, D.C., to court for having fired him when he left the priesthood and married. Maguire, a member of the original board of directors of NAPR, claimed that he had been discriminated against by being deprived of employment for religious reasons at an institution funded in part by the federal government. Maguire was given a cash settlement before the case was brought to court.

McGoldrick thought the issue was worth testing. He argued, as Maguire had intended to do, that mandatory celibacy was a violation of the Bill of Rights. A priest who marries is deprived of the right to exercise his profession, has no due process, no pension, and no severance pay.

McGoldrick was not unmindful of the principle of separation of church and state. But he asked:

> Does the separation clause give an organized religion the right to demand anything it wishes and to inflict disabilities upon that religion's members and officials, which disabilities flow over into civil life? If so, then it would seem that a religion could go to the extremes of demanding infant sacrifice of its members and ministers and the courts could not intervene.

The response from the American Civil Liberties Union in April 1972 dashed hopes that this approach to eliminating mandatory celibacy would succeed. Paul N. Halvonik, the legal director of the ACLU, pointed out in a letter to McGoldrick that the First Amendment guaranteed the free exercise of religion. Although some behavior such as ritual slaughter could not be permitted, other practices that one may not like are not thereby unconstitutional. He argued:

> It would, to my mind, be a gross invasion of the Catholic Church's First Amendment rights were the Federal Courts to begin participating in decisions about the proper job qualifications for priests. Churches are not labor unions and they are not private businesses. Churches are, unlike those other institutions, given a special protection by the First Amendment.
>
> I think the Catholic celibacy rule is foolish; I think the exclusion of women from the priesthood is foolish. That is only a partial list of my disagreements with the Catholic Church. But, as long as the Catholic Church goes its way and lets me go mine, I do not see how I can fairly request

the government to force the Church to adopt ideas I
consider more congenial to a modern society.[7]

McGoldrick abandoned the notion of challenging the constitu-
tionality of mandatory celibacy, but he did probe one further legal
possibility, namely, suing the Church for job discrimination. He
claimed that in various parts of the country bishops were blocking
the secular employment of resigned priests. McGoldrick said:

> If a priest applies for a job at some state social agency and
> they are about to give him a job, it is possible that the
> agency will get a telephone call from the bishop asking
> them not to do it. I believe this happened in Tennessee.[8]

Although McGoldrick did not follow up on this idea, in the late
eighties FCM took the case of Daniel Patrick Duffy through the
California courts. As will be related in chapter 10, Duffy was fired as
a state prison chaplain upon the intervention of the local bishop.

McGoldrick's Legacy: The Call to Freedom

By the fall of 1973, rather than spearheading a worldwide movement
for ministerial renewal, SPFM was financially bankrupt and ideo-
logically fragmented. A disillusioned McGoldrick faded into the
peace and security of his private life, remarking to his wife, Cappy,
"I have done as much as I could do." He had left the Jesuits only a few
years before, with little more than the clothes on his back and a
passion to bring to the entire Church the enhanced sense of freedom
that he experienced within his own life. But there comes a time to let
someone else attempt to carry forward the cause.

In the popular inspirational novel *Joshua*, neighbors ask Joshua, a
modern-day Jesus, What do you mean by religion? The response
might have been written by McGoldrick or any of the others who
shared the dream of a renewed Christianity. Joshua answered:

> God never intended that religion become what it is today.
> Jesus came to earth to try to free people from that kind of
> regimented religion where people are threatened if they
> don't obey rules and rituals invented by the clergy. Jesus
> came to teach people that they are God's children and, as
> God's children, they are free, free to grow as human
> beings, to become beautiful people as God intended![9]

Robert Duryea: From Politics to Pastoral Ministry

At the September 1972 convention in Los Angeles, Robert and Lu Duryea succeeded Roméo and Vicki DiBenedetto as national executive secretaries and served in this capacity for two years, bridging the transition from SPFM to FCM. All of the hundreds of letters that Bob wrote during the period were signed "Bob & Lu," a tribute more to his love for his wife than evidence of active collaboration. Bob was well into his forties when he married Lu, a woman nearly twenty years his junior. He had found a treasure and celebrated it continuously.

With wit and common sense, Duryea maintained critical links with the far-flung executive board. Furthermore, he was a model of the kind of daring behavior that many felt was needed if ministerial breakthroughs were to occur. In a November 1972 letter to the board in which he introduced himself as new executive secretary, Duryea said:

> Briefly, we are a happy, heterosexual couple, with one seven year old boy. I had been a priest of the Archdiocese of San Francisco for 25 years, and married for the last seven of those years, before being zapped by the rusty guillotine of Canon Law. Now I am co-leader of a small, healthy Sunday community. I am marginally busy with a private counseling practice, which leaves me free enough to do this (we think) very important work for SPFM. Lu is very busy as R.N. in charge of the Progressive Care Area at the hospital where we met.

Duryea had gained considerable local notoriety when it was disclosed in 1971 that he had served for seven years as pastor of St. Peter's Church in Pacifica, California, while married and the father of a five-year-old son, named after the reigning Pope Paul. Hundreds of parishioners petitioned Archbishop Joseph McGucken to allow Duryea to retain his pastorate. Instead of being retained, he was excommunicated.

Personal Witness to a Married Priesthood

Once elected to the board of SPFM, Duryea took every opportunity to publicize the organization in the context of his own unusual personal experience. He appeared on the Mike Douglas television show, and articles about him were carried in several California newspapers.

In April 1973, the conflict with the bishop now two years behind him and also having found support and fellowship in SPFM, Duryea could reflect:

> Being publicly excommunicated is a very freeing experience. When you are completely washed out of the whole picture, there are no more pretenses to keep up. You can say what you want and nobody can hurt you.

But he had been hurt. He was one of those rare Catholic priests who had experienced serving as a married priest and who was convinced that his ministry was, if anything, enhanced by the fact that he had a partner. All his life he had been a parish priest and long remained eager to be restored to that position for which he felt most qualified and which had afforded him so much joy.

After being replaced at Pacifica, Duryea shared with an Anglican priest the leadership of a group of fifty people who met each Sunday in the co-op market in Sunnyvale, California. The congregation consisted of people who were turned off by their own parish churches and who were searching for something more satisfying.

Duryea resisted with difficulty the temptation to return to Pacifica and to set up an alternative Catholic parish as former parishioners there had invited him to do. He wrote:

> I might go back as a leader of a group who wanted what we had before. The thought of leading an underground or something like that was very distasteful before. But the changes in the Catholic world are no longer underground. The leadership of the Roman Catholic Church is not going to listen to voices that feel change is necessary.[10]

These pessimistic words were written in the spring of 1973, by which time, like many other free ministers, Duryea was becoming convinced that the moment for change was passing and that the alternatives now were either to cease and desist or to go it alone.

Fortunately for him, just as his enthusiasm for free ministry began to crumble, Duryea's personal career situation solidified. He was hired in September 1973 as a counselor in the newly created Fremont Youth Service Center. Over the years he has been promoted to deputy director, then acting director, and finally director of a staff of eight. In 1990, Duryea reached age seventy and was planning to retire from the agency after eighteen years of service.

Spiritually, the years between 1973 and the present have been turbulent and unsatisfying. From being the joyful troubadour of free ministry, Duryea became bitter and angry. For years he avoided formal religion and considered himself an agnostic. Lu never shared his bitterness and in recent years has helped Bob to move beyond his anger and rejection of religion. Once again he calls himself a Christian but is not sure what he believes. He is saddened by the thought that he has deprived his two children, now young adults, of their Christian heritage.

Defining the Role of Executive Secretary

At the 1972 convention, McGoldrick had been reelected president. In October he wrote a candid letter to Duryea, with whom he would have to work in close collaboration. The letter, which was largely a job description for the executive secretary, revealed some of the problems of a loose-knit organization such as SPFM. McGoldrick described frankly the difficulties he had encountered the previous year when the DiBenedettos held the position.

Perhaps confusion and tension were unavoidable because the secretary's address was the SPFM "national office." Accordingly, correspondence was directed there rather than to the president. From McGoldrick's perspective, the DiBenedettos had exceeded the role of secretary and entered the realm of policy making, which McGoldrick felt belonged to the board under the direction of the president. Roméo DiBenedetto had been sending out lengthy "epistles" that McGoldrick felt were both usurping the role of *Diaspora* and dictating strategies and agendas that did not represent group consensus.

On the other hand, McGoldrick did not want Duryea to feel that he was to be little more than a clerk, and so he added, "Your role is creative, however, and not merely administrative." But how was one to be "creative" without crossing the line of setting policy? It was inevitable that a professional in a "national office" would make decisions on his own initiative when consultation with the board was time-consuming and expensive. In terms of day-to-day business matters, the secretary *was* the organization. As will be seen, this problem would cause pain for Duryea when he attempted to work with the new officers elected at the 1973 convention. Chapter 13 will

relate how in 1990 a similar tension ruptured the relationship between the CORPUS board and its paid secretary, Terence Dosh.

Organizational Crises Continue

In January 1973, Duryea wrote to *Diaspora* recipients indicating
that SPFM was $1,000 in the red and asking for some sign of sup-
port for the movement and hopefully a contribution. A few months
later, he reported that only one out of six of the people contacted
had responded.

An even more serious crisis emerged when McGoldrick, concerned
about the fate of the proposal for an international meeting, asked
Duryea to contact once again the men in Chicago who had volunteered
to serve as a committee. The same group also had volunteered to host
the 1973 convention, and the area vice president, Vincent Eckholm,
had offered to establish SPFM archives at the University of Illinois.
Much responsibility had been vested in the Chicago group. Unfortu-
nately, not only did they not follow through on the international
meeting, as already mentioned, but the archives never were activated
and the offer to host the convention withdrawn. As Duryea wrote to
McGoldrick, "Big pretensions, then not a word of follow-up."

As a consequence, a tone of anxiety pervaded the correspondence
during the first half of 1973 as the leaders searched for a location for
the convention. Finally, in May, the New York vice presidents, Gerald and Marita Grudzen, offered to host the convention in New York.

Not all of the crises were organizational. There was also much
going on in the personal lives of men who recently had changed
careers, married, and were in the process of starting families. Perhaps
the most striking coincidence of all was that, in 1972–73, the wives of
all the executive board members as well as of Grudzen and Manseau
gave birth to daughters. The correspondence included references to
breathing exercises, babies being late, parents kept up at night, and,
not least of all, the increased expenses entailed in supporting growing families. Duryea, who was fifty-two when his daughter was
born, frequently alluded to how poorly his private counseling practice was doing. McGoldrick suggested delicately that he might not be
able to attend the New York convention because of financial constraints augmented by the birth of his second child.

To Change the Church or to Serve the People?

Although Duryea was very conscientious as a national official, his
heart was on the local pastoral level. Besides conducting a service

each Sunday for a small community, he tried to organize a First Friday group at his house for resigned priests and their wives. He believed that the key to free ministry was serving people on the local level. In this respect, he was at odds with McGoldrick. The perspectives of these two men embodied a central tension within the movement, namely, between those who saw SPFM as an agent for changing public consciousness and Church regulations, and those who saw it largely as a support network of people engaged in direct pastoral service.

McGoldrick's view of SPFM was elaborated in a January 1973 letter addressed to the "Dear Brothers and Sisters of SPFM." The letter reflected on the movement and on his role within it. It also revealed the penchant he, like Bianchi, had for *asking* questions and his difficulty in *answering* them. He said that some of the questions he had been asking himself were:

> Do we represent anything real? Who or what authenticates our meaning, our efforts, our statements, our witness? Have we already served any legitimate goal-in-the-Spirit that we may have had and should we now close the book?[11]

This soul-searching would continue in a series of letters that concluded with the 1973 convention at which McGoldrick's term and, in a sense, his agony would end. There was a striking parallel between Gene Bianchi's position at the end of his two years as president and Bernie McGoldrick at the end of his. Both men were conflicted. They had invested two of the prime years of their lives in a cause and had gained painfully meager results.

McGoldrick attempted to clarify his position by posing and answering a set of sixteen questions that he called "criteria of discernment." On his own Mount Horeb in the Sierras, he had gone through a protracted assessment of himself and of free ministry. Now he needed to share with his colleagues the fruit of his reflections. What he concluded was that SPFM was mainly an idea and that the task of the group was to spread that idea. Once the world had heard and hopefully accepted the idea, then the objective would have been achieved and the little group could fold its tent. He cited surveys that found that the idea of ministerial reform, including a married priesthood, had been widely accepted. Therefore, he concluded, SPFM had achieved its goal.

Duryea's Alternative View

While McGoldrick espoused, at least in the later phase of involvement, a consciousness-raising role for SPFM, Duryea promoted an alternative view. In an April 1973 report to a European correspondent, he said:

> In the past half year we have noticed certain trends: SPFM can count fewer financial supporters and people interested enough to subscribe to *Diaspora*. This is because, I think, the ones who espouse any liberal cause in the hope of a real change-oriented attack upon the institutional church have cooled off and gone elsewhere. Those who have been willing to invest time and effort in the search for honest ministry have turned away from the political push for some kind of reinstatement in the church, because the temper of the U.S. hierarchy is totally closed and fearful. Consequently, much more is happening on the level of personal, local ministering.[12]

In March of 1973, when Duryea told the board that he had begun to invite people to his house for informal get-togethers, he added: "We feel that this kind of thing, at the moment at least, is the most important function of SPFM." He had just met with his fellow Californians, McGoldrick and Durkin, and came away convinced that the idea of a political victory in the Church was futile and that the impact of SPFM on Catholic consciousness was minimal.

Breaking the Mold of the Past

Despite his misgivings, Duryea continued to provide for the board a channel for the group's identity exploration. He did so with wit and good cheer. A July 1973 letter titled, "Re: The charmingly transitory nature of things," attempted to capture the zeitgeist of the day:

> I search for words to summarize the important trends of thought to which we must address ourselves at the N.Y. convention. I take refuge in the fact that the church is people, and that in '73 people are more articulate, more honest, and not very puttable into boxes—to be labeled "ins," "outs," "activists," "institutionalists," or "transcendental communitarians." . . . at each convention-time we find ourselves less inhibited by the ecclesiastical mould

(mold!) in which we were cast. We find ourselves looking with increasing conviction to the personal experiences of the year that is ending.

So off to New York went Duryea. A group picture shows a smiling, aging man with a thin face and bushy sideburns, the man behind the hundreds of letters of the past year that, like glue, had held together the fragile network.

Duryea returned to California, answerable to a new leadership, and one that he did not know very well. He continued to act as he felt his position required but soon found that he had fallen into the trap of his predecessors, the DiBenedettos. His initiatives were judged to have exceeded his authority.

On November 13, signing himself "Mildly troubled," he wrote to the board:

> In the past few weeks I have felt confused and troubled by the ever-present vagaries of the Communication Problem. Crises have arisen over money, the ballot, the change of name, the printing of new stationery. I have used "executive privilege" and made quick decisions, that have almost infallibly been wrong, it seems.

Knocked Off His Horse

Despite growing discouragement, the Duryeas felt duty bound to attend the 1974 convention in Chicago and to bring to a smooth close their two years as executive secretaries. As they planned the trip, Bob wrote his final official letter, one that served as his farewell address to FCM and in effect to the movement. He wrote:

> Yesterday I made reservations for Lu and myself to fly to Chicago. I took time to wonder why I felt such pleasing anticipation. Simply, I was looking forward to seeing friends again. I have little to bring to the convention: no theology, no political action programs, no social action programs. I cannot claim that I have been part of the accreditation work, or the drive to open ministerial training to women (and to all) on an ecumenical basis. I am happy with all these things because they rise from the hearts and minds of those I love.... All Lu and I will be bringing to the convention is ourselves, with a few experiences of what

"church" has been for us during the past year. . . . We will also bring our share of a dream.[13]

However, the Duryeas were not to bring their "share of a dream" to Chicago. When asked in 1991 to reflect on his free ministry days, Duryea vividly recalled a major turning point:

Lu and I were preparing for the Chicago convention in '74 and we sat in bed one Sunday morning talking about it. We realized that we didn't want to go. It was like St. Paul being knocked off his donkey, only backwards. All the excitement and optimism suddenly had drained away and the fight to reform HM Church seemed pointless.[14]

Once again, a free minister was abandoning the movement. But there were others to take his place as there have been throughout the years. In particular, William Manseau, the subject of the next chapter, remained convinced that fresh leadership would propel the movement into a more successful trajectory.

8

The Fellowship of Christian Ministries

I have risked my life several times, at knife point and at gun point, out of obedience to the Gospel. I have endured and accepted years of widespread misunderstanding and heckling by peers in the priesthood, public disgrace and recrimination for daring to be a witness to the need for social and ecclesial change because I know what the Gospel has done for me personally. . . . I have lived in Roxbury for five years with its rats and hatred and rotten buildings and stinking hallways, with its people struggling to make it, to live, to have a moment of love; so many of them having to drug themselves high with pills or booze just to escape, just to have a sense of breathing easily.

I had become convinced beyond the shadow of any doubt that obedience to the gospel of Christ was our only hope and the obedience required was total. Only the freed Gospel of Jesus incarnated in the lives of ordinary men and women can hope to rescue our times from its mad dance of death. I believe that God is freeing his Gospel for his people and that he is empowering many of its ministers.

William J. Manseau, July 1973

By 1973, dramatic changes were transforming the Catholic Church. Like a sleeping giant, it was awakening and shaking itself free of the stiffness and lethargy of several centuries.

Liturgical reform had revolutionized the Mass. Popular devotions such as benediction of the Blessed Sacrament, novenas, and Forty Hours devotion disappeared almost over night. The rosary and other prayers to Mary lost favor.

Lay participation increased dramatically from lectors and Eucharistic ministers at Mass to directors of religious education to principals and superintendents of Catholic schools. No longer were parishes and diocesan offices the exclusive domain of priests.

Church teachings were deeply affected by the progressive transformation of Catholic consciousness. A sense of mortal sin, of hell and of the devil, had dissolved and with it the practice of frequent confession. The content of faith became more streamlined, less cluttered with the accretions of the ages. Christ became a central figure and the Scriptures rather than the catechism were looked to for guidance.

However, while the updating of the Church proceeded rapidly in many respects, in two areas it had come to a halt, namely, ministerial freedom and human sexuality. Conservative elements controlled the Vatican. They demanded of bishops, priests, and religious conformity to their directives and made it increasingly clear that optional celibacy for priests was not open to reconsideration. They remained unyielding on contraception, divorce, abortion, homosexuality, and other aspects of human sexuality that were undergoing dramatic reconsideration throughout the world.

It was in this context that the free ministry movement found itself stalemated. Much potential lay support for the cause was co-opted by the wider role given the laity in the Church. Catholics who had expressed their discontent by joining underground churches, often serviced by married priests, now found that revitalized local parishes once again satisfied their needs.

Married priests were marooned on a shrinking island, their cries for help ignored by hierarchy and laity alike. The awful truth that they were alone forced them to reconceptualize their vision and restructure their organization. What was needed most urgently of all was a leader who would not be deterred by failure nor distracted by personal considerations.

Leadership for a Revamped Movement

Such a leader emerged at the SPFM convention at a Jesuit-run retreat center in Staten Island, New York, on the Labor Day weekend of 1973. The principal architect of the new vision and structure was William Manseau, a married priest from Massachusetts.

Manseau had a long apprenticeship for assuming the presidency. He had been attracted to SPFM in 1969 when he and Mary, his wife of a few weeks, attended in Boston a talk on optional celibacy by Eugene Bianchi, who had just been elected as the first president of SPFM. Bianchi invited the newlyweds to the November convention in Washington, D.C. At that meeting, Manseau was elected to the executive board, beginning what would be a lifetime of dedication to the cause of free ministry. Neither economic hardship, health problems of his wife, the failure of many of his projects, nor the loneliness and isolation of championing what to most seemed a futile quest ever dissuaded Manseau from fidelity to what he felt was his calling.

Manseau went to the 1973 convention with the intention of running for the presidency of the floundering group. He arrived with a detailed action program for a reoriented free ministry and was determined to jettison the name Society of Priests for a Free Ministry, which many had come to feel was obsolete.

Influence of a Secular Institute

Manseau had been born to French-speaking parents in Lowell, Massachusetts, in 1936. He did not learn French because of the strong anti-French bias of the English-speaking population, especially the Irish, who dominated the Catholic Church in the area. While in the seminary for the archdiocese of Boston, he did not join the French Club in order to avoid being classified as a French-speaking priest.

After ordination in 1961, Manseau worked as a parish priest for eight years, primarily in the inner city, as he recalled in the excerpt from a letter to Bernard McGoldrick that begins this chapter.

Besides this pastoral experience, Manseau credits a French-speaking group with having been a major factor in shaping his priestly identity and his sense of the new direction that Christianity should take. In 1962, he was introduced to the Secular Institute of Pius X and, in particular, to the New Hampshire unit of the lay community that had been founded years before by Henry Roy, cousin of the Cardinal Archbishop of Quebec. Henry Roy had established the Young Christian Workers and Young Christian Students in North America and had attracted lay people to what impressed Manseau as a powerful evangelical spirituality. Roy told the lay members of the institute that they were priests in neckties.

Manseau was profoundly influenced by what he experienced, including the joyful spirituality of married people. He concluded that a committed Christian life in the world was where the true vitality of the Gospel was to be found and that he could be a more effective priest by living in the midst of the people, not in a semimonastic celibate life-style. He decided that he was called to be a married priest and to contribute to the shaping of a new ecclesial ministry. He would be a "worker-priest" ministering to small communities of believers who wanted to support and engrace one another.

Such pastoral work and small group spirituality were far removed from the experience and interests of academic free ministers such as Bianchi and McGoldrick. What happened on Staten Island in 1973 was that the pastoral-spiritual orientation challenged the faltering theological-political approach. McGoldrick was burned-out and had announced that he would not run again for the presidency. No theologically oriented candidate emerged and so the pastoral approach, led by Manseau and his close collaborators, Gerald and Marita Grudzen, carried the day.

With this shift, SPFM/FCM would progressively deemphasize the effort to change the Catholic Church. Instead, it would become a professional organization, providing credentials for men and women, principally married priests, who wanted some formal institutional legitimacy for their ministerial work.

This does not mean that the original institutional reform thrust of the movement disappeared. It was kept alive in a new organization, the Corps of Reserve Priests United for Service (CORPUS), founded in 1974 and which will be discussed in the next chapter. For many free ministers, FCM and CORPUS have worked in tandem; FCM providing a minimal institutional structure for functioning as Catholic ministers and CORPUS serving as the vehicle for sustaining the hope that eventually the Roman Catholic Church could be changed.

Agenda for a Renewed Movement

In effect, Manseau began his campaign for the presidency of SPFM early in the two-year period (1971–73) during which he served as pastor of the Dunstable Congregational Church in Massachusetts.

He wrote frequently and extensively about this experience, which was for him a model of how a Catholic priest might continue his ministry after leaving the official priesthood. As an "ecumenical pastor" granted "dual-standing ministerial membership" in the United Church of Christ, Manseau remained a Catholic yet was able to minister to a congregation comprised of people of diverse denominational backgrounds.

Armed with the status afforded him by his unique ministry, he attended the 1972 SPFM convention in Los Angeles. There he made proposals that would become the basis for his presidential platform the following year.

First, he urged the formation of a "professional ministerial credentials committee." This was the genesis of what would become the Certification in Ministry program, destined to be the principal appeal of FCM. Second, Manseau proposed a "committee on ecumenical relations." Manseau assumed the chairmanship and undertook a mission to forge links with various denominations in an effort to connect disenfranchised Catholic priests to some formal ecclesiastical entity. His carefully crafted letters to Protestant leaders elicited equally carefully crafted rejections.

Finally, at the 1972 convention Manseau presented six resolutions on "trans-traditional ministries" that, in effect, specified some concrete projects for the two committees already approved. It is clear that the resolutions, which were duly approved and effectively ignored by the organization, embodied Manseau's lived experience with the Dunstable experiment. He envisioned the development of a mechanism for certifying "trans-traditional ministers," publishing a directory of such ministers, and fashioning procedures for staffing what he called "contract-parishes," that is, communities of Christians that wanted "de-institutionalization" and would be in the market for the kind of worker-priests who would be listed in the trans-traditional ministerial directory.

This was Manseau's agenda. However, McGoldrick was still president, and his major project was the sponsoring of an international free ministry meeting in Geneva. Accordingly, what meager resources SPFM had were devoted to this soon-to-be aborted venture.

Seizing the Initiative

Thus, the stage was set for what might be called a "palace coup." Manseau and the Grudzens did two things. First, when the Chicago group withdrew, they offered to host the 1973 convention. In practice, those who hosted a convention controlled the program and also had the advantage of being able to augment attendance from their home area. Second, Manseau undertook a letter-writing campaign, making it clear to key people that he was a serious candidate for president and that he had in mind a new direction for the organization.

Whereas neither Bianchi nor McGoldrick had done any local free ministry organizing before assuming the presidency, Manseau had worked hard to develop the New England region. In the fall of 1971 he had convened "the first N.E. regional SPFM-sponsored get-together" at his church in Dunstable. Fifteen married priests and their wives attended. A second such regional get-together in May 1972 drew twenty married priests. Manseau had asked several men to serve as "local coordinators" under his leadership and in July 1972 held a meeting with these area coordinators. By that time he had drawn up a New England SPFM directory that contained sixty-five names of people who were either members or had "manifested serious interest" in the group.

The information in the previous paragraph is taken from a six-page, single-spaced report that Manseau sent to the SPFM executive board in mid-1972 detailing his year of "creative initiative and response." Four of the pages were devoted to an account of his position as ecumenical pastor, with lengthy excerpts from the constitution of the United Church of Christ. He wanted to establish the ecclesial legitimacy of his position and to offer it as a model for others. No SPFM region was organized more thoroughly or led by someone who invested more energy in promoting the cause of free ministry.

Fund-raising Plan

That energy included ambitious fund-raising activities. In late 1972, Manseau sent to the SPFM board, "and interested friends," a twenty-four page, single-spaced set of letters and attachments that documented his plan for raising money for free ministry projects. Two years before, Durkin had proposed raising $36,000 for a national office and for "development." Manseau was certainly aware of Durkin's futile effort, but nonetheless now proposed to raise between $96,000 and $130,500 for the same purpose, including a budget of between $4,000 and $6,000 for each of ten "regional offices."

Not unmindful of his own proposals, which apparently had been forgotten by others as soon as approved, Manseau's funds allocation included $30,000 for a planning and development office that would "design and negotiate into reality the platform resolutions on Trans-Traditional Ministries adopted by the Los Angeles Convention."

Manseau did send professional-looking proposals to foundations, including the Clement Stone Foundation, but no money ever was raised. However, since copies of everything he did were sent to board members, the SPFM leaders became aware of the New England vice president's continuing commitment at a time when others were becoming discouraged.

There were some misgivings. For example, Bob Duryea, in responding to what he called Manseau's "opus," while admiring his "energy and ability," cautioned that Manseau's leadership "be wide enough to accommodate the pluralistic community that is dear to us." There was concern on the part of the board that Manseau's emerging leadership was in a direction with which they were not fully comfortable. This concern became most evident in a strikingly intense and analytical series of letters that McGoldrick termed "our summer correspondence."

The "Summer Correspondence"

On June 19, 1973, Manseau reported to McGoldrick on the plans that he and the Grudzens had been making for the September convention. He said that their reading of the sentiment of the people in the New England and mid-Atlantic regions was that SPFM should cease its confrontational stance, vis-à-vis the Church, and instead focus on providing people with

> opportunities to serve and to be affirmed in that service without having to expend precious energy and life on a whole lot of nonsense.

Manseau went on to say that he was considering proposing to the convention that SPFM change its name to the National Catholic Ministerial Association and

> move from a confrontation/contestation posture to a resource development, service-oriented association. It is very important that we deal with the familiar, the recognizable, the non-antagonistic if we ever expect to have any success with the rank and file priest, religious and lay person.

Manseau concluded his letter with the words, "I am available for national office should there be a need and I have the competence."

Within a week McGoldrick responded with a letter of even greater length. He was piqued by Manseau's reference to his approach as "a lot of nonsense" and proceeded to craft a letter that had all the earmarks of a lecture that a seasoned political scientist might deliver to a novice student:

> Your model is very pastorally oriented, Bill. That is both good and essential. But it is far from the total picture of both gospel life and ministry. I still see here some of what we discussed last year in L.A., that is, a certain tension between the pastoral and the intellectual ministries. I repeat that I do not mean by that that your own approach is not an intellectual approach to pastorality. It is highly articulate and intelligent. I am referring rather to the ministry of social, political, economic and cultural criticism in which many of your brothers and sisters find themselves engaged by virtue of their full-time profession in higher education.

McGoldrick went on to question the certification proposal as "a married form of semi-clericalism." He also drew attention to his own hopes for an international alliance of reform groups, an idea not included in Manseau's plan. He gave a mini-lesson in Church history on the significance of dissent for institutional change. In a word, McGoldrick politely, but firmly, rejected the Manseau Plan, concluding with words that showed McGoldrick's understanding of a social movement and his fear that Manseau would transform a movement into a professional organization. He wrote:

> We would seem to have in SPFM the classical dimensions and gamut of slightly rightist-to-centrist to somewhat leftish-to-radical positions on ideology that one finds in groups that are movements more than they are associations or organizations. A coalition of these inclinations might serve us well. The adoption of an entirely non-conflictual model would not seem to me to fit the facts of our times.

Again, within a few days Manseau replied with the most impassioned letter in his extensive files. He accused McGoldrick of "misinterpretation/misrepresentation" of his position. Manseau was angry. But he was also determined to pursue what he saw as his mission. He announced that even if McGoldrick reconsidered his decision not to seek the presidency again, he, Manseau, was a candidate.

A Flurry of Campaign Letters

As an indication of just how badly Manseau wanted the presidency, he sent throughout the spring and summer a series of letters to Bob Duryea, seeing in Duryea the kind of grass roots minister he felt was exactly what the organization needed rather than the ivory tower intellectuals who had led it thus far. The largest mailing was his July 14 letter, to which he appended thirteen enclosures, including a twenty-one page curriculum vitae. As was customary, copies of this detailed account of his life were sent to a number of others.

Finally, on August 21, just ten days before the convention, Manseau sent a letter to his mailing list, presenting himself and his platform for ratification by the membership. He had recruited the Grudzens as his vice presidential running mates and had asked Bob and Lu Duryea to continue as executive secretaries. So, having made alliances, he brought to the convention a strong candidacy, especially since no one else had expressed interest in the position.

For his part, McGoldrick did not believe that Manseau had the stature appropriate for the presidency of SPFM. In a lengthy letter late in June, which served as a sort of farewell address, McGoldrick recommended Frank Bonnike, Rosemary Radford Ruether, and Phil and Liz Berrigan as attractive candidates. All had national reputations and could enhance the image of the organization by their high profile names as well as by their creative ideas. However, there is no evidence that any were interested in the position.

A Handful of SEEDS

Bearing sixteen pages of reports and proposals, Manseau went to Staten Island on that torrid Labor Day weekend in 1973. The weather wasn't the only thing that was hot. The meeting itself among the one hundred participants would be on rather heated terms. The *National Catholic Reporter* article on the convention reported:

> The intentionally loose organization of the convention produced some confusion among delegates, and the

discussions often broke down into acrimonious exchanges and outbursts of temper and frustration.[1]

One who did not lose his temper was Bill Manseau. He calmly read his proposals and, in the end, prevailed. It was clear from the sharp divisions in the group that the only alternative was dissolution of the organization.

The key to Manseau's plan was what he called "A Handful of Seeds." As a good teacher, he had found a device—the acronym SEEDS—to capture the elements of his proposed program. Briefly, they were:

- Service program: assisting individuals and groups through counseling, teaching, preaching, healing, and organizing.
- Enablement program: establishing a ministerial certification program and collaborating with seminaries and universities in providing professional competency for men and women ministers.
- Education program: informing the public of the availability of the new ministers, using the public media and other forms of communication.
- Development program: establishing house-church communities as a local expression of the Church.
- Spirituality program: acknowledging the need for a vibrant spirituality, unspoiled by the negative experiences of the past.

No Requirement for Church Approbation

Manseau's plan was a significant departure from earlier free ministry self-definitions in that it did not call for any relationship to the Catholic hierarchy. Quite the contrary, Manseau argued:

Theologically, it appears to us, that it is now commonly accepted that the ministerial powers of Christ are not encapsulated in the Papal, Episcopal or Sacerdotal institutional offices in the way previously believed, but are there radically as they are present in the ministerial activity of any who act faithfully in the name of Christ.

Free ministry had reached its logical limit. *Anyone* who acted in the name of Christ could be a minister—or could they? Actually, what Manseau's plan did was transfer the power to certify ministers from the hierarchy to his organization. If the bishops would not validate ministry, then he would establish a mechanism that would. FCM would evaluate credentials and grant or deny certification.

Manseau had argued that McGoldrick's policy of confrontation with the hierarchy made many people uncomfortable. Yet others were uncomfortable with this plan which, in effect, established a separate ecclesiastical structure. Words such as *sect* and *schismatic* were used in reaction. Membership in FCM reached an all-time low as Manseau led the remnant into uncharted waters.

Eugene Bianchi, the first president of SPFM, attended the convention. He was quoted by *National Catholic Reporter* as wondering whether or not such groups as SPFM and the National Association of Laity were "movements that are no longer moving." McGoldrick, the outgoing president, was more conciliatory, stating that "what you are asking SPFM to become is what it already is."

What it already is? No one seemed sure of what it was. But Manseau knew what he wanted it to be. An article in the *Boston Globe* a few days after the convention quoted him as saying that during the coming year, while working toward a doctor of ministry degree, he would develop a methodology for "a private-practice Catholic ministry." He did not foresee the bishops accepting this free ministry in the near future but used St. Paul's words that "there is only one Spirit, but a variety of ministries" to provide a theological basis for his plan.[2]

A Revamped Agenda

Manseau's vision for the organization, now officially renamed Fellowship of Christian Ministries, was summed up in the Associated Press report of the convention, which appeared in various newspapers throughout the country. Manseau said that the reconstituted group represented

> the shift from confrontation with the official church to the search for newer forms of ministry, the more active participation in the group by women and a trend toward a more ecumenical ministry open to the other churches.[3]

These three elements would be mentioned over and over again as the guiding principles of FCM:

1. It was a group of people who were developing "newer forms of ministry." Just what they were was never made clear. Perhaps the greatest disillusionment of the movement was that dissatisfaction with the traditional parish structure did not lead to the creation of vigorous alternatives such as "intentional communities," or as Manseau called them, "generating communities."

2. It was becoming clearer that sexism was a much more radical problem in the Church than priestly celibacy. FCM saw itself as well-positioned to champion the cause of women's equality. Women assumed at least symbolic leadership roles in FCM, and "women's issues" became a standard component of conventions.

3. The Church had all but abandoned the postconciliar enthusiasm for ecumenism. FCM felt that here also was a dimension of reform to which it could contribute. Certainly Christ did not bless the scandalous divisions that had separated his followers for centuries.

The Chicago Generating Community

Having been awarded a fellowship to study at the Chicago Theological Seminary, Manseau and his family moved to Chicago shortly after the convention. Here he went about the task of attempting to implement this tripartite program. It seemed so urgent and so right. There was every reason to be confident of success.

As a project for a course during the fall semester, he proposed organizing what he called a "generating community" that would be composed of "disenfranchised clergy" from several denominations. He began the paper in which he presented his plan with a "thesis," which in a few words captured his idea not just for his course project but for FCM as well:

In the present circumstances of the American Church and Society, a local, ecumenically oriented, new form of the Church made up of 'tent-making' disestablished clergy is an appropriate and necessary instrumentality to assist the existing churches in fulfilling their ecumenical ministry.[4]

Manseau contacted representatives of several Chicago ministerial associations and organized a group designed to be a three-year experiment in "an intentional community of local disestablished clergy" who would attempt to develop a mode of "Christian witness and mission which will . . . relate effectively to modern secular man." The group was formed—met periodically—but ceased to function once Manseau left Chicago. At the end of the three-year period, it disbanded, not having met in nearly a year.

Organizing the 1974 Convention

Manseau also took it upon himself to organize the 1974 FCM convention. It is clear from the voluminous correspondence surrounding what would be the first post-SPFM gathering that Manseau did virtually all the planning himself and that he intended it to be a model of the kind of refurbished organization he was shaping. His year in Chicago, working on the doctorate, was a period of nearly full-time service to free ministry.

Over the 1973 Christmas holidays, the Manseaus returned East and continued to develop the close working relationship with the Grudzens that would be the key to the survival of FCM. Together, they hammered out the certification program, made what seemed like promising connections with Protestant churches, advanced the cause of women's equality in ministry, promoted the idea of "base communities," and strove to raise money for the perennially nearly bankrupt organization.

Seeking a Broader Appeal

A major concern of the convention planners was how to attract a larger number of people to the annual event, which afforded FCM its major vehicle for publicity and recruitment. Attendance at the previous four gatherings had never reached one hundred fifty, but Manseau was confident that a strong program would draw a larger response. Accordingly, he decided to sponsor a one-day, freestanding conference to be held in conjunction with the convention, with the hope of drawing local people who were not necessarily interested in free ministry.

For such a program to succeed, two things were needed. First, there had to be a "big name" keynote speaker. In this case, it would be the prominent theologian, Rosemary Radford Ruether. Joining her on the program, titled "Ministry after Watergate," would be John C. Schwarz, a former Jesuit, and Charles M. Olsen, a Protestant minister and director of Project Base Church. All were to deliver papers on aspects of ministry.

The other need was to get the conference brochure into the hands of potential attendees. By the spring of 1974, Manseau had developed numerous links with reform-minded individuals and groups in the Chicago area. Perhaps the most important was the Association of Chicago Priests (ACP), composed of active and inactive clergy. Among the "inactive" priests was Frank Bonnike, former president of NFPC.

The leader of the ACP, William Hogan, an active priest, was enthusiastic about the conference and sent the brochure to the five hundred fifty men on the group's mailing list. The cover letter, signed by Bonnike, Hogan, and thirteen others, said that one of the short-term goals of the ACP was to understand more fully what was meant by ministry and to explore ways to make it more meaningful. The FCM conference was recommended as a way to work on this objective. The tone of the letter was close to a cosponsoring of the conference. Bonnike and Hogan did attend, together with fifteen other ACP members, including Frank McGrath, who with Bonnike and others, would within a few months establish CORPUS as a new component of the free ministry movement.

Dramatic Role of Women

Despite Manseau's efforts, fewer than one hundred people participated in the weekend and if some attended in order to hear Ruether, they were disappointed when she did not show up. However, what they did get was perhaps even more challenging. The paper that Ruether had prepared was read by Alla Bozarth-Campbell, an Episcopal priest, who for several years maintained a relationship with FCM as a member of the advisory board and through attendance at conventions. Bozarth-Campbell had been ordained earlier in the summer together with ten other women in a controversial ceremony in Philadelphia. Just days before the FCM convention, the Episcopal House of Bishops had declared the ordinations invalid. What the conference attendees had to deal with then were not just the radical ideas of Ruether but a living example of the struggle for the equality of the sexes in the ministry. It was the most vivid vignette possible to illustrate what FCM was all about: a Protestant woman priest reading a theological paper and later participating in an experimental liturgy.

As is often the case, what gained media attention, and long remained vivid in the memories of convention participants, was an event that happened somewhat spontaneously, namely, for the first time women publically presiding at the Eucharist. The service was conducted on Sunday morning at a wooden table in a dormitory building at North Central College, Naperville, Illinois, near Chicago. The following morning a large picture accompanied a *Chicago Tribune* article about the convention.[5] The picture showed a married priest offering the chalice to Bozarth-Campbell.

The article related what in 1974 was still very shocking, namely, that

> those who actually performed the rituals, who said the prayers of the traditional celebrant and held the wine and bread toward heaven, were five married priests, a Presbyterian minister, and three former nuns.

SPFM had advocated the ministerial equality of women from its earliest days, but as long as it was trying to win acceptance from the Catholic hierarchy, the liturgies had not included women among the celebrants. Now, with the reaction of the bishops not a primary concern, women could assume any position and serve any function on an equal footing with men. Henceforth, FCM would deliberately include women, a group who had been excluded from positions of leadership in the Church even longer than married men.

The Joy of an Older Priest

The picture in the *Chicago Tribune* showed the youthful Bozarth-Campbell receiving the Eucharist from the hands of an elderly man who was wearing a Latin American poncho over his white shirt, tie, and suit jacket. He was Frank Pleasant, and his story illustrates another dimension of free ministry and another type of person whose life was enriched by the inner freedom to which FCM summoned those who had lived in the shadows of guilt and shame for many years.

Pleasant, ordained for the archdiocese of Pittsburgh in 1939 before many free ministers were born, had left the priesthood in 1949 and married in 1952. Choked with emotion, he told the small congregation gathered around the table for the convention liturgy that the Mass was the first he had celebrated publicly in twenty-two years. It has been said that one rebel is looked on as crazy, two as conspirators, and three as a movement. Pleasant, fifteen years before his time, had been considered odd, if not crazy, for wanting to continue his ministry after marriage. Now he was part of a movement.

Years before Vatican II, Pleasant had established a relationship with Cardinal John Wright, then bishop of Pittsburgh. He told Wright how much he missed his ministry and how he longed to be able to exercise it again in some way. Wright was sympathetic. Pleasant also developed his ideas on married priests under the pseudonym Victor Venete in an essay that appeared in *Married Priests and Married Nuns*.[6]

When Vatican II was announced, Pleasant wrote a letter addressed to Pope John XXIII and gave a copy to Wright. The letter called for amnesty from excommunication for all priests who had married without a dispensation, rapid granting of dispensations for those who sought them, recognition of the ministry of married priests, and the liberalization of the rule of celibacy.

Complying with the wishes of his wife Ann, Pleasant himself requested and was granted a dispensation so that their marriage of more than a decade could be validated by the Church. Ironically, it was during the laicization process, which he experienced as degrading, that Pleasant was further radicalized. In particular, he was irritated by the requirement that he promise never to say Mass. The prohibition precipitated a much greater desire to celebrate the Eucharist than he had experienced before. Occasionally at home he would do so. However, he had never done so in public. Here he was now not only pictured in a Chicago newspaper but shown on television and mentioned in wire service articles around the country.

Confrontation with Cardinal Wright

The strangest part of the story of Frank Pleasant occurred at O'Hare Airport in Chicago as he and Ann were boarding the plane to Pittsburgh after the FCM convention. They met Cardinal Wright, who had seen the *Tribune* article. Wright was furious. In a letter to Manseau, Pleasant described this chance meeting with his former bishop:

> I went to stand in front of him. It was I who went to meet
> him, full of courage, not exactly to have a confrontation,

> but willing to come out in the open as an honest man, not as an enemy. But he staged a confrontation and I accepted the challenge. I never saw his eyes so burning with anger, his lips contracted in disapproval, his face so red with emotion. . . . He called me a liar and a hypocrite. . . .

Pleasant defended himself, saying that he still loved being a priest and felt that the invitation by Manseau to concelebrate the Mass was, in a way, making up for all those years during which he had been deprived of his ministry.

When Ann Pleasant offered her hand to Wright, he refused to take it. It must be added that by the time the plane arrived in Pittsburgh, Wright had regained his composure and spoke kindly to both Ann and Frank.

Pleasant said that his affiliation with FCM made him feel more free and more determined to start a "home church" as soon as possible. The Pleasants attended several other FCM gatherings before his retirement. At each of them Frank stood out from the crowd not just because he was so much older than the rest but because of the smile of contentment that irradiated his face.

Ecumenical Efforts

The presence of Bozarth-Campbell and Charles Olsen at the convention were but two of the numerous efforts by Manseau to forge links with Protestants. FCM, together with NFPC, joined the Steering Committee of an Interfaith Coalition for Ministry, a venture more impressive in its title than its achievements. The materials published by SCICM attest to the existence of a Protestant "free ministry" movement. The Protestant version of the movement set in clear relief that the central issue was not celibacy but rather the felt need on the part of many ministers for greater self-determination.

For example, an essay, "The Hidden Priesthood," by H.A. Woggon, an Episcopal priest, appeared in the November 1973 SCICM newsletter and sounds strikingly similar to what Catholics were saying. Woggon had worked for seven years as a full-time minister. He then moved from what he called an "occupational priesthood" to a "functional priesthood." During the week he worked as director of an alcoholism program in Asheville, North Carolina, and on Sundays served without pay as a supply priest to St. Mary's Church, where his family attended service. He preferred this new style of priesthood, one that was more hidden on weekdays and more open on Sunday.

Manseau's efforts to make FCM more ecumenical did not bear much fruit. One of the first women to be certified was a New York Protestant friend of the Grudzens, Mary Alice Warner. She was an example of both a woman and a Protestant who felt at home in FCM. However, few others joined her, and never was any corporate affiliation with a Protestant denomination or school of theology realized.

The New Constitution

It is informative to compare the SPFM constitution of 1969 with that adopted by FCM at the 1974 convention. The earlier group's preamble began with the words:

> We are priests and people striving to be open to the Spirit of a New Pentecost and to embody that Spirit in a church that is Christian.

Although following the same format, the newer group's opening words reflect a significant change of perspective:

> We are Christian men and women striving to be open to that same Spirit that was in Jesus Christ, the Spirit of a New Pentecost, and committed to the embodiment of that Spirit in a variety of Gospel ministries.

"Priests and people" had given way to "men and women" and "Church" was now "ministries." Clericalism had been eliminated as had the need to be organically connected to the institutional Church.

Also, although both constitutions stated that their purpose was the renewal of the Church, SPFM defined renewal in terms of "communicating with existing Church groups," while FCM saw the task in terms of being "a community of love and concern, a communicating network fostering life models of home churches to give visible presence in society of the real mystery of the church catholic."

House Churches

The goal of establishing "house churches" has remained central to the free ministry vision. Enthusiasm about it led one member to suggest that the official Church was dying, and that when it expired, the new house churches affiliated with FCM would be there to carry forward the Gospel of Christ.

In 1975 Manseau was dreaming of such small, home-based communities when he organized that year's convention at Eastern Michigan University in Ypsilanti. The gathering was hosted by the Plymouth House Church at Ann Arbor in order to provide a model of what was possible. Manseau envisioned a national network of such communities, with FCM providing guidance and coordination. With characteristic optimism, he announced in his presidential address that several new communities had sought membership in FCM. As a matter of fact, few communities have ever affiliated with FCM, and members of the organization itself have had little success in establishing vigorous communities.

Continuing Commitment to Free Ministry

In 1976, after three years of effort, including the planning of three conventions, Manseau turned the presidency over to the Grudzens. Bill assumed the title past president and remained on the executive board. His wife, Mary, became secretary-treasurer. Eventually, Mary ceased being active in the movement, devoting herself to her work, her family, and the local Catholic parish, where she served on the parish council and in the religious education program.

For his part, like a number of other early SPFM veterans including McGoldrick, Manseau progressively redirected his energies away from FCM and toward CORPUS. He may have spearheaded the move to disassociate from the institutional Church, but he found that such a direction offered no hope for the social recognition of his priesthood, always his primary goal.

Manseau loves the altar and the pulpit. For several years after leaving FCM leadership positions, he served as part-time minister of St. John Chrysostom Anglican Catholic Church of Nashua, New Hampshire. The Anglican Catholic Church had broken away from the larger Anglican Communion in protest against such changes as the ordination of women and a liberal position on homosexuality. So, paradoxically, Manseau, who had welcomed one of the first women priests to participate in the 1974 FCM convention, ten years later ministered to a congregation that rejected them.

Today, Manseau is a pastoral psychotherapist in Nashua. However, he insists that he has another very important occupation. He says that he is "in practice, through the Roman Catholic Church, assisting in the transformation of ministerial priesthood."

In his office is a closet filled with traditional Mass vestments. Nearby is a small room equipped as a sacristy. In the center of the room is an altar adorned with all the accoutrements for worship. On the wall are pictures of himself and some colleagues, dressed in the vestments.

9

CORPUS: The Corps of Reserve Priests United for Service

For free ministry you need free persons.

Frank Bonnike, telephone interview, 1990

One of the best-known priests in the United States in the early seventies was Frank Bonnike of the Rockford, Illinois, diocese. For more than two years as president of the fledgling National Federation of Priests Councils (NFPC), he served as point man for clerical activism. In 1972, shortly after being reelected president of NFPC, he suddenly resigned the post. The following year, he resigned from the priesthood itself in order to marry.

Because of his national prominence, Bonnike's resignation drew considerable media attention. The *Chicago Tribune* headlined its report with words that captured the essence of Bonnike's life: "Priest quits, but still wants to help." The "wanting to help" would take two forms, personal and organizational. Bonnike would continue to exercise a priestly, even if non-Eucharistic, ministry as a hospital chaplain, and he would found the Corps of Reserve Priests United for Service (CORPUS), which would play a pivotal role in carrying forward the free ministry movement.

Nontraditional Route to Priesthood

Bonnike attributes his dissatisfaction with the clerical life-style and his leadership skills to his own unusual route to priesthood. During the forties and fifites, almost all priests emerged from the lockstep assembly line of Catholic schools, minor seminaries, and virtually cloistered major seminaries. There was little exposure to the broader society or to ideas that were not strictly orthodox.

Bonnike, born in 1923, attended Northwestern University and majored in business. He then served in the Navy for three-and-a half years during World War II. As a business officer, he traveled to every naval base in the country, dealing with admirals and captains, and, as he says, "seeing them with their pants down." Working so closely with top military officials helped to prepare him for dealing confidently with the Church's hierarchy. During most of his time in service, Bonnike was engaged to be married, a fact to which he would allude more than forty years later in his homily at the 1988 CORPUS conference in Washington, D.C.[1]

After the service, Bonnike worked for several years and then entered the seminary as a "delayed vocation." He studied at the Catholic University in Washington, D.C., which provided him with national contacts and a broader view of the Church than that obtained by priests trained in diocesan or regional seminaries.

During his twenty years as a priest, Bonnike had a variety of experiences. He was the first priest intern at the American Institute for Family Relations in Hollywood and with this training was assigned to conduct pre-Cana and Cana conferences. At various times he was a chaplain at the Illinois State Reformatory, the superintendent of a Catholic high school, and the pastor of two parishes. His leadership ability was widely recognized, and several of his colleagues thought that it was likely that he would become a bishop.

The National Federation of Priests' Councils

During 1968 several events occurred that heralded the beginning of a new direction for Bonnike's career. In February, three hundred priests met in Des Plaines, Illinois, to form the NFPC. In May, delegates from 127 of the 162 senates and associations of priests in America assembled at the same Chicago-area location for the first annual NFPC "delegates assembly." The priests represented more than thirty seven thousand of the sixty thousand Catholic priests in the United States. One of the members of the steering committee was Frank Bonnike.

A Chicago priest, Patrick J. O'Malley, was elected president, to be succeeded two years later by Bonnike. Chicago would be the national headquarters for this first-ever national organization of lower clergy. Many would refer to NFPC as a clerical labor union, since the group was a striking challenge to the age-old structure of the Church in which bishops, like medieval lords, held absolute authority over their vassal-like subjects. One of the group's leaders, Rev. W.F. Graney, called the formation of NFPC a manifestation of "democracy entering into the life of the Church." He said that the federation would give priests a common voice on national issues.

In July of 1968, the fast moving organization published its first newsletter. In a front page statement, President O'Malley said:

> In these days of collegiality and coresponsibility, none of us can afford the luxury of sitting back to let the total responsibility of improvement, renewal and reform fall on the shoulders of other men, no matter how capable or devoted they may be.

These "other men" were, of course, the bishops. With youthful enthusiasm, O'Malley was claiming for priests a voice in the government of the Church. He expected the bishops to welcome this offer of help. He, and Bonnike after him, would find that the bishops would listen to them little more than they would listen to the resigned priests represented by SPFM.

The basic tension soon became evident. On the one hand, the priests were an "opposition party" to the bishops. On the other hand, they were the subjects of and representatives of the bishops, not independent professionals. Much of the early NFPC leadership was rather militant, believing that a respectful but assertive stance, vis-à-vis the bishops, was appropriate. The October 1969 NFPC board issued "A Statement of New Directions" that said that the entire Church must participate in the decision-making process and that NFPC would move toward "systemic change in Church structure," even if the process entailed "tension, confrontation, and, at times, conflict."[2] Bonnike vigorously pursued this strategy.

Heightened Expectations

Forecasts that major changes were imminent heartened Bonnike and his reform-minded associates. For example, the Jesuit magazine, *America*, looked into its journalistic crystal ball in the first issue of 1970. Thirteen editors forecast what the next decade would bring. An article on the priesthood predicted that

> By the middle of the decade a new and volatile element will have entered the staid galaxy of ecclesiastical authority: the priest's wife. The Roman Catholic Church will decide to make clerical celibacy optional. The consequences will be many—not the least of which will be a new respect for marriage, an increase in the number of priests and an enhanced dignity for the celibate vocation. More important, perhaps, the message of the gospel of freedom and commitment and fidelity will be more credible from those who are more clearly free in what they have chosen to be.[3]

Confident that decisive leadership would produce historic results, Bonnike resolved that the 1971 NFPC House of Delegates would be the great turning point in the lives of Catholic priests.

Collaboration with Bianchi

Bonnike had participated not only in the establishment of NFPC but of SPFM as well, having attended the 1968 NAPR symposium. His conscious plan was to serve as the link between the canonical priests and the married priests and thereby advance the liberation of a clergy he believed to be bound by antiquated restraints.

His commitment to a married priesthood was similar in its intensity to that of Carl Hemmer, a founder of NAPR. Bonnike, however, had the advantage of a position of strength as elected leader of a substantial constituency. He was also a skilled political operator and believed that an alliance with those priests already married would add clout to his efforts. Accordingly, shortly after his election as president of NFPC in 1970, he began an extensive correspondence with Eugene Bianchi, president of SPFM. It would continue with Bianchi's successor, Bernard McGoldrick, and would include also the executive secretary of SPFM, Tom Durkin, and later Bob Duryea. A major theme of the correspondence was how to develop a strategy for getting SPFM admitted as a constituent member of NFPC. Such membership would lend credence to the claim of married priests that they were still priests entitled to participate in clergy organizations.

The close tie between SPFM and NFPC is reflected in correspondence between Bonnike and Bianchi in November 1970. Bonnike begins a letter with the words, "We are getting to be regular 'pen pals!'" He goes on to make a striking, even disturbing suggestion. Bianchi had sent him the draft of an article on free ministry that Bianchi proposed to submit to *The New York Times Magazine*. Bonnike was enthusiastic and wrote:

> The more I think about the article the more I wonder if its effectiveness could be limited, were it to come out under your signature. I am sure you realize that I am not up tight about anything when I say this, but I am simply interested in obtaining the greatest possible acceptance for the article. I hesitate to suggest this, but perhaps the article could go out under my name or any other active priest, with a complete understanding that you would receive all the financial benefits. I am presuming that the article will say nothing about my wife and children!

Bianchi's response was that he felt Bonnike was overcautious and that he might be "selling the bishops short by indirection, if you imply that they would not be able to take reasonably-presented ideas just because my signature was attached."

Bianchi may have rejected Bonnike's idea for the article, but he certainly had received the unequivocal message that in Bonnike he had a strong ally, one who apparently saw no ethical problem in the proposed deception.

The article eventually appeared in *Catholic World*. Bonnike was so pleased with it that he ordered three hundred copies so that one could be included in the packet of each participant to the March 1971 NFPC House of Delegates in Baltimore.

Then, he invited Bianchi, as president of SPFM, to address the Baltimore convention as a participant in a panel on "Creative Ministries." Bonnike heard Bianchi organize his reflections around two words: *freedom* and *love*. These were words that would speak with increasing urgency to Bonnike as he struggled to bring greater freedom and fuller opportunity for love into the priesthood, which he felt crippled the development and stifled the spirit of men.

Bianchi attempted to activate in his listeners a yearning to be free and to love. The following statement, spoken at the Baltimore convention, appeared in the March–April 1971 issue of *Diaspora*:

> I have experienced in my present mode of life a *greater freedom* for priestly service than I knew before. What I am attempting to communicate is a somewhat elusive sense of being my own man, of making decisions that imply a fuller personal commitment and risk. This sense of freedom resonates in the way I now teach and write, and it pervades the choices I make to speak at this peace rally or participate in that demonstration. . . . I no longer have that feeling of always being an institution man, of having to portray certain institutional value-judgements before I express my own freely-chosen inner values.

And on the topic of love, so central to the Christian message and so circumscribed by the vow of celibacy, Bianchi said:

> One of the chief old arguments against a married priesthood stated that such a minister would not be able to devote himself sufficiently to the full discipleship of ministry. Yet I discover just the opposite to be true. A loving relationship with my wife makes me freer for ministry. The growth experience of marriage has both its pains and joys. But the intense affectional center that it provides helps me to overcome the exaggerated loneliness and frustration that in the past was a hindrance to my ministry.

Bianchi believed that his talk swayed the delegates to a more liberal stance than they had originally intended. In a letter to the SPFM board after the NFPC meeting, he said that when Bonnike presented his "strong requests for change in the priesthood," the mood of the gathering was not supportive. But two days later, when Bianchi spoke, the climate seemed to change. At the last minute Bianchi inserted a thought that had occurred to him as he reflected on the setting for the meeting. Alluding to the Baltimore Council, he said that a hundred years ago the bishops had met there to determine the pace and pattern of American Catholic life for decades to come. Bianchi suggested that now the initiative had shifted to the priests. He speculated that what moved the priests was the challenge that they were the new plenary council of Baltimore; they could speak a new word of hope, write a new page in American Catholic history. I urged them not to miss their moment in history, that they stood at a crucial watershed.

The Moment of Truth

Resonating with the sentiments expressed by Bianchi, there emerged from the convention a "Statement on the Priesthood" that would be appealed to for several years as the Magna Carta of free ministry, a document issued not by men who had abandoned their ministry but by priests toiling in the vineyard and faithful to their vows. It was the "moment of truth" statement.[4]

Alluding to the words of Ecclesiastes, "There is an appointed time for everything . . . a time to tear down and a time to build . . . a time to keep and a time to cast away . . . a time to be silent and a time to speak . . . ," the statement said that now was the time for renewal, the moment of truth. The last words of the seven-page document, of which Bonnike was principal architect, were: "That moment is now!"

What was so desperately needed that it prompted the authors of the statement to declare with such urgency and passion that "there may never be another moment like this within our lifetime?" It was a call for a radical restructuring of the Church.

With undiplomatic daring, the manifesto opened with a direct attack on the bishops: "First, we speak to the problem which most seriously troubles priests today, the lack of leadership from those in authority . . .!"

The statement went on to say that "a bishop alone does not bear the responsibility for the ministry of the local Church," but rather shares this responsibility with his priests, religious and laity. One way to share responsibility was for bishops to be selected only after "broad consultation with priests, religious and laity" and that they serve a limited term of office. One wonders how Bonnike and his associates ever expected that the bishops would give a sympathetic hearing to such bold demands.

Under the heading "Church Structures" and echoing the SPFM position, the statement insisted that new forms of ministry were required to respond to the needs of the day. They included "non-geographical apostolates, co-pastorates, self-supporting ministries, team approaches, and an expanded sharing in ministry by the laity, including an official ministry by women."

The section titled "Celibacy," after paying homage to the "charism of celibacy," went on to say:

> We are convinced that the present law of mandatory celibacy in the western Church must be changed . . . . We ask that the choice between celibacy and marriage for priests now active in the ministry be allowed and that the change begin immediately . . . . In a spirit of brotherhood, we ask that priests who have already married be invited to resume the active ministry.

High Hopes Quickly Dashed

The "moment of truth" statement was sent to all the bishops in the United States. The accompanying cover letter noted that it had been adopted by a 193-18-3 vote of the House of Delegates. The bishops were urged to use the material in their upcoming meeting and also at the October synod in Rome, "as a helpful, honest, constructive presentation of the concerns of USA priests."

Bianchi wrote to Bonnike, referring to the Baltimore gathering as "an historic turning point in Catholic clergy history" and attributing the outcome to "the dynamic leadership" Bonnike had provided. Nearing the end of his two years as president of SPFM, Bianchi was given what would be his greatest reason to be optimistic. He said to Bonnike, "I'm sure the bishops will try to resist in one way or another the NFPC mandates. But I don't think there is any turning back at this point."

Just a few months later, Bianchi would deliver his "Does SPFM Have a Future?" paper. A year after that Bonnike would resign as president of NFPC. The bishops would have stonewalled the "moment of truth" statement.

By hindsight it is clear that the high watermark of the free ministry movement occurred in March 1971. Never again was the momentum for change greater. NFPC and SPFM had issued nearly identical agendas. Each group had as leader an intelligent, spiritual, and articulate man who presented to his constituents and to the bishops the most convincing arguments possible. Each communicated his message with respect, but also with strength. Each appealed to Vatican II, to the changing world, to the decline in vocations, and to the centrality of freedom and love in the Gospel. It would seem that the case was unassailable. What then went wrong?

Grass Roots Reaction to NFPC

One of the founding members of the NFPC was the Rev. John Fagan of the diocese of Brooklyn, who represented the New York Province on the executive board. His experience can serve to illustrate the dynamics of what was happening in the Catholic priesthood in the early seventies.

Fagan had been elected to the Brooklyn Priests' Senate by people of his own age group in a diocese that consisted of one thousand priests. At that time—and to the present—he has held a high visibility position as executive director of Little Flower Institute, a child care agency. Also, he has been an unflagging supporter of married priests, many of whom had been or became his friends. Whereas Bonnike would resign the priesthood and join the ranks of the married, Fagan remains within the structure, providing a respected link with the hierarchy. His challenge in 1971 was to "sell" the NFPC and its "moment of truth" to the Brooklyn Senate.

An eighteen-page, single-spaced appendix to the minutes of the December 13, 1971 meeting of the Brooklyn Senate provides a near-verbatim account of the discussion that occurred relative to NFPC. What was at stake was not agreement or disagreement with the national group but the far more critical issue of continued affiliation. Each senate in the country was free to disassociate at any time, withdrawing with its resignation its share of the NFPC budget. Thus the national group was constantly vulnerable.

Fagan explained the purpose and achievements of the NFPC and then listened to the reactions of his fellow senators. One of the senators listed under the ominous heading "against affiliation" was the Rev. Anthony Bevilacqua, a diocesan official and future Cardinal Archbishop of Philadelphia. Bevilacqua's comment was brief but telling. He said:

> I am opposed to affiliation because 1) I found so many priests opposed to affiliation during the visitations of Operation Listen; 2) I see this opposition based on the actual record of NFPC.

Several senators referred to "Operation Listen." Senate members had been urged to consult their constituents on senate matters, including affiliation with NFPC. Many priests had an obviously negative attitude toward the national group, seeing it as too radical.

In terms of the specific issue of clerical celibacy, many of the senators referred to the fact that the Brooklyn Senate had voted *against* optional celibacy and had instructed its representatives to the house of delegates to comply with their decision. However, when the vote on the "moment of truth" was taken, the Brooklyn delegates voted in the affirmative. One senator's challenge to Fagan on this matter cut to the heart of representative government:

> We sent delegates to Baltimore stating that we opposed optional celibacy. They voted for the final statement against our wishes. Their vote didn't represent us. That is what I am against.

Fagan responded by saying that the delegates did not feel bound by the senate vote, and that in the context of the sentiment that emerged in Baltimore and considering the entire "moment of truth" statement, they had voted as they felt was appropriate.

After a lengthy and sharp debate, the Brooklyn Senate voted to maintain its affiliation with NFPC. However, it was clear from the tone of the discussion that Bonnike and his associates did not represent the priorities of the majority of Brooklyn priests.

Evidence for this can be found in another statement by Bevilacqua at that same senate meeting:

> Let me cite for example Frank Bonnike's participation in an international peace symposium, pictured with North Vietnam delegates and saying that there is no persecution in the North. Did he speak to refugees to South Vietnam before offering the statement? Further, in all four issues of *Priests USA* [newsletter of NFPC] I have seen recently, there was only one anti-abortion statement. I see a lack of perspective and consistency.

The 1971 Roman Synod

Much hope was focused on the fall 1971 synod in Rome. It was felt that bishops from underdeveloped countries as well as liberal bishops from Holland and elsewhere would push for optional celibacy. Cardinal Suenens in his March meeting with Bianchi in New York had said that he hoped that the synod would decentralize the question of priestly celibacy, allowing regional hierarchies to settle the issue for themselves.

However, the synod slammed the door in the face of those advocating change. Bonnike himself spent weeks in Rome lobbying for
favorable action on proposals for optional celibacy and other issues
he considered vital. The *Boston Globe* reported that Bonnike "reacted
angrily to the Roman Catholic Church's latest display of intransigence on the question of priestly celibacy." Bonnike complained,
"We have no vote. We feel a little like the blacks when white
legislators make decisions about them, or sort of like the poor must
feel when the rich pass legislation affecting their lives." Neither did
he endear himself to the American hierarchy when his anger and
disappointment led him to add, "We want strong leadership, leaders
which priests and laity help to select. We want leaders who serve by
listening to the priests and people."[5]

Roman Rescript on Dispensations

The next blow to Bonnike's hopes came in June 1972. The Sacred
Congregation for the Doctrine of the Faith issued a rescript on
procedures for handling requests for dispensing men from their
priestly obligations. This document would be the last straw for
Bonnike. Not only would Rome not consider a married priesthood,
but it was subjecting those who sought release from their vows to
what he, Bonnike, considered a degrading process. As he said in a
letter sent to a number of people, including several SPFM officers:

> We are told that we should never react to something when
> we are angry. Three weeks have passed since I saw the
> rescript, but my dismay, discouragement, and disappoint-
> ment have not subsided.

While enlisting support for what would be a foredoomed effort
to have the rescript retracted, Bonnike continued his hectic schedule
of travel on behalf of ministerial reform. He refers to himself as a
workaholic. In a 1990 interview, he said that while a college student
he supported himself by working five jobs and that throughout
his life he had always worked incessantly. Never was this more true
than during his tenure as president of NFPC. His report to the
executive board in Tampa, Florida, in November 1972 lists dozens of
meetings that he had attended, including the SPFM convention in
California. In retrospect, Bonnike said that this obsession with work
shielded him from dealing with his deep need for an intimate
relationship.

Nevertheless, despite almost continuous travel, he did meet and fall in love with Janet Proteau, a music teacher. Within a year he applied for "reduction to the lay state," ironically becoming subject himself to the provisions of the despised Roman rescript. The pain Bonnike experienced at officially relinquishing the priesthood, while in his heart embracing it more tightly than ever, is suggested in his letter critiquing the rescript:

> The rescript treats priests as if they were boys rather than brothers who are professional men in pain. These priests are truly in pain, precisely because they have to give up their priestly ministry in order to exercise a human right which is God-given.

A Bittersweet Resignation

During the first week of September 1973, while SPFM was meeting in New York and transforming itself into FCM, Bonnike in Chicago was writing another letter to his friends, this time explaining in tender detail how he hoped to combine the love for a woman and the love for the priesthood. He was fifty years old when he announced that he could no longer live as a celibate. He used the letter to promote once again his conviction that marriage in no may was an obstacle to priestly service and that a loving relationship could actually help enhance one's ministry. He renewed his pledge to the service of the Gospel:

> I would like to do work which is as priestly as possible and am, God and the church willing, hoping some experimentation can take place in this regard. Furthermore, I would gladly serve the Church and God's people at the altar as a married priest should the present law be changed.

A "Lay" Catholic Chaplain

Providentially, at the time of his resignation, Bonnike was in a training program to be certified as a hospital chaplain. Cardinal Cody of Chicago allowed him to continue in the program and also to work at Lutheran General Hospital, Park Ridge, Illinois, in the ambiguous position of a priest who was a lay Catholic chaplain. This would be the setting for Bonnike's personal pastoral ministry for more than ten years.

His understanding of that ministry is explained in an article published in 1975. After describing the care provided at a hospital, Bonnike asked when such care could be considered pastoral. His answer was that care becomes pastoral "when the primary focus is upon God as a living, dynamic reality in life." He then posed the more critical question of who is the appropriate minister of such care. At the time, most pastoral ministry was provided by ordained clergymen. Bonnike argued that the key to effective spiritual care for the sick is qualities that are not restricted to the ordained such as

> a committed, lived faith; a sensitivity to the spiritual na- ture of people; . . . awareness of one's own feelings, needs and motivations, [together with other] skills which enable a chaplain to perceive needs more clearly and help others more effectively.[6]

Bonnike was contributing to a theology of ministry that in the following decade became more widely accepted, resulting in the transformation of hospital and college chaplaincies and even parish staffs into teams comprised of celibate priests, religious men and women, and married and single lay men and women. Competence and not ordination became the primary criterion for employment.

Nevertheless, a few ministerial activities considered critical to the Catholic way of life remained in the hands of the ordained. To celebrate Mass, to anoint the sick, and to forgive sins were sacramental actions reserved for priests. It was the determination to open these dimensions of ministry to married men that spurred Bonnike to return to the issue for which he had crusaded as president of NFPC: recognition by the Church of the ministry of married priests.

The Establishment of CORPUS

A year after his marriage, Bonnike invited several married priest friends and their wives to the home that he and Janet had established in a Chicago suburb. The guests were Frank and Sue McGrath, Tom and Pattie Hund, Bill and Teddi Nemmers, and Jim and Joan Wilber. This group, joined later by Joe and Rosemary Marto, began to meet on a regular basis. From this small community a new, and eventually the dominant, free ministry organization would emerge.

It was Janet Bonnike who originated the acronym CORPUS: Corps of Reserve Priests United for Service. The initial idea for CORPUS was a simple one: to compile a list of resigned priests who were available to serve the Church once again. These men would constitute the "reserves," waiting to be summoned to active duty.

Actually, the idea was not original. The previous year, the NFPC at its House of Delegates convention had voted

> to let its personnel committee serve as a clearing house for registering the names of priests who have been laicized or are in the process of being laicized and who desire a full- or part-time church-related ministry.[7]

By that time, Bonnike had resigned from NFPC. But the idea reflected his continuing, though diminishing, influence. The resolution also included the plan to "prepare a list of the names of parish councils, institutions, and religious and diocesan personnel boards seeking the services of such men."

Both these ideas, a list of married priests willing to serve and a complementary list of Church agencies willing to utilize their services, would become central to the mission of CORPUS once it became clear that NFPC would fail to implement the proposal.

Nevertheless, Bonnike did make one last effort to enlist the support of NFPC. Just as Eugene Bianchi had presented the message of SPFM at the 1971 House of Delegates in Baltimore, Bonnike presented the CORPUS agenda to the NFPC meeting in St. Petersburg, Florida, in 1975. Of the seven points he suggested "for incorporation into your resolutions and actions," the first was that the still cherished 1971 "moment of truth" statement be reaffirmed. But it was too late. Despite Bonnike's knowledge of the organization and the ties he had to many delegates, the fact was that he had left the brotherhood and would be listened to no longer. The scattered fellowship of resigned priests would be his new constituency. The effort to organize and lead them would become the primary concern of his life.

Early History of CORPUS
In 1978, Frank McGrath, one of the "facilitators," summarized the early history of CORPUS.[8] He related how difficult it had been to compile a list of resigned priests. The facilitators had written to all American dioceses and most religious orders seeking help. Few responded. The problem was not so much antipathy to CORPUS as the fact that authorities did not keep records of the whereabouts of their former members.

Nevertheless, by June of 1976, some seventeen hundred such priests had been contacted. Over six hundred subscribed to the CORPUS statement. Based on such a response rate, McGrath concluded that "at least one-third of the resigned/married priests remain committed to their priesthood and are ready and willing to serve the Church."

The men had been sent a "Dear brother" letter that wished them well in their new lives and invited those who were interested in being listed in the "reserves" to join CORPUS. The letter was conciliatory and respectful. It bore no trace of the anger and pain that Bonnike had expressed the year before. Even as FCM was establishing its separatist certification procedures and attempting to affiliate with Protestants, the CORPUS approach was one of humble willingness to serve as the Catholic bishops saw fit.

Relationship of CORPUS to FCM

There is some disagreement as to whether or not CORPUS was founded as a reaction against the direction FCM had taken. William Manseau, elected president of FCM in 1973, felt that it was. He is quoted as saying:

> This move by FCM to a wider vision and a broadening perspective, . . . while a challenging and valuable move in itself, occasioned a large number of the membership to disagree with that strategy, and in my view, that shifting of positions gave birth to the Corpus movement.[9]

Bonnike, on the other hand, insists that each group has its unique and distinct function and that he established CORPUS in order to keep the issue of a married priesthood in the forefront of public consciousness. He points to the fact that he has remained a member of FCM and indeed is certified by that group and appreciates the status such certification affords him for officiating at marriages. Further proof that Bonnike is comfortable with FCM is his personal long history of ecumenical involvement. In fact, in a situation similar to that of Manseau in Massachusetts, he served for a time as ecumenical pastor of an Illinois congregation. His point is that there is room for more than one organization in the movement.

Despite such an explanation, some tensions have existed between the two groups, with more conservative CORPUS subscribers insisting that FCM was too radical, and some FCM members considering

CORPUS too conservative, merely wishing to graft a married priest-hood onto a deeply flawed ecclesiastical structure. As early as 1975, an editorial in the FCM newsletter struck a conciliatory tone in an effort to allay fraternal squabbling. It argued that diversity within the ranks of married priests was to be expected and that the two groups

> are necessary to reflect the different attitudes of the inac-tive priests, but hopefully they will not work at cross purposes and thereby dilute the momentum of the recon-ciliation process.[10]

As a matter of fact, there has always been a broad overlap of membership in the two groups, despite the philosophical differences. CORPUS supporters focus their energies on "reinstatement" into the Roman Catholic clergy, while FCM supporters believe that Christi-anity is entering a new major phase of development, one that will produce a radically new type of Christian minister.

More Activist Tendencies Emerge

For the first ten years of its existence CORPUS consisted of a post office box in Chicago and the small group of facilitators led by Bonnike. These men compiled the list, sent out occasional mailings, issued periodic press releases, and regularly reminded the bishops of their presence.

However, as in any movement, some people became restless with such a low-keyed, even subservient stance and advocated more direct action. As early as 1976, the CORPUS statement was revised in order to include reference to the need for action on the local level. Explaining the change, the newsletter said:

> Please continue to send us names and addresses so that we may reach as many resigned/married priests as possible. However, we do feel the emphasis must shift from collect-ing names to more direct action—such as establishing models of resigned/married priests actually involved in Church work.[11]

McGrath's *Clergy Review* article also reflected this desire to remain loyal to the institutional Church while at the same time nibbling away at the frontiers of ministry. It said:

Careful to avoid involvement with any other causes, COR-
PUS is a single-focus organization—utilization of married
priests. In promoting this cause, it plans no protests, no
demonstrations, no public celebrations, no demanding
ultimatums. It does plan . . . to encourage models of
ministry by married priests and to alert the laity about the
availability of married priests to serve their needs. The
approach of CORPUS is seen as direct, respectful and
honest, but also firm, forceful and political.[12]

Fifty Facts and Insights

Reflecting growing impatience with the lack of response from the
Church, CORPUS in the eighties became progressively more asser-
tive, sounding like the SPFM of the late sixties, and, in effect, moving
more firmly into the mainstream of the movement. For example, in
1980, the facilitators produced the most celebrated publication that
CORPUS would issue, *Fifty Facts and Insights about Priests Who Marry*.
In addition to the "facts and insights," the four-page paper contained
"Seven Actions You Can Take." The actions included:

1. If your parish is closed or services reduced due to a
   shortage of celibate priests, keep telling the bishop that
   the parish must be kept open and the services supplied
   whether the priest be celibate or not.
2. Ask a married priest to preside at an occasional liturgy
   in your home.
3. Help us to establish ministries for priests who have
   married by telling us of bishops who might accept the
   help of married priests in administering some parishes.
4. Tell us of hospitals, nursing homes, colleges, military
   installations, and apartment complexes that might be
   eager to have a Catholic chaplain.

These suggestions for action are elements of the CORPUS contribution to the free ministry movement. With minimal organization,
the Chicago group gained increased recognition and respect as the
voice of ministerial reform. However, the voice spoke in a whisper
and was heard by relatively few. Like FCM, CORPUS became
increasingly marginalized. The bishops found that such groups
offered no real threat to their position and were best ignored.

In 1990, Bonnike would say that the period from the midseventies to the mideighties was a quiet time in terms of the movement. The numbers were not there. People were not hurting yet. There was little sense of emergency. Married priests were looked upon benignly but without a sense that their services were needed.

Lengthening Shadows/Glimmers of Hope

It is late in the day, and shadows gather. Although retired as a hospital chaplain, Bonnike is still at work, ministering to the Church in a variety of ways. He has an 800 number for his various enterprises, including an agency to help priests get tax-deferred pensions and appropriate insurance. His goal, as always, is to help men to be more free and thus more alive and more Christian.

Family responsibilities contribute to Bonnike's sense that his work is not over. For three years after their marriage in 1973, Frank and Janet tried to have a child. Finally, they adopted an infant girl. As fate would have it, two years later, with Bonnike fifty-seven years of age, Janet gave birth to a son. So, while he long since passed the traditional age for retirement, Bonnike still has children to see through high school and college.

Chapters 13 and 14 will describe the second phase of the CORPUS story, one which began late in 1984 with the hiring of a full-time executive secretary and includes the formation of a national board, the adoption of a constitution, and the selection of officers for what would now be a bona fide organization. Bonnike supported this restructuring, hoping that at long last the "moment of truth" had arrived and that a concerted mobilization of resources was required. As he reached sixty-five, he knew that the time had come to turn over the reins to younger men.

Still Saying "Yes" to Priesthood

At the first National Conference on a Married Priesthood, sponsored by CORPUS in 1988, Bonnike was invited to preach at the closing Mass. His moving homily included the antiphonal-like participation of the congregation of four hundred. He said:

> The Lord called us to presbyteral service among the people. And we said, [At this point, the congregation shouted, "Yes!"]. Later He called many of us a second time, and this time to marry, to be a co-servant with another, and we said, [The congregation shouted "Yes!"]. He calls us today to

presbyteral service and to marriage, and what do we say?
[The congregation shouted "Yes"].[13]

In words suggesting both the suffering of a man who still wanted to be a priest and the wisdom gained from that suffering, Bonnike exhorted his listeners "not to hate the Church for the violence done to our liberty, identity, or maturity. Our mission is to forgive, to reconcile . . . otherwise we can never grow or be at peace."

He concluded his presentation to an audience that revered him not only as a founding father of CORPUS but as an inspiring role model for a restored priesthood with the words: "We now proceed to the sacrifice of the broken Body and spilled Blood of Jesus, where memories count the most; the present is celebrated; and the future is dreamed and resolutely planned."

However, Frank Bonnike did not himself proceed to the altar to offer the sacrifice. He walked to his place at the side of the sanctuary and watched as an "active" priest presided at the Eucharist. Three years later, as CORPUS became more and more confrontational, he concelebrated with other married priests at the New York conference to be discussed in chapter 14.

Aware that the limits of the human life span were working against him, Bonnike has said that even if he could never be a canonically approved priest again himself, he would be at peace knowing that he had helped to make it possible for others. Long ago, Moses led the people through the desert, and when at last the Promised Land was in sight, he had to remain behind, but died in peace, knowing that he had fulfilled his mission.

Part IV

Experiments in Free Ministry and the Role of Women

10

FCM Certification and the Ecumenical Catholic Diocese

It is clear, then, that a Catholic Chaplain's duties require him to perform Roman Catholic rites, services and instruction. Pursuant to the prohibitions of the establishment clause, only the Roman Catholic Church may determine who is fit to do these things.
Superior Court of State of California, January 1989

As the years passed and the Roman Catholic Church refused to change its restrictions on sacramental ministry, free ministers devised new strategies to bridge the gap between themselves and the Catholic people. Even though they could not obtain ecclesiastical status, they were able to procure legal status. Two mechanisms for legitimacy were devised, both of them emerging from the small but determined band of married priests who comprised the leadership of FCM. One, certification, entitled men and women designated by that legally constituted religious group to function in its name as ministers, including officiating at marriages. The other, the Ecumenical Catholic Diocese, went further, duplicating the very structure of the Roman Catholic Church by ordaining priests and consecrating bishops. There can be no doubt that certification and the ecumenical diocese provide people with credentials that the state recognizes under some circumstances. However, although a number of free

ministers welcome these mechanisms for reestablishing some socially recognized clerical identity, their existence has produced
minimal impact on the institutional Church.

Two men can serve to embody these approaches to legitimacy.
Daniel Duffy, in a protracted battle with the state of California and
the Catholic bishops, attempted to be recognized as a Catholic prison
chaplain, basing his claim on certification by FCM and faculties from
the Ecumenical Catholic Diocese. The other, Peter Brennan, is the
originator of the diocese and its primary bishop.

Duffy v. the State of California

Daniel Patrick Duffy was ordained an Oblate of Mary Immaculate
priest in 1967 at the age of thirty-three. The following year, he was
expelled from the Oblates because of his relationship with a woman
in Japan, where he was a missionary priest. He married in 1970 and
was later divorced. In 1979, he married Janice, a non-Catholic, who
has remained his staunch support throughout the series of economic,
legal, and health problems that he has experienced. There are no
children.

In 1984, Duffy obtained a position with the California Department
of Corrections as a "Catholic chaplain." Shortly after his appointment,
state officials became aware that Duffy was no ordinary Catholic
priest when he applied for health insurance for his wife. Upon being
apprised of the situation, Bishop Francis Quinn of Sacramento requested that Duffy be dismissed because he was not, as required by
the state job description, "an ordained priest, duly accredited by and
in good standing with the Roman Catholic Church, and approved by
the Bishop of the diocese in which the institution is located."

However, Duffy had not claimed to be approved by the *Roman*
Catholic Church but rather by FCM and the Ecumenical Catholic
Diocese of the Americas. He maintained that he was a *Catholic* priest
although not possessing credentials from the *Roman* Catholic Church.
Duffy sued to be reinstated.

The case, which would be in litigation for seven years, contained
weighty constitutional implications and was perhaps the most serious
challenge free ministry has presented to the Church. Aware of these
implications, the California bishops united and utilized their extensive
legal resources in their determination to win.

After the decision by the California Corrections Department to
dismiss Duffy from the chaplain's position, the case went first to an

administrative law judge, who, in two separate hearings, sided with Duffy and overturned the decision of the Corrections Department. The judge, James C. Waller, ruled:

> The appellant (Duffy) argues that permitting the Roman Catholic Church, and specifically the Bishop of the Roman Catholic Diocese, to approve the person appointed Catholic Chaplain for the institution is unconstitutional in that it indicates a preference for one Catholic denomination over another and creates an excessive entanglement between church and state. . . .
>
> The appellant's argument has merit. The specifications for Catholic Chaplain must be broadened to include other Catholic denominations. The appellant cannot and was not appointed a Roman Catholic Chaplain. However, he was properly appointed a Catholic Chaplain and should be reinstated. The prisons need qualified religious leaders as Chaplains. They do not have to be members of any particular denomination.[1]

These words of Judge Waller follow almost verbatim the testimony given by FCM leader Gerald Grudzen who, as expert witness for Duffy, argued that "many groups consider themselves Catholic without considering themselves Roman. Historically, there is pluralism in the definition of Catholic."[2]

Buoyed by this victory, which was appealed by the Catholic Church, Duffy and his free ministry associates were eager to pursue the case further. Particularly helpful was James M. Mize of Sacramento, an FCM member and Duffy's lawyer throughout the protracted proceedings. Mize worked on a pro bono basis, incurring considerable personal expense.

Despite confidence that both free ministry and Duffy were on the verge of a significant victory, an unbroken sequence of setbacks began. First, the state personnel board overturned Judge Waller's decision. The case was resubmitted in 1988, and once again the board decided against Duffy.

Finally, in 1991, the California Supreme Court ruled against Duffy. A summary of the arguments on both sides can serve to illustrate the complexity of the American principle of the separation of church and state and the care with which the court attempted to navigate its way through the swirling currents of conflicting rights.

Duffy challenged his dismissal on the grounds that state law violated the Establishment Clause by limiting employment to persons of a particular religion and by subjecting candidates to the approval of the local bishop. He argued also that his dismissal violated the Equal Protection Clause of the Fourteenth Amendment by discriminating against him on the basis of creed.

In rejoinder, the court held that the case was governed not by the Establishment Clause but by the Free Exercise Clause, to wit, that a prisoner has a right to reasonable access to ministers of his religion and that only the bishop can determine who is qualified to minister to Roman Catholic inmates. Requiring that the bishop approve Roman Catholic chaplains does not constitute excessive entanglement with religion. In fact, a policy interfering with the bishop's determination of who ought to be a Roman Catholic priest would create far more entanglement. The court also rejected the equal protection argument, pointing out that Duffy was not a Roman Catholic priest and hence not qualified to perform for Roman Catholic inmates the essential duties of a Roman Catholic chaplain.[3]

In an interview after the 1991 decision, both Duffy and his wife said that they had wanted to appeal the case to the U.S. Supreme Court but that they lacked the resources to do so. Mize was not able to continue and the Duffys had no personal assets on which to draw. They contacted CORPUS, but neither that group nor FCM was in a position to carry to the nation's highest court what would have been the movement's most striking legal challenge to what it considered the Roman Catholic hierarchy's excessive religious hegemony.

A Man's Livelihood

At the 1985 hearing, Judge Waller had urged both sides to reach an agreement. He suggested that, as a compromise, Duffy might be given a chaplaincy at some state prison without the title of Roman Catholic chaplain. The diocese of Sacramento indicated some willingness to accept such a settlement. However, Duffy insisted that he was a Catholic priest and wished to be hired as such. In gambling that he would win the case, Duffy assumed considerable personal financial risk. And indeed he experienced difficulties. In a letter to *Diaspora* he thanked the FCM members of northern California for their "spiritual and financial support to my family through some bad times."[4]

Duffy did assume another position with the state of California. A newspaper recorded his experience in moving terms:

What the Rev. Patrick Duffy does is still done behind walls—in a criminal holding tank void of sanity and filled with needs. The ministry that Duffy loves and lives for, however, isn't there.

Instead of ministering to the needs of inmates at the state prison in Susanville, a job Duffy was fired from. . . , the Catholic priest has spent the past two years doing social work at the Atascadero State Hospital, a facility for the criminally insane.[5]

Even this work had to be relinquished in 1990 when Duffy suffered several strokes that left him partially disabled. In a phone interview that year, his speech slurred by the strokes, he expressed confidence that his health would be restored enough for him to resume his chaplain's duties if the Supreme Court decided in his favor. However, after the 1991 decision, both Duffy and his wife said that his health had deteriorated to the point where, even had he won, he would not have been able to resume the position. Duffy said that he had wanted to continue the case for the sake of others.

Comparing the Bonnike and Duffy Cases
Frank Bonnike had served openly and for many years as "Catholic chaplain" in Lutheran General Hospital in Chicago without objection from Roman Catholic Church officials. What was the difference between the two situations? From the point of view of the Church, the difference was substantial. Although both men were Roman Catholic priests who were now married, Bonnike's position was that of lay Catholic chaplain whereas Duffy was attempting to be a *priest* chaplain. Occasionally, in emergency situations, Bonnike used his priestly powers to administer the sacraments. This was in accord with Canon Law. Duffy wanted to administer those same sacraments on a regular basis, as part of his job. This was not acceptable.

Origin of Certification Program
Although not anticipated by the founders of SPFM, it soon became clear that frequently the exercise of religious ministry requires credentials. In the July–August 1970 issue of *Diaspora*, Charlie Sullivan, SPFM representative-at-large, mentioned that he had encountered problems of "clerical identification" while attempting to visit imprisoned Vietnam War protesters in Minnesota. He wondered about

"the feasibility of SPFM issuing certificates attesting to the clerical status of its priest members."

In 1972, William F. Nerin, an Oklahoma SPFM member and a pastor of the Catholic experimental community of John XXIII, wrote to Tom Durkin expressing his view of the direction in which the Church was headed. His words are typical of the views of free ministers at the time and included the suggestion that certification was needed. Nerin wrote:

> I think that in the future alternate institutional forms of life will gain a secure foothold and perhaps within thirty years either the old institutions will collapse or will be so ineffective that the new forms will attract people of vitality. There seems to be no stemming the tide at this point. Here in Oklahoma we are losing our finest priests. Some are willing to continue in some kind of ministry, which is a new twist for some of the guys leaving, and they are willing to try it locally.
>
> In view of this, what sort of apparatus do you have, if any, to authorize the credentials of a former priest in such a way that he can be considered legitimate by IRS . . . as well as perform marriages. If there is no apparatus for this, I think one should be established.

And indeed William Manseau did have such an idea. He proposed it at the 1972 SPFM convention in Los Angeles. In 1973 it was one of the planks in his SEEDS proposal, and after the 1974 convention in Chicago he announced that five people had been certified.[6]

The five were Manseau himself, Gerald and Marita Grudzen, Harold Furblur, and Peter Brennan. The four men, all of whom had been ordained priests, were "recognized as full ministers." Marita Grudzen was certified for a "ministry of pastoral care," which enabled her to witness marriages but did not include "such priestly functions as presiding at the eucharist."

In summarizing the work of the 1974 convention, Gerald Grudzen wrote:

> The Fellowship ratified a new constitution which reflected the shift it had made from being a lobby group for married priests within Roman Catholicism to a religious society with its own program of ministry. Professional certification

> for men and women seeking recognition of their ministries
> and a network of generating communities to support the
> training and placement of such ministers will mark the
> national outreach of FCM for the coming year.[7]

The "network of generating communities" never materialized,
but certification did, saving FCM from almost certain demise. By
1990, some one hundred FCM men and women, one-third of all dues-
paying members, would be certified. Most would be married Catholic
priests who wanted the certification for the legality of the occasional
marriages at which they officiated.

The legitimacy of FCM certification was put to the test in the late
seventies at the United Nations Chapel in New York. Several men,
including Louis Gioia and Henry Fehrenbacher, were officiating at
marriages there and identifying themselves as FCM Catholic priests.
The chancery of the archdiocese of New York attempted to stop the
practice. Through the intervention of Paul O'Dwyer of the New York
city council, FCM was able to get the city clerk to accept the validity
of marriages performed by what were called "ecumenical Catholic
priests." However, in 1992, the issue resurfaced when an official in
upstate New York challenged the validity of a marriage performed
by an FCM-certified minister.

Theological Rationale for Certification

In a 1983 letter to a married priest requesting information about
certification, Grudzen explained both the rationale behind certification
and the specific requirements to be certified. He established the legal
basis for certification by indicating that FCM was "a 501c3 religious
corporation," recognized nationally as an organization "which em-
powers its members to engage in alternative forms of religious
ministry."

For the theological rationale, Grudzen referred to an article in
which the married priest theologian Robert C. Scharf provided a
justification for the certification program using extensive citations
from Edward Schillebeeckx and, in particular, his book *Ministry*.
Schillebeeckx wrote:

> Against the background of existing church order, new and
> perhaps urgently necessary alternative possibilities can
> usually be seen only through the medium of what must
> provisionally be called "illegality". . . . Christians can

develop a practice in the church from below, from the grass roots, which for a time can compete with the official practice recognized by the church, but which in its Christian opposition and illegality can eventually nevertheless become the dominant practice of the church, and finally be sanctioned by the official church.[8]

Is Ordination Necessary for Ministry?

Scharf raised the further question of the need for ordination. Obviously, married priests were already ordained, but what about the practice FCM had initiated of certifying nonordained men and women? Scharf again appealed to Schillebeeckx in arguing that Christian ministry was not limited to those ordained by bishops. In fact, for the first thousand years of its history, the Church left open the question of whether or not ordination was absolutely necessary. It would seem that "the call of the community" and not ordination was the essential requirement.[9]

In his 1983 letter, Grudzen further bolstered his case for certification by adding:

> We also have discussed this program at length with Hans Küng, Bernard Cooke and Anthony Padovano, utilizing them as theological consultants. All of them have basically concurred with the direction we are taking.

Grudzen firmly established the legality of certification in California by obtaining its validation from the attorney general of that state. A letter from the attorney general said that in the eyes of the state, an FCM certified member had the same standing as a Roman Catholic priest or a Protestant minister in good standing. The key to the ruling was that FCM was "a legitimate faith community capable of endorsing its members for ministry." On the other hand, a priest, married or not, who was *not* in good standing with his bishop or who was not certified by FCM did not have any legal status and hence could not witness marriages or be recognized legally as a minister.

Requirements for Certification

Manseau envisioned the certification program as functioning in tandem with a training program. FCM would train as well as certify people for ministry. The training program never materialized, and the certifying process soon became a pro forma acceptance of virtually all who applied. It was difficult to reject anyone, since FCM, in attempting to be an umbrella covering the widest possible spectrum of people, had found it impossible and, in the minds of most leaders, undesirable to specify a basic set of beliefs to which members must subscribe or a level of education they must have attained.

The FCM executive board meets twice each year, once during the winter and then in conjunction with the annual convention in the summer. The certification of members consumes much of the time. The several regional vice presidents present the applications to the board, adding whatever personal knowledge they may have of the candidates. Since most are resigned Catholic priests, there is little discussion of their training or background. Many applicants have no history of involvement in FCM activities.

Although the question of their membership in a faith community is raised, few applicants participate in a "basic Christian community" in the sense intended by the formulators of the program. Most FCM certified members hardly fulfill Schillebeeckx's definition of ministers as people called to service by a community.

Certification as Professional Credentialing

At one time Manseau used the analogy of a "professional organization" to explain what he had in mind by certification. He himself belonged to the American Association of Pastoral Counselors. Others belonged to the American Psychological Association. In such organizations, members typically are independent practitioners. Once attained, membership requires little more than the paying of dues. Participation in the running of the association is welcome, but not required.

FCM soon found that most certified members were treating their status as that of a professional organization. They would pay the annual dues and submit a brief report but not participate in the leadership of the organization or attend the annual convention or the occasional regional gatherings. Several certified members told the author that they felt no need for "community" or "networking" with other FCM members. In general, they wanted certification in order to officiate at marriages, typically of couples impeded by divorce from marrying in the Catholic Church.

Liability Implications

During his tenure as FCM president (1980–84), Paul Schlesinger, a hospital personnel director by profession, warned frequently of the legal implications for board members of certifying professionals. Conscious of malpractice suits from his hospital position, he warned that if a certified member were sued for malpractice, the board also, as certifying agent, could be sued. Schlesinger was uncomfortable serving on a board that did not have board of directors' insurance.

Fortunately, in the seventeen-year history of certification, no member has been sued. This lack of litigation may have lulled the board into a remarkably casual approach to certification. Typically, with the passage of time, professional organizations make admission requirements more stringent. FCM has made them less so. The board remains uninsured and hence exposed to liability.[10]

Peter Brennan and the
Ecumenical Catholic Diocese

Besides his FCM certification, Daniel Patrick Duffy based his claim to be a Catholic chaplain on the fact that he was affiliated with the Ecumenical Catholic Diocese of the Americas. At the center of this aspect of the story is Peter Paul Brennan, who broke new ground in an effort to find a viable channel for the exercise of a free ministry.

To a certain point, Brennan's life followed a typical pattern for an Irish-American Catholic boy interested in the priesthood growing up in New York City in the fifties. At age thirteen, he entered the residential high school seminary of the Franciscan Friars of the Atonement, followed that with a year of novitiate, and then in 1964 completed a bachelor of arts degree at St. Pius X Seminary, in Graymoor, Garrison, New York. At this point, after nine years with the Graymoor Friars, he transferred to the Long Island Rockville Centre Diocese and studied theology at St. Bernard's Seminary in Rochester, New York, and then at the Seminary of the Immaculate Conception in Huntington, New York. In 1967 Brennan withdrew from the seminary, one year before ordination.

He began a career in education with the New York City public school system, working in various positions over the years. Currently, he serves as assistant principal for English in a New York high school.

The public schools not only provided Brennan with a career but also with a wife. During his first year of teaching, he met Marie Therese Kirby, a fellow teacher. They were married during the summer of 1968 at the United Nations Chapel. Like Brennan, Marie had a background in religion, having been a member of the Religious of the Sacred Heart of Mary. The Brennans have three children, the first born in 1971. They have lived at the same address in West Hempstead, Long Island, for twenty years, an address used by Brennan as the official center for all his ministerial ventures.

Certainly this history is not particularly noteworthy. However, there is another dimension to Brennan's life that marks him as an unusual figure in the free ministry movement. Most free ministers were ordained priests first and then married. Brennan married *before* he was ordained a priest. More than that, he subsequently had himself consecrated a bishop. He has done what few free ministers have ever done: He has ordained priests and even consecrated a bishop.

In a 1991 interview, Brennan said that since he was six years old he had wanted to be a priest. He left the seminary not because he changed his mind about the priesthood but because he could not make a commitment to celibacy. His continuing and uninterrupted interest in priesthood is supported by the fact that immediately upon leaving the seminary, he enrolled at St. John's University, where in 1970 he received a masters degree in theology.

When in 1972 he was ordained a priest by Richard Arthur Marchenna, coadjutor archbishop of the Old Roman Catholic Archdiocese of North America, Brennan saw this step as a natural progression from the training he had received for many years.

The archdiocese did not have any ministries available, and thus Brennan had to find a congregation in which to minister. He did so in Harlem. The parish of the Good Shepherd was affiliated with the African Orthodox Church (A.O.C.), which was similar to the Old Catholic in its emphasis on traditionally Catholic-like rituals. Brennan served there as priest-in-charge from 1976 until a fire the following year destroyed the building. The congregation, which consisted of a few elderly people, had no fire insurance and was forced to unite with another African Orthodox congregation. Though Brennan's pastorate came to an end, he continues to be in communion with the A.O.C. and holds a seat in their House of Bishops.

Legally, FCM Becomes a New Church

Paralleling Brennan's efforts to develop a ministry within the African Orthodox Church was his role in FCM. On the one hand, because of his background, Brennan has always considered himself a Catholic and has wanted to minister as a Catholic. On the other hand, he was not adverse to affiliation with structures not in union with Rome.

He exemplifies the school of thought expressed by Grudzen in the Daniel Patrick Duffy case that there can be pluralism within Catholicism, including organizational and jurisdictional pluralism. With this mentality, Brennan and others rather quickly transformed FCM from a protest group within Roman Catholicism into an independent religious organization. What made this step inevitable was the institution of certification in which Brennan played a significant role.

Not only was Brennan among the first to be certified, but at the 1974 convention he and his wife Marie succeeded the Duryeas as national secretary-treasurers and served in that position for two years.

One of Brennan's tasks was to submit FCM's annual report to the state of New Mexico, where SPFM had been incorporated since shortly after its inception. To the September 1975 report, Brennan attached a Notice of Change of Name as well as a copy of the new constitution. His report included a paragraph that was designed to ensure the organization's continuing status as a tax-exempt religious organization and that suggested the group's emerging self-understanding. He said:

> We are most accurately described according to our purposes, activities, and operations as a church, and as an association or convention of churches, and as a religious order.

Registration of Sacramental Actions

In 1976 the executive board position of registrar was created, consistent with the group's sense that it had become a separate religious organization. If certified members were baptizing and performing marriages, then there should be some central place where such actions could be recorded. Accordingly, registers were purchased and baptismal and marriage certificate forms were printed. The first and as it turned out, only registrar was Peter Brennan.

The project did not receive much support. Over the years, only six or seven people utilized the services of the registrar, especially Joseph O'Rourke, who had married the Brennans at the United Nations Chapel. When O'Rourke was challenged by the New York City clerk for witnessing marriages, it was Brennan in his position as FCM secretary-treasurer who submitted the documentation necessary to clarify O'Rourke's status.[11]

The FCM board minutes reveal that the position of registrar was eliminated in 1980. By that time Brennan, while maintaining his certified status, had ceased to be active in the group and, in the 1991 interview, said that he learned that the position of registrar had been eliminated when it no longer appeared on the organization's stationery. About sixty marriages and fifteen baptisms had been recorded in the registers that are still in Brennan's possession.

Brennan Is Consecrated a Bishop
The traditional route to ministry for Catholics has not been certification, but *ordination*. And for ordination, a bishop is needed. Despite his support for certification, Brennan next took what might have been the most daring step in the history of the free ministry movement: He had himself consecrated a free ministry bishop and made himself available to ordain people who wished to be priests, be they male or female, married or single, seminary-trained or not.

On June 10, 1978, Brennan was consecrated by Richard Thomas McFarland, bishop of the Holy Orthodox Catholic Church in America at Our Lady Queen of Heaven Orthodox Catholic Church in Mastic Beach, New York. The program for the consecration contains an "Order of the Service," which includes such traditional components as "Reading of the Apostolic Mandate and the Oath," "The Prostration and the Litany," and "Book of Gospels on Shoulders and the Imposition of Hands." The program also explains the origin of the Holy Orthodox Catholic Church in America. Its claim to Apostolic Succession comes through the African Orthodox Church, with which Brennan was already associated.

Should There Be FCM Bishops?
Brennan used two strategies in an effort to have himself accepted as a bishop. The second, the establishment of his own diocese, gained the most attention. However, before taking that step, he attempted to have FCM incorporate an episcopacy into its organization.

Shortly after being consecrated, he proposed to the FCM board that a bishops' advisory committee be established to be of service to "communities or individuals who may desire the presence and ministry of a compatible bishop." This suggestion was presented at the October 1978 convention in Phoenix but referred back to Brennan for "further development."

Ambivalence with regard to the role of bishops in the free ministry movement was reflected in the actions of William Manseau. At the April 1978 FCM board meeting at the Grudzens' home in White Plains, New York, two months before Brennan's consecration,

Manseau reported that in January he had visited two men affiliated with the "Catholic Church of the East, Bishop John in Phoenix and Archbishop Michael in San Francisco." Manseau reported that these men were "interested in providing a ministerial base for married Catholic priests who were pentecostal in spirituality and theology." Manseau went on to "wonder" what would happen if several FCM members were to be consecrated bishops by the Eastern Catholic Church and then proceeded to ordain married laypersons who showed "ministerial competencies." The minutes show that Manseau's idea met with a "mixed reaction."

The Ecumenical Catholic Diocese

Undeterred by the cool reception with which his episcopal status was greeted by FCM, Brennan tried another approach. In 1979 he founded the Ecumenical Catholic Diocese of Long Island, to serve as the legal framework for his personal ministry. For several years after establishing the diocese, Brennan did little to develop it. Then in 1983 he made what would be the one serious effort to transform his paper structure into a living reality.

On December 10, prompted by Raymond Kelly, a resigned Maryknoll priest, Brennan hosted a meeting in his home. Also present were Rocco Caporale, Joseph Fradale, Gaylord Shimnoski, and John Kenny, all of them resigned Catholic priests. The group agreed that "the needs of the Catholic community at large were such that a new vision of the Church and Catholicism was required."[12] It was decided that the Ecumenical Catholic Diocese of Long Island would be transformed into the Ecumenical Catholic Diocese of the Americas (ECDA). The literature listed Brennan as Ordinary of the ECDA, Fradale (also a bishop) as Vicar General, and Caporale as Chancellor. To complete the trappings of the Roman Catholic Church, both bishops appended D.D. to their names. Caporale, the only one with an earned doctorate, used Ph.D.

The Second Coming of Rocco Caporale

Like a Phoenix rising from the ashes of free ministry, Rocco Caporale, whose "Blueprint for a Liberating Structure" of 1969 had been a seminal essay in the emergence of the movement, now authored the paper that presented the rationale and agenda for the ECDA. In fifteen years he had not lost his fire but now, significantly, redirected the flames. Caporale, who had been one of Brennan's teachers at St. John's University, was a founding father of the ECDA, just as he prided himself in being a founder of SPFM. The results of his efforts in the eighties, however, would be even more disappointing than they had been in the sixties.

The ECDA paper was a development of Caporale's earlier writings and, to some extent, a repudiation of them. In any case, the paper and the ecumenical diocese would be a challenge to the direction that FCM and CORPUS were taking. FCM had set up a nonhierarchical, nonclerical structure as its framework for ministry. CORPUS, at this point, had established no structure whatever, content to lobby gently for Church reform. Brennan and Caporale offered a third alternative: duplicate the Roman Catholic Church's own structure.

While agreeing that it was possible to reform the Church from within, Caporale argued that the stalled post-Vatican II reform movement now demanded a more frontal attack. He saw a clear need "to establish an institutional alternative, a church-like organization characterized by all the features of institutional catholicism. . . . I envision a nationwide, non-territorial church organization such as a diocese."[13]

Although in his "Blueprint," Caporale had urged a reform movement from *within* Catholicism, he now insisted that a "church form" was needed, not a voluntary movement. As he put it: "Institutions last; movements do not." The new Church or diocese would have a hierarchy of bishops whose "apostolic succession can be validated." There would be priests, married and single, male and female. The congregations, which would be ecumenical, would be "house churches." There would be no test of faith; the diocese would be open to all who professed "the fundamental tenets of Christianity."

Despite Brennan's earlier rejection by FCM, Caporale's paper proposed a link between the ECDA and the free ministry organization. It might have been nostalgia for the group he had helped establish that motivated Caporale to advance the foredoomed plan. Disconnected from FCM for many years, he was not aware of the group's weakened condition or its antipathy toward bishops. Be that as it may, he envisioned the ecumenical diocese functioning as a congregation within FCM and "under the leadership of FCM members."

It is difficult to imagine a workable authority structure in which "bishops" would be answerable to "FCM members." Nevertheless, Caporale hoped once again to have a role in the movement, urging it to accept an episcopacy empowered with "the ability to validly transmit that priesthood to which FCM members have endeavored to remain faithful."

FCM's Rejection of ECDA

Accordingly, Brennan and Kelly applied for FCM chapter status. In August 1984, they flew to Chicago to attend the convention at Barat College in Lake Forest, Illinois, confident that they had created an important new dimension for the movement. However, they made three mistakes that would shatter their dream.

First, in 1984 the presidency of FCM was shared by Paul and Susana Schlesinger, Chicago residents. They had planned the convention but had not been privy to the establishment of the ecumenical diocese nor to the intention of the promoters of the diocese to publicize it at the convention. Furthermore, Paul Schlesinger was the first FCM male president who had not been a priest and had no desire to be one. Neither he nor Susana had any sympathy for the trappings of a hierarchy and supported a more congregational direction for FCM.

Second, without authorization of the FCM leadership, Ray Kelly had issued a press release to the effect that the diocese would be announced formally at the convention. Sensing a major religious conflict, Associated Press sent the story out and it was picked up in several cities, including Chicago, where a reporter contacted the office of the archbishop to inquire about this rival diocese to be announced at Barat College, a Catholic institution. Archbishop Bernardin was out of the country, and one of the auxiliary bishops said that he knew nothing about it but would look into the matter.[14]

When the Schlesingers and the other convention attendees arrived at Barat, there was considerable confusion. It was expected that representatives of the archdiocese might appear or that Barat officials would bar them from holding the meeting. Furthermore, Kelly had said in the press release that there would be a press conference on Sunday morning.

After lengthy discussion, Schlesinger assured the Barat administration that there would be no press conference and that no rival diocese was going to be established. The convention proceeded but with a high level of tension.

The third mistake of the diocese was not to have Rocco Caporale, the most articulate spokesman, present. Kelly's manner of speaking was abrasive, and Brennan, although conciliatory and diplomatic, struck some as endowed with an episcopal demeanor from which they were attempting to disengage themselves. In any case, the petition of the diocese for FCM chapter status was tabled and never resubmitted.

Subsequent History of the Ecumenical Diocese

Having been rejected by FCM, the diocese, legally established as a tax-exempt religious organization, went its own way and became one of the numerous small groups that gather like flies around the giant Roman Catholic Church, causing minor irritation but offering little threat to its power.

That even splinter groups splinter is evidenced by the experience of the three men who have been bishops of the Ecumenical Catholic Diocese. At the 1984 FCM convention at Barat College, Brennan met Patrick Joseph Callahan of California, who like Brennan, had been consecrated a bishop by a prelate of the Old Catholic Church.

Subsequently, Callahan visited Brennan in New York. The two agreed to divide the diocese, with Brennan the "Bishop in New York" and Callahan the "Bishop in California."

The titles in quotation marks are the ones used in a March 1985 letter to Francis Quinn, the Roman Catholic bishop of Sacramento, with reference to the Duffy case. At that time Brennan and Callahan were cooperating in the effort to have Duffy reinstated as a prison chaplain. The tone of the letter is that of episcopal peers discussing a jurisdictional conflict. Brennan and Callahan inform Quinn that Duffy "is currently functioning under faculties from our diocese." They grant Quinn "permission" to provide Duffy with Roman Catholic faculties, explaining to the bishop of Sacramento that

> The Ecumenical Catholic Diocese allows priests to minister to other Christians including Roman Catholics who are in need of spiritual support. Thus, our priests are quite flexible and versatile in service to the church community.

Bishop Quinn did not accept the proposal of his episcopal colleagues.

Whereas in March 1985 Brennan and Callahan were working together, by October of the same year Brennan was instructing Duffy to "avoid communication" with Callahan who had "suspended" Duffy. Brennan assured the anxious Duffy: "You have my full protection and support. I made the original promise and will stick with you even if it means losing Callahan."

And indeed Brennan did "lose" Callahan whose offense was that he had been dunning Duffy for money and had threatened to write to the California state personnel board informing it that Duffy had been suspended from the diocese.

While this was going on, Brennan, together with his Long Island neighbor, Robert Penaskovic, a former Franciscan priest, was hosting the 1985 FCM convention at Hofstra University. There was some apprehension that Brennan might generate controversy once again by introducing the ECDA proposal. However, sensing that the group was not interested, he did not do so.

Reaching the consensus that episcopal ordination was not essential for full Christian ministry, FCM has since proceeded with its own certification program. The practice of not requiring ordination in order to exercise the full range of ministerial function is FCM's most significant departure from Catholic tradition and its most striking contribution to the free ministry movement. It is both a rejection of the claims of the hierarchy for exclusive control of the Church and a model for a more democratic ecclesiastical organization.

Brennan's Continuing Ministry

Besides his affiliation with Bishop Callahan in California, Brennan consecrated Gus Sicard of Texas to be a third bishop for the ECDA. However, in 1991, Brennan reported that he had not had contact in some time with either associate and that the diocese was dormant. At one time or another, about a dozen priests, most of them resigned Catholic clergy, have been affiliated with the ECDA. Typically, as is true of FCM's certification, they needed credentials for employment purposes as chaplains or to witness marriages. Two men who had not been priests were ordained by Brennan. Although he is willing to ordain women, none has applied.

In the basement of his house, which he calls Christ House Ecumenical Center, Brennan has a fully equipped chapel, where for many years he offered daily Mass. He never had more than two or three people as his congregation. On occasion, he still celebrates Mass with his family. His ministry today is a thriving business officiating at marriages, mostly of divorced Catholics. Brennan performs some one hundred fifty marriages a year. Generally the service is held in a catering hall. When a couple contacts him, he invites them to attend a wedding he is to perform and talks with them afterwards. This is the extent of their premarital instructions.

Certification v. Ordination

Two alternative routes into the world of free ministry have been constructed: certification and ordination. To be certified simply requires that an application be completed and accepted by the FCM board. There is no ceremony, not even the expectation that the candidate be present. It is impersonal. Most board members do not know the man or woman being certified and that person does not know them. Hopefully, the candidate has been "called" by a community to bring to them the Gospel and the Sacraments of Christ. In practice, few of the people certified by FCM have a true communal affiliation. Many are simply freelance marriage ministers. Like teachers or social workers, they have been certified but feel little emotional attachment to the certificate that was mailed to them or to those who sent it.

Ordination, on the other hand, entails the laying on of hands by a bishop and the calling upon God to invest the candidate with the power of Christ. A bishop embraces the new priest in a communal ceremony, with candles, incense, and music to dramatize what is happening. Wearing special vestments for the occasion, the prelate breathes into the face of the candidate the warming Spirit of God. There is a sense of connectedness with the church of the millennia through a successor to the Apostles who welcomes another person to that awesome fraternity of martyrs, saints, scholars, missionaries, and pastors. Yet ordination to the ecumenical diocese has not produced a loyal and supportive band of disciples. Like other efforts before them, certification and ordination have not been able to revitalize Christianity or offer a convincing alternative for ministerial validation.

Both these mechanisms do provide a sense of identity and approbation. Men who had been ordained priests in the Roman Catholic Church need only certification to feel that once again, in some peripheral way, they belong to the company of ministers. Those never ordained, like Brennan, need the more traditional ritual of ordination in order to feel secure in their priestly persona.

In any case, a concrete aspect of the free ministry movement has been this search for legitimacy. Some have found it in the Episcopal Church or another mainline Protestant denomination. Others, not willing to relinquish some identification with their Catholic roots, have turned to FCM or the ecumenical diocese.

It would be tempting to picture Peter Brennan celebrating Mass by himself in the basement of his home or marrying people in catering halls and feel either pity or sadness. Likewise, it would be easy to feel sorry for Dan Duffy pursuing in vain his quest for a prison chaplaincy. An alternative reaction would be to imagine Brennan and Duffy as representative of the many sincere men who, rejected by the Catholic Church for wanting greater freedom in their lives—including the freedom to marry—are forced to wander down strange and lonely paths in search of a ministry.

11

The Search for Community and Constituency

Christian ministry cannot be separated from Christian community.

Gerald Grudzen, *New Age Catholicism*, 1979

While the free ministry movement has focused on the reform of the clerical profession, it also has stressed the larger issue of the reconceptualization and reorganization of the Church itself. In particular, the traditional parish with its array of organizations has been judged incapable of shaping a vital personal spirituality, let alone transforming the world. Free ministry calls for a radical rethinking of the way that the followers of Christ attempt to deepen their faith and to foster peace and justice on a rapidly changing planet. A buzzword for this search has been *community*.

FCM has been convinced from its inception that it would be futile to graft a "liberated priesthood" onto an obsolete ecclesiastical framework. However, although there has been general dissatisfaction with the old, there has been little success in fashioning viable new models for Christian living. One model that has been tantalizing in its appeal—but frustrating in the efforts to implement it—has been the *base community movement*. The movement has played an impressive role in the revitalization of life in Latin America. Since the early seventies base communities have become the most powerful engine for religious and social renewal in a number of countries, Brazil in particular. In 1991, four thousand representatives of base communities in Sao Paulo held their ninth statewide conference and were praised by Cardinal Paulo Evaristo Arns as "the social and spiritual conscience of our society."[1]

Few have worked harder to promote the idea of community and to form base communities in the United States than Marita and Gerald Grudzen, key leaders of FCM since it broke from its narrowly clerical moorings in 1973. To a large extent, FCM itself is the community that the Grudzens have fashioned.

Genesis of a Love Relationship

Marita Reilly joined the Maryknoll Sisters in 1958 at the age of eighteen, following a Chicago childhood in a traditional Catholic family. In 1966, while working in the infirmary at the Motherhouse convent in New York, she was assigned to help a twenty-six-year-old Maryknoll deacon prepare sermons for the convent patients. As they worked together and organized a Bible study group in the convent, they realized that they were in love.

The deacon, just a few months from ordination to the priesthood, was Gerald Grudzen. Like Reilly, Grudzen was the product of a midwestern Catholic family and entered Church service immediately after high school. He enrolled in the Detroit archdiocesan minor seminary with the idea of becoming a parish priest. However, attracted to foreign mission work, he transferred to Maryknoll in 1962.

The couple thought that their love would enhance their Church work and initially saw no conflict between love and the celibate life.

After ordination in the summer of 1967, Grudzen was assigned to Bolivia, while Reilly remained at Maryknoll. Not just their love but the ferment of the times fed into a radical reevaluation of their lives. New ideas were transforming the young couple's sense of their vocations.

Vatican II had given Grudzen an interest in ecumenism as well as a broad conception of the role of the priest. However, in Bolivia he found that his colleagues still saw priesthood in terms of ritual and narrow denominational concerns. He experienced the shock shared by many of those trained during and after the council when assigned to work with men and women with preconciliar thinking.

For her part, Reilly experienced a growing inclination toward "community" rather than "institutional" life. She and three other sisters had been praying together, forming what would be called an *intentional community*. They requested that they be assigned as a group, rather than as individuals. When their request was denied by their Maryknoll superiors, they decided to leave and to attempt communal life outside the convent walls. At that moment, Reilly's major concern was how the move might affect Grudzen. She did not want him to feel that he should leave the priesthood.

Nevertheless, Grudzen, deeply affected by Reilly's decision and reviewing his own feelings, flew to New York immediately after she left Maryknoll. Years later, Reilly would recall, "There was so much joy in being together, everything just flowed from there." The two were married less than a week later, on December 29, 1967. Grudzen had been a priest for six months.

New Age Christians

From the beginning of their life together, the Grudzens knew that although they had left the institutional Church, they were nevertheless called to ministry. They felt that a community of believers was the best context within which to live the Christian life. For most of the first five years of their marriage, they shared what they called "an experiment in communal living" with the women who had left Maryknoll with Marita.

The early experiences and ideas of the Grudzens are recorded in two books that Jerry published privately during the seventies. In *Genesis of the Christian Experience*,[2] he credited Teilhard de Chardin as the inspiration for the direction their lives were taking. He felt that a new stage in human development had arrived; that human life was evolving into a higher form of spiritual awareness and an enhanced capacity for love. He believed that "traditional ecclesial structures were not adequate" to serve the needs of men and women who were moving into this "New Age." Although the Christian religion possessed a vital core of beliefs and practices, they were encased in increasingly obsolete institutional forms. Grudzen saw the intentional community in which he lived as a model for the future. Communities of men and women—married and single, working in the mainstream of life—would replace single-sex religious communities.

A few years later, having moved from New York to California, the Grudzens were exposed to the New Age religious movement that they found congruent with their ideas of Church and spirituality. More than that, Jerry saw FCM, of which he and Marita were now copresidents, as an example of the creative possibilities for combining a Catholic heritage with the spirit of the new age. Accordingly, he titled his second book, *New Age Catholicism: A Life of Service in the World.*[3]

Although the Grudzens themselves were no longer living in community but in a comfortable house in a middle-class area of the rapidly growing city of San Jose, the idea of community remained central to their vision of Christianity. Community members need not live together, they believed, but should meet in one another's homes for prayer, mutual support, planning social justice projects, and the breaking of bread. Christian ministry would flow from and be guided by these base communities or house churches. There was no need for a cultic priesthood, still less for a hierarchical superstructure. Christ would be present within the small groups of his followers who would serve as a leaven in the world.

Free Ministry in New York

All this lay ahead. For the first eleven years of their marriage the Grudzens lived in New York, where they continued their education, established new careers, and gave life to their two daughters. They also became deeply involved in the free ministry movement.

Drawing from her experience in the convent infirmary, Marita entered what would be a lifetime career in health care and health care administration. She obtained credentials as an inhalation therapist and worked in a New York hospital. Jerry was employed as a counselor for a teen center and pursued graduate work in history at Columbia University, where he had earned a masters degree in church history while in the seminary. Grudzen credits these studies with a significant role in his spiritual evolution.

The Grudzens became aware of the free ministry movement in 1969 when they heard about "underground" liturgy groups meeting in convents and Protestant church halls in Queens, New York. Here were priests, married and single, sisters and lay people, worshiping together in a spirit of joy and freedom. They identified immediately with the experience.

Among the participants in the group were Joseph and Ann Bukovchik (or Buko). Joe, like the Grudzens, had belonged to Maryknoll. Ann had been a member of the now defunct community,

Daughters of Mary Health of the Sick. The two had met at a language school in Tokyo in 1967 and now, two years later, were the central figures in an event that would jolt those present into a totally different perception of what Catholic worship could be. In a convent living room, even though celibate priests were present, Joe Buko was invited to preside at the Eucharist. Using a free-form prayer and holding with deep reverence the sacramental bread and wine, Buko led the group of fifty people in worship. By the side of this young man stood his beautiful wife Ann, eight months pregnant with the first of their four daughters. The Grudzens thought, "Why not us?"

Another member of the Queens group was Joe Burns, already a prime force for free ministry in the New York area and soon to be elected executive secretary of the fledgling SPFM. Burns recruited the Grudzens, who the following year became vice presidents for New York. In 1973 they worked with Bill Manseau to organize the national convention that transformed SPFM into FCM.

After three years as Manseau's national vice presidents, the Grudzens became the first copresidents, serving in that capacity until 1980. Since then, they have remained prime factors in the survival of the organization. Besides the informal leadership provided by both, Jerry has served as development director and chairman of the board. They have been the glue that has held together the fragile FCM network. Jerry never misses a board meeting or a convention, where he provides a calm but strong presence expressing hope for a better future to the reduced and aging band of free ministers.

Journey Across America

In a letter written to his friends and colleagues just before the climactic 1973 convention, Grudzen reviewed his personal and family history. Most of all, he revealed the hunger within his soul for ministry and the conviction that growth and change, personal and institutional, were needed. His concluding paragraph was, in effect, the preamble to the rest of his life. He wrote:

> My hopes for the future are bound up with our continued growth in ministry and mission. Please join with us in helping to fashion a "new heaven and a new earth" for ourselves and our children. May the witness of our pilgrimage encourage you to embark upon a similar journey

which makes us one people joined together by our common desire to love and serve the Lord.

The metaphorical references to "pilgrimage" and "journey" in June 1973 became reality for the Grudzens in July 1978 when Jerry, Marita, and their daughters, Corita, five, and Simone, three, undertook a three-month, cross-country trip that was to have significant implications for them personally as well as for the free ministry movement. Their careers were not progressing, and they felt no attachment to the East Coast. California, on the other hand, was a magnet for adventuresome people ready for a fresh start. An important aspect of their journey would be to explore the possibility of relocating to the West. If the Grudzens were at a standstill personally, so also was FCM and the movement by married priests to have some organized impact on the Church. The journey would be a missionary trip for free ministry.

Agenda for a Movement

Grudzen announced the transcontinental venture in a front-page open letter in *Diaspora*.[4] He reviewed the ten-year history of free ministry, recalling the five years that the organization had been known as the Society of Priests for a Free Ministry and the five years as the Fellowship of Christian Ministries, the past two years of which he and Marita had served as copresidents. Grudzen enumerated what he considered the major achievements. His list is informative in showing how a key figure perceived the movement on the eve of undertaking what he hoped would be a major organizing effort. He wrote:

> Within the past five years a great variety of programs have been initiated as expressions of the dynamic communal life we are sharing. Certification for ministry, Priestly Ministries, career development, disability insurance, international assistance to Bangladesh and Honduras, spiritual renewal, inter-religious dialogue, women in ministry, and network building for alternate Christian communities are just some of the specific program divisions of FCM. Our publication, *Diaspora*, reaches 2,500 readers every two months. We have almost tripled our membership in the past two years from 100 to 300 men and

women. About 40 members have been certified, including three women.

There is no reference to the priesthood or to the Roman Catholic Church. In Grudzen's mind, free ministry had freed itself from the institutional Church and was developing ministries on its own.

The phrase "program divisions" not only provides some insight into Grudzen's growing interest in the terminology used by the business and public relations worlds but also indicates his vision for the organization he was attempting to energize. Although each item on Grudzen's list had some basis in reality, most were either the projects of individuals or little more than ideas. Bangladesh, for example, refers to an impressive humanitarian project of Grudzen himself while the allusion to Honduras pertains to the efforts of Gus and Noreen Cadieux to help poor people in Central America. Organizational applause greeted these ministries, but they were hardly FCM "program divisions."

Phrases like "spiritual renewal" and "network building" suggested the general objectives of free ministry rather than existing programs. To a large extent, Grudzen was presenting his agenda for FCM, rather than its past achievements.

Reduced Membership

If one accepts the figure that there were 2,500 *Diaspora* readers and 300 members, then only 12 percent of the people receiving the publication were interested enough to send in the modest membership or subscription fee. Eventually, thousands of names would be culled from the mailing list after several efforts to elicit a receptive response.

In January 1974, Bob Duryea, executive secretary at the time of the change of the group's name, interpreted the dramatic decline in membership to disillusionment with organizations. People were weary of government in the wake of Vietnam and Watergate and they were weary of the institutional Church in the face of the growing resistance of the Vatican to reform. The attitude was, "Just leave me alone. Let me get on with my life."

At work also may have been what Schillebeeckx would describe as the rapidly spreading spirit of secularism.[5] Whereas in the pre-Vatican II period Catholics lived in a cultural world that took the supernatural for granted, now, for many, the world of the spirit had evaporated like a mist touched by the morning sun. The council had thrown

Catholics of the developed countries into the mainstream of modern life, which did not so much ridicule or persecute religious faith as find it puzzling and irrelevant.

Whatever the reasons, the world of free ministry declined precipitously after 1973. In 1978, as a result of the Grudzens' visit to thirty cities and making personal appeals to scores of people, some new life was infused into the movement but even that did not last. While numbers are not the only measure of a movement's vitality, they are instructive. Since 1979, paid membership in FCM has declined 25 percent, although it has been rising gradually in the past two years. (See Table I.)

Table I: FCM Membership (1979–1991)

Year	Number of Members
1979	332
1981	264
1982–3	254
1985	240
1987	275
1989	227
1990	234
1991	250

(Source: Official Directories)

Indicative of the role FCM plays in the lives of its members is the steady increase in the proportion who are certified. In the 1985 directory, fifty-one members were listed as certified. In 1989, it had risen to eighty; in 1990, to ninety; and in 1991 to one hundred twenty five. Half of the current members are certified. While there is declining interest in other items on the FCM agenda, interest in legal credentials for officiating at marriages remains high. Despite the record number of certified members in 1991, only twenty-three people joined Jerry Grudzen at the 1991 FCM convention in St. Louis—the lowest turnout in the group's twenty-three year history.

Recruiting a Leadership Core

Not knowing what lay ahead and possessing little more than hearts filled with hope and a list of names, the Grudzens left New York in 1978 on the journey that would shift the focus of their lives and of free ministry from the East Coast to the West Coast. It would also clarify the strategy of FCM, which would be to develop a religious world separate from the Catholic Church but always hoping for an eventual convergence. Those not prepared to disavow the direct effort to change the Church of Rome would gravitate toward CORPUS or leave the movement altogether.

The immediate and urgent objective of the Grudzen trip was to encourage people to attend the annual FCM convention in Phoenix, Arizona, during October 6–8. This was the latest in the year that any FCM convention was held, and it was in a part of the country little touched by free ministry. While hoping to develop the area for the movement, the Grudzens were concerned that attendance might be embarrassingly low.

The first stop on the trip was Syracuse, New York, where the Grudzens met Frank and Mimi Woolever, a married priest couple who offered to organize and host the 1979 FCM convention. The Grudzens then moved on to visit with their families in Chicago and Detroit. In St. Louis they enlisted the help of Anne and Bill Lally, who had participated in the establishment of NAPR many years before and whose dedication to the movement is attested to by the fact that they have been principal organizers of three conventions in the St. Louis area: in 1981, 1987, and 1991.

In Indianapolis the Grudzens met Jim and Mary Catherine Dooley, who would occupy FCM board positions for many years. Similar fruitful contacts were made in Denver, San Antonio, Los Angeles, and elsewhere.

In 1990, reflecting back on that 1978 journey, Marita said that the most precious aspect for her was the sharing of the day-to-day lives of so many people. Each place they went, they spent a few days with a local family, eating meals, going for walks, watching the children play—all the normal activities of the domestic world of people like themselves: making the transition from priesthood and religious life to family and secular careers yet wondering if, somehow, they might yet serve as ministers.

This sense of community, of warm personal relationships, would be the one strong strand that would bind free ministry leaders to one another for the lean years ahead. Even when no one seemed capable of answering satisfactorily the question, "What is FCM?," the core members would travel cross-country for the annual convention.

The Children of Married Priests

For several families, such as the Grudzens, the Lallys, the Weirs, the Schutziuses, the Ruanes, and the Clarences, the convention was the only time of the year when their children saw one another. During the seventies, the need was for child care, while the parents attended sessions. In the eighties, the concern was for program components designed for the eight to ten young people who were in attendance. By 1990, many of the children were young adults, moving on to college and to the challenges of life. But certainly these annual encounters with other FCM families added a valuable dimension to their lives, including for some a not unpriestly zeal to be of service to the world. Denominational loyalties might be tenuous—as with their parents—but the essential thrust of compassion for the less fortunate and belief in the power of the individual to make a difference was prominent.

Joseph Fichter, S.J., a sociologist now in his eighties whose research in the late sixties had helped Carl Hemmer and NAPR establish that a majority of Catholics were ready for a married priesthood, surveyed the teenage children of married priests in 1990. His source was the CORPUS directory, which perhaps yielded a more conservative sample than if he had contacted FCM teenagers or the children of other married priests not included in the directory. What Fichter found was a high level of Catholic commitment on the part of the boys and girls, a striking 28 percent of whom were considering a Church vocation, compared with only 1 percent of American college freshmen. Fichter suggested, perhaps with tongue-in-cheek, that the shortage of vocations to the priesthood might be solved in part by the children of married priests.[6]

Women Lead the Liturgy

When the men and women recruited by the Grudzens assembled in Phoenix for the 1978 convention, the uncertainty as to the direction FCM should take was illustrated by an unplanned occurrence that created considerable controversy. While some found it shocking and an affront to their Catholic sensitivities, others saw it as the work of the Spirit. The central figure was Alla Bozarth-Campbell.

At the 1974 convention, Bozarth-Campbell, the then newly-ordained Episcopal priest, had received Communion from the hand of Frank Pleasant, a married priest, but had not celebrated the

Eucharist herself. Now in 1978 she joined several male married priests in presiding at the altar. All were wearing liturgical vestments available at the Franciscan Renewal Center where the convention was being held and to which the local Catholic bishop, James S. Rausch, had, in a letter to the organizers, welcomed the participants, unaware that they would enact such an unorthodox liturgy.

As it happened, during the liturgy someone in the front row of the chapel asked what "these people in vestments were doing there." It was a challenge to the continuation of dependence for worship on ordained clerics. Bozarth-Campbell, assigned to recite the Eucharistic Prayer, spontaneously invited three lay women to join her.

Anthony Soto, the husband of one of the women, related what happened next:

> After a moment's hesitation, Sr. Alla announced that she was sharing the priestly symbols with her companions at the altar as an act of empathy for the frustration felt by women denied the priesthood. She proceeded to place her stole on Phyllis Soto, her cord around Jessie Garibaldi, and her alb over Marita Grudzen.[7]

Some onlookers were shocked and offended. As a sign of protest, one of the male priests dramatically removed his vestments. However, most participants experienced this liturgy as a powerful representation of what free ministry was all about: the equality of the sexes, the ecumenicity of community, and the lack of necessity of ordination for worship.

The *National Catholic Reporter* gave extensive coverage to the convention and in particular to the liturgy. A picture showed the four women at the altar with Bozarth-Campbell about to place her stole over the shoulders of Phyllis Soto. Above the women, on the wall of the chapel were the words, "Send us your Spirit of love and peace, and we will renew the world."[8]

The role of women in free ministry will be examined more fully in chapter 12. Shortly after the dramatic liturgy in Phoenix, Marita Grudzen, Jessie Garibaldi, Phyllis Soto, and Sarah Segovia traveled from San Jose to Baltimore for the second Women's Ordination Conference. These shared experiences of late 1978 helped to fashion between Marita and her Hispanic friends a sense of sisterhood that would strengthen her resolve to work for the full integration of women and minority members into the ministry of the Church.

The Phoenix as Symbol

From the ninety people who attended the convention a leadership core was formed that would work with the Grudzens for the following decade in quest of a workable formula for ministerial renewal. Years later, Jerry and Marita would acknowledge the tenth annual convention as the moment when the movement was reborn. Certainly it was at Phoenix that the Grudzen stamp was firmly implanted on FCM.

The image of the phoenix, the mythical bird that rose to new life from death, has long been a Christian symbol for the Resurrection of Christ. Grudzen used it to represent the rebirth he hoped was taking place from the ashes of the organization to which he had invested so much of his resources during the preceding five years. Indicative of this hope was a poem he had written for the 1978 convention brochure:

> ### *Phoenix Bird*
> Resurrect! Come Forth!
> Your ashes have turned to flapping wings,
> Your heart is beating strongly
> Your eyes are open to new horizons
> The world is enlivened by your presence.
> Ready for flight
> the sky awaits your gracious curves and dives
> the sun is rising in honor of your ascent
> heavenward.
> Nature comes alive to greet you
> And all humanity finds hope in your rising.

The phoenix has remained a powerful symbol for Grudzen. Several years after the Phoenix convention, he commissioned an artist to fashion a large metal sculpture of a phoenix. It is located today in the center of a fountain in the lobby of the historic building in downtown San Jose, which Grudzen manages for a group of investors. Every day as he goes to his office, he sees this reminder of his family journey of 1978 and of his continuing hopes for FCM.[9]

Maryknoll-inspired Projects

The Grudzens did not restrict their ministerial concerns to the reorganizing of FCM or to the United States. Prompted by their continuing contacts with and affection for Maryknoll, they under-took several ambitious projects. One was Milk for Bangladesh, another was Maryknoll-in-Diaspora, and a third was an effort to link the North American free ministry movement with its counterpart in Latin America.

Milk for Bangladesh. In 1974, a famine in Bangladesh touched the hearts of many, including the Grudzens. Responding to an appeal from a former Maryknoll colleague in that suffering region, Jerry founded Milk for Bangladesh, which raised $25,000 and several hundred thousand pounds of milk and other food for the crisis-plagued country. The project continued for several years, with declining public response. In 1978, Grudzen abandoned the venture, donating funds collected to a CARE project for Bangladesh.[10]

Maryknoll-in-Diaspora. Over the years, hundreds of men and women had left what was officially known as the Catholic Foreign Mission Society of America. In 1977, the Grudzens contacted many of their former associates and established a loose-knit organization designed to capitalize on the skills present in this extensive body of former missioners. Grudzen said that the goals of Maryknoll-in-Diaspora included "fashioning human development programs, advocacy on behalf of the poor and oppressed, and alternate forms of relevant ministry."[11]

Grudzen and his associates—Raymond Kelly and Gregory Rienzo, in particular—hoped to establish a free ministry affiliation with Maryknoll, offering their services to mission projects in such fields as mental health, education, and business. Grudzen envisioned FCM acting as an umbrella agency that would provide coordination and technical assistance to Maryknoll-in-Diaspora and other specialized free ministry groups.[12] On several occasions, prompted by Grudzen's dual leadership positions, Maryknoll-in-Diaspora meetings were held in conjunction with FCM conventions.

In time, Maryknoll co-opted Grudzen's group, setting up its own structure and publishing a newsletter, *Interchange*, which served—and still serves—as a vehicle for former Maryknollers to maintain contact with one another. However, no formal participation in Maryknoll mission work has developed.

Latin American connections. Early in 1973, the Grudzens made the first of several trips to Latin America where they met with representatives of the married priests' movement. Once again the Maryknoll connection played a role. It was a missionary in Caracas, Venezuela, Rev. Steven Wood, a classmate of Grudzen, who served as host to

Jerry and Marita and who volunteered to coordinate free ministry activities in the area.

Some of the people with whom the Grudzens met had attended the 1972 FCM convention and thus were familiar with the North American movement.[13] The idea of publishing a Spanish-language edition of *Diaspora* was explored, and Sean Walsh on one occasion prepared what was to be a one-page insert for *Diaspora*. Financial constraints and the evaporation of the tenuous links with Latin American married priests resulted in the plan being abandoned.

Comunidades de Base

The contacts the Grudzens had with Latin America contributed to their interest in the theology of liberation and the ecclesial structure called *comunidades de base* or base communities. Early in 1973, Grudzen wrote:

> As we struggle to evolve new patterns of ministry here in the U.S., it is important that we learn from our brothers in Latin America. They are looking to us for new modes of ministry and we can look to them for a theology of ministry rooted in the needs of oppressed peoples.[14]

Why should North Americans look to Latin America for "a theology of ministry rooted in the needs of oppressed peoples?" How are North Americans "oppressed?" Bernard Cooke addressed this question in a spring 1986 *Diaspora* article.[15]

He argued that more attention would have to be paid to "the distinctive oppressions that are part of North American life" and that if base communities were to be formed, they must be tailored to the social reality of North American life. A "liberation theology" for North Americans must flow from "our own indigenous reflection about God's saving action in our lives." The Third World model was not directly applicable to the American social and cultural milieu.

In Cooke's mind, no permanent base communities were possible without a concerted effort on the part of theologians and pastors to provide a solid "intellectual/spiritual formation." He recommended as a model the observe-judge-act pattern that had been promoted by the Young Christian Workers several decades before.

It is precisely here, in the area of formation, that FCM has been unable to make a contribution. Although Grudzen was convinced that there were areas of oppression in American life, especially in terms of the condition of minority groups and women, he was unable to institute a process of formation within the free ministry movement that would communicate this conviction effectively and prompt the establishment of vigorous liberation theology-inspired groups.

Models of Base Communities

Certainly the Grudzens had a ready-made, even providential opportunity for base community development when they moved to California in 1978. There they found several freestanding communities of Mexican-Americans who would be mentioned over and over again in the years ahead as models for the anticipated blossoming of grass roots Christian communities. The Grudzens themselves worshiped with these people, loved them, admired them, and encouraged them. But the groups not only did not stimulate the development of similar structures in the Anglo community, they did not even lead to growth among Mexican-Americans. By 1991, only one Mexican-American group was officially linked with FCM, the Comunidad de Ministerios Cristianos of which Anthony and Phyllis Soto were leaders.[16]

What attracted the Grudzens to the Hispanic groups was that, although married priests were included, men did not dominate. Women also presided at the liturgies. They did not claim, however, that these liturgies were the same as the Catholic Mass. Further, the groups sponsored lay formation programs called *Cursillos*, weekend courses in Christianity modeled after a format found to be effective, especially among Hispanics, by the official Church.

The groups were quite independent of the institutional Church, baptizing their own children and celebrating marriages. It was here that Grudzen and FCM came in. Through certification the unaffiliated Hispanic groups were offered both a sense of connectedness to something larger than themselves and also a legal status for their marriages. Several of the small group members are certified, including both women who celebrated the liturgy with Marita Grudzen and Alla Bozarth-Campbell at the Phoenix convention.

Role of Mexican-Americans in the Movement

Middle-class Anglo-Catholics do not feel oppressed personally and culturally the way that some Mexican-Americans do nor do they experience the deep "systemic poverty" of the Third World poor. It was hoped that the FCM-related Hispanic groups would serve as a bridge between the cultures and evolve a base community format that would respond to the distinctive needs of North Americans. On the one hand, they could help their Anglo brothers and sisters to become conscious of subtle but pervasive dimensions of social and religious oppression. On the other, because of their linguistic and cultural compatibility, they could link the Latin American world with the United States. Married Anglo priests and their wives, such as the Grudzens and their Mexican-American counterparts, the Sotos, were positioned for a fruitful collaboration. Some modest efforts were made.

At the FCM conventions held in California (Berkeley in 1983 and 1986 and San Jose in 1990), the Soto group did fashion a liturgy that featured Hispanic symbols, including artifacts from Mexico, where the Hispanic communities explained to the the non-Hispanic participants their life-style. However, no ongoing relationships were established, not even with the Anglo groups in northern California. Time constraints and distances were cited as barriers to more frequent contact. In effect, the two worlds of Hispanics and Anglos remained separate, with only the Grudzens serving as a bridge.

In terms of international linkages, several joint Anglo-Hispanic initiatives were undertaken. For example, the theme of the 1986 FCM convention was "Basic Christian Communities in the U.S." The keynote speaker was Guillermo Cook, director of the Latin American Center for Evangelical Studies in Costa Rica. Cook followed up his participation by inviting FCM members to come to Latin America and see base communities for themselves.

In the summer of 1987, Jerry and Marita, together with Anthony and Phyllis Soto and Mary Catherine Gibson Dooley, joined a large group on a trip to Guatamala, Nicaragua, and Costa Rica. They discovered that most of the base communities were connected to the institutional Church, which in many areas had shifted from a position of supporting the status quo to one of advocacy for the poor. To a large extent, reform elements within the Church had negated the need for noninstitutionally approved groupings.[17]

Non-Hispanic Small Communities

There are several small Grudzen-related, if not FCM-affiliated, Anglo communities in northern California. Most core members are married priests who, under the Grudzens' leadership, have attempted various outreach activities, including the sponsorship of free ministry retreats. Such retreats had to be canceled due to insufficient registration. However, commencing in 1990, participants in these groups have conducted several camping trips that combine family vacation activities with spiritual renewal. Grudzen said that these experiences were spiritually invigorating and also served as a mechanism for attracting new supporters of the free ministry movement.

The group with which the Grudzens are most closely associated is based in Berkeley and led by Judy and Henry Clarence. Judy, a librarian, has been editor of *Diaspora* since 1988. Henry is a former Benedictine priest and retired book publisher's representative. The Clarences have worked closely with the Grudzens, playing a major role in planning the 1983 and 1986 conventions, both of which were held at Pacific Lutheran Theological Seminary, which is within walking distance of the Clarences' home.

Another married priest couple, Patricia and Daniel Curtin, belong to a group based in Stockton, California. Both Curtins are certified FCM members, have attended several conventions, and hosted a board meeting in February 1990 in the nursing home of which Dan is the administrator. The Curtins have been involved with the Grudzens in FCM of California, which has caused some confusion for the national board. Jerry Grudzen explained the incorporation of FCM in California as a legal step taken in anticipation of possible sponsorship of low-income housing or other projects that might be eligible for funding. Although no projects have materialized, in 1991 Grudzen was in the early stages of developing a training institute in ministry under FCM of California auspices. It would be housed in vacant office space in a building he manages. Grudzen did not suggest such an eventuality, but it is possible that, should the national FCM group disband, its California namesake could continue. Much of the organization's potential for survival and growth is found in northern California, that is, in the Grudzens' area.

Other Efforts to Stimulate Base Communities

In 1986, Walt Melfi of Charleston, South Carolina, who tried for years without success to form a base community in his area, summarized a report of Guillermo Cook, which noted that conferences on base ecclesial communities had taken place recently in England and in Australia for the purpose of discussing how these communities, so powerful in parts of the Third World, might be made relevant to the "affluent church." Cook argued that, properly adapted to First World conditions, the base communities could be powerful forces in "the reevangelization of our own stale churches."[18]

In March 1990, Melfi, Anthony Soto, Bill Manseau, and FCM president Joseph Ruane attended a National Consultation on Base Communities and Home Churches in North America in Salem, Massachusetts, that brought together two hundred people, mostly Protestants, from several countries.[19] Once again Guillermo Cook was a speaker and reported that whereas there were more than two hundred thousand base communities in Latin America, only a few hundred had been formed in the industrialized world. The critical factor was judged to be sociopolitical. First World Christians do not feel that the conditions of their lives require the radical reconsideration of the Scriptures that routinely take place in Third World areas. The process of *conscientization*, or making people aware of their needs and the needs of the world, is much more difficult in a context of political freedom and economic well-being.

Base Communities—A Dead End?

For more than fifteen years, the Grudzens have been convinced that the base community is a powerful mechanism for religious and social transformation. Yet, despite conferences and articles and workshops, little headway has been made. Free ministry had hoped by now to be able to present to the institutional Church a national network of alternative communities that would provide leadership and energy for a renewed Christianity. Married priests were to be important factors in the process while working as equal partners with all segments of the community. Younger adults were expected to be attracted to a form of religion that responded to their need for meaningful interpersonal relationships as well as for Scripture-generated responses to economic and social injustice. It just didn't happen.

When asked in 1990 what they considered their most significant contribution to free ministry, the Grudzens answered that it was the development of small communities. They believe that many Christians hunger for emotionally satisfying worship and service groupings and continue to point with pride to the groups in the San Jose area, undeterred both by the fact that few groups have emerged elsewhere and that all such groups struggle to survive and undertake few societal transformation projects.

The 1978 FCM directory listed eight community memberships and the 1991 directory just five, none of which appeared on the 1978 list. Only one was represented at the 1991 convention, and that was the Comunidad, represented by Anthony Soto, who also is FCM vice president for the West and is expected to attend board meetings in that capacity.[20]

Continuing Grudzen Influence

The Grudzen impact on FCM is evident in the membership pattern. In 1979, just as the Grudzens moved to California, that state had thirty-seven members. New York, which they were about to leave, had fifty-six. By 1991, those numbers had changed dramatically. Now there are seventy with California addresses and only twenty-five in New York. Total membership has declined during these eleven years, making the increase for California even more pronounced, from 11 percent of the members in 1979 to 28 percent in 1991. Most of these members reside in northern California, are affiliated with small worship groups, and are known personally by the Grudzens.

One of the northern California members, Daniel Mesa of Salinas, played a significant role in the Grudzens' transfer to the West Coast as well as to their association with Mexican-American communities. Mesa heads a minority economic development agency and hired Grudzen as a community economic developer. Within a few years, Grudzen had acquired the skills and made the connections that enabled him to establish his own business, the Grudzen Development Corporation.

Basically, what Grudzen does is to put together the complex package required to build or rehabilitate properties. He is very patient, at times nursing a project along for years only to have it fall through. Because of the tax credits available for projects, which include either housing for the poor or the preservation of historic buildings, he is able to obtain financial backing. His challenge is to work with banks, government agencies, real estate people, and lawyers to the point where a proposal can be presented to investors and construction begun.

Over the years, Grudzen himself has been able to take very little money out of the corporation and has had to refinance loans and find additional backers in order to forestall bankruptcy. Marita's position in the health careers department at Stanford University provides some steady income as well as health insurance for the family.

Attention has been paid to Grudzen's secular employment both because he sees it as a ministry in itself, and because it has honed skills that are transferable to his more strictly religious projects. One of his dreams is to build housing for the poor and elderly that would include components for enriching and humanizing their lives. Nothing would please him more than to be able to create housing where free ministers might be available to serve the residents.

Real estate development requires patience and optimism. There is considerable financial risk. The odds against significant success are staggering, especially for a small entrepreneur. It is precisely these qualities that Grudzen possesses and that are needed to keep the "business" of free ministry alive when "the market" seems bad. While many people have fallen away from the cause and others see FCM as little more than a credentializing agency, the Grudzens continue to tout base communities and to offer the little clusters of people in the San Francisco Bay area as models for what can be done with FCM leadership throughout the country.

Dancing for God

One of Marita Grudzen's interests has been dance. At several meetings, she added graceful movement to the liturgy, evoking with her body a sense of the Spirit of God flowing through the group and summoning it to life. She has long been an advocate of holistic medicine and a firm believer in the power of the loving heart to heal the wounded body. Her smile, passion for the interests of women, and obvious joy in the great number of friendships she has made through the free ministry movement have been critical, if often unrecorded, elements in the survival of the cause.

Both Jerry and Marita Grudzen are God's dancers. Their projects may fail, but they keep on dancing. There is much talk of charisms. The Grudzens have the charisms of hope, friendship, and passion for a renewed Christianity. If eventually free ministry bears more visible fruit, it will be due in large measure to the insistence of Jerry and Marita that, despite appearances, it was a good time to dance.

12

Women in Free Ministry

In the more spontaneous communities the contextual nature of ordination can be more informal so that whoever is the natural leader of the group or, perhaps on a shifting basis, members of the group can exercise priestly roles.

Rosemary Radford Ruether, 1967

Free ministry is a man's world. Most of the principal actors in the movement have been men who resigned from the official priesthood. They comprise a brotherhood. Their training, ordination, and ecclesiastical work have forged a strong bond among them. Furthermore, the process of leaving the priesthood, with all the stress associated with such a radical departure from a life to which they had pledged permanent fidelity, has added another layer of commonality and rapport. Finally, their paradoxical stance of wanting to resign from the priesthood yet remain priests sets them apart as a group from all other segments of the Church. They are no longer accepted by the hierarchy as priests yet refuse to assume the status of laymen. They reside in a no man's land of ambiguous identity. They need one another for reassurance that their lives have made sense and that their vision has substance.

Many free ministers would object to the preceding paragraph, insisting that women have always played an important role in the movement and that the goal is not their own personal reinstatement

223

so much as a reform of ministry and the elimination of the caste-like distinction between cleric and layperson. In particular, they would point to the collaboration of their wives. However, notwithstanding the obvious supportive role of many wives and official statements to the effect that free ministry is open to all, the movement has been essentially a male clerical phenomenon. The story might have been different had attempted coalitions with lay and religious organizations been successful or if it had been possible to attract a substantial number of nonclerics to the cause. This has not happened. After twenty-five years, free ministry is still predominantly a project of married priests.

However, there were two moments when women did occupy significant positions. One was in the earliest stages of the movement when the theologian Rosemary Radford Ruether lent her formidable intellectual resources to SPFM. The other was in the late eighties when Mary Jane Schutzius as president of FCM attempted to redirect the movement away from its male clerical focus. Neither woman was able to establish a true alliance of equals between men and women.

Rosemary Radford Ruether, Adviser to SPFM

In a July 1973 letter to SPFM President Bernard McGoldrick, Bill King, the *Diaspora* editor, wrote:

> I am *very much* in favor of Rosemary Ruether being approached to take on the presidency of SPFM.... Rosemary knows SPFM and its thrust. She is not an ordained priest. She has national visibility and creative thought and she is a woman.

King's enthusiasm for Ruether was well founded. She had been a highly visible and dynamic member of the SPFM advisory board since the earliest days of the society. The extensive correspondence between her and Eugene Bianchi attests to her deep commitment to the movement as well as to the creative leadership that she provided. However, that leadership would remain on the level of ideas, not in an organizational office. Like Bernard Cooke, Ruether knew that her gift was to be a theorist for Church renewal, not a free ministry practitioner or institutional functionary.

Although Ruether now describes herself as a feminist theologian, her involvement in the free ministry movement in the early seventies was not in terms of advocacy for the rights of women in the Church. That would come. Her initial goal was to overcome the stranglehold that the hierarchy had on Catholic people, male and female.

Ruether was instrumental in putting together in April 1971 an SPFM-sponsored conference in Detroit that was designed to equip the American Catholic bishops with the free ministry agenda in preparation for the fall synod of bishops in Rome. She was joined on the panel of speakers by Gregory Baum and James J. Megivern. In addition, Bernard Cooke prepared a paper for the meeting, which was held at Sacred Heart Seminary in Detroit. Ruether's talk articulated a set of ideas and strategies that would reappear in her espousal of the Women-Church movement in the eighties and again in the "Pastoral Letter from Catholics Concerned about Fundamental Renewal of our Church," which she prepared in 1990 for Call to Action.[1]

The core idea was that a coalition of reform-minded groups must present to the bishops the unambiguous message that their control of the Church violates the will of Christ and can no longer be tolerated. Her conviction that the power of the bishops could be countered only by power from reform groups was already well established when, on January 2, 1971, she wrote to Bianchi, expressing concerns about the April conference. She said:

> I am afraid that there is a certain kind of mood that passes itself off as "moderate" and therefore "trying to remain in dialogue with existing authority," but in fact simply lacks imagination, creativity and foresight into the needs and emerging possibilities of the times. As a result, its so-called "moderation" is merely dull and speaks to no one, whereas, with creative boldness, it could attract both those who are looking for new things *and* force those in authority to take notice. I'm concerned that our conference be of the latter, not the former variety.

Ruether had identified a fundamental feature of the free ministry movement, perhaps its tragic flaw, namely, that the leaders tended to be conciliatory. Ruether, although a Catholic, had not been shaped in the Catholic subservience to the hierarchy and, more clearly than the clerics with whom she worked, understood that the basic issue was power and that power, even in the Church, would never be relinquished voluntarily.

Call for a Pastoral Council

The specific strategy for gaining power that Ruether had in mind, which she presented in the January letter to Bianchi as well as at the April conference and once again at the September SPFM convention in New York, was the summoning of a national pastoral council that would bring together all "the creative forces in the American church." Ruether revealed her vision in no uncertain terms when she went on to say:

> Convergence is there, ready to be discovered. That would be very exciting. It would be important. It would attract a lot of people. It would scare the bishops because it would look like power to be reckoned with. We should declare ourselves the church, and invite the bishops to join us; not belligerently, but as though to state the obvious. It seems to me that unless we kind of get on the stick with that kind of boldness of conception, the conference won't be worth doing.

It would turn out that her boldness was too radical for most Catholics, even the most dissatisfied. However, there is no denying the audacity of her ideas as well as their prophetic aspects. Ruether would use much of the same fervor and reasoning in her appeal to women in the eighties.

A Manifesto for Change

Ruether's 1971 paper was a comprehensive formulation of the radical free ministry vision, an extension of Rocco Caporale's 1969 "Blueprint for a Liberating Structure," and in large measure the perspective that would fashion FCM in 1973. The substantial failure of FCM to implement Ruether's ideas after nearly twenty years of effort can mean either that liberals did not have the necessary commitment or resources to carry them out or that Ruether in 1971 presented a plan much too utopian to be realized. What follows is the first paragraph of her sweeping vision for Church reform.

> The liberal wing of the Catholic Church, particularly in the United States, is faced with a fundamental task of survival in the face of what will be at least a generation of negative leadership from Rome and the American hierarchy. Both

the behavior of the bishops at their Spring meeting and what can be expected from the Synod at Rome gives us no reason to think that any lines of institutional support will be forthcoming from these sources. In effect, the official leadership has become negative leadership, determined to destroy the progress stemming from Vatican II, and the liberal church must develop its own ongoing organizational structure that can survive as a parallel structure for some decades to come, in a way that will (a) have its own mandate to act independently in the development of ministries and communities, (b) will refuse to be defined as schismatic and will maintain constant openness to the hierarchical church for whatever opportunities for authentic relation to them may develop, but without dependence upon them, and (c) will look forward to its own new organizational structure as the authentic future of the church which should itself eventually take over and become the proper parliamentary and elective body of the American Catholic Church. To do so does not suggest any kind of tactic of force or exclusion of others, but simply an organic growth in which it proves itself to be the most viable leadership structure which is generating the most important ideas and activities and which will gradually draw into itself the mandate to be the central leadership body through that fact. That fact has still to be historically proven, needless to say. That the structures which are presently being developed in the liberal church, such as priests' associations, a lay association and organizations of religious should build up representative bodies from the grass roots and grow to the point where they can logically be seen as the elective and parliamentary body of the American church is not some unheard of idea, but corresponds exactly to the principles of Vatican II and is the way in which other modern churches, including hierarchical churches such as the Episcopal Church are presently governed.[2]

Like a gauntlet thrown before what she hoped were courageous warriors, Ruether offered this daring program to Bianchi and the SPFM members. They, however, were not prepared to pick it up. Bianchi himself had indicated his uncertainty in a January 1971 letter to Ruether, in which he expressed his reaction to her planned frontal attack on the institutional Church. He wrote that he wanted to

> steer between two possible shipwrecks. . . . One would be the wreck of sounding too kooky to the people we want to attract; this is my conservative strain. The other wreck would be to come on in a stodgy manner, being so moderate that no one pays attention; this is my liberal-progressive bent.

As it turned out, the main danger was the shipwreck of SPFM itself and the entire fragile network of liberal Catholic groups. Neither the April conference nor the September SPFM convention drew many people and, in particular, did not attract leaders of organizations ready to form the envisioned coalition that would in turn summon a pastoral council.

Growing Frustration with SPFM

Ruether herself soon grew frustrated. In a March 1972 letter to Bernard McGoldrick, Bianchi's successor as president of SPFM, she complained that the groups with which SPFM was attempting to bring about a convergence were "undoubtedly too hung up on preserving their own identity, much threatened by change, and consolidating their own meager empires, to relate to us at this time."

Ruether went on to advise that SPFM pursue an alternative strategy to the ill-fated convergence. The alternative was to decide upon one or two projects that would demonstrate the "innovative aspect of our *raison d'etre.*" The next convention, she argued, should focus on developing new ministries that would offer visible accomplishments to these other groups, leading them, perhaps, to "want to relate to us because we are where they want to be."

At that September 1972 convention in Los Angeles no such new ministries were planned. Instead, under McGoldrick's leadership, SPFM continued the quest for convergence, this time on an international level. The ill-fated call went out for an International Congress on Ministry and Social Change to be held in Geneva, Switzerland. Several committees were established, including one chaired by William Manseau to seek ways to relate to Protestant churches. Ruether attended the convention and saw that SPFM was more interested in forming committees and calling meetings than in engaging in actual free ministries. She would make one further attempt to influence the married priests group and then turn to other more promising segments of the dissatisfied Catholic population in her campaign for reform.

At times, Ruether used the stationery of the Howard University School of Religion where she was teaching. On other occasions she used the SPFM stationery on which she was listed as a member of the advisory board. For several years she invested considerable energy in working with SPFM. Besides writing and speaking for the group, she attempted to raise funds through contacts that she had, including the Institute for Ministry Development. She attended meetings with the Bishops Liaison Committee on Priests, with Joe Burns, Gabriel Moran, Gregory Baum, and others in the New York area. In March 1971, she was a speaker at Emory University in Atlanta and held one of several meetings with Bianchi, a member of the Emory faculty. At all these meetings, she was the only woman participant.

Defining Christian Ministry
Ruether's last substantial contribution to the organization, now called FCM, was a paper on the meaning of Christian ministry. The paper was printed in *Diaspora* in two installments.[3] The editor noted that the essay was "a working paper for the 1974 conference." It is the longest article ever to appear in *Diaspora* and, based on the centrality of its topic, quite likely the most important.

There is no evidence that groups of free ministers used the paper as the basis for discussion, but nevertheless the ideas it contained became part of the thinking of the movement and anticipated the writings along similar lines of theologians such as Schillebeeckx and Cooke and even some of the analysis of Hans Küng.

Basically, what Ruether argues is that "the essential ministry is the ministry of the *Laos*, or 'the people.'" She examines the traditional categories of *laity* and *minister* and concludes that there is a profound misunderstanding of the terms and that this misunderstanding must be corrected if the Church is to be reformed.

The purpose of ministry is to witness to and serve Christ,

> transforming the world into that Kingdom of God where God's will is done on earth. It was to found this ministry of the Church to the world that Christ came into the world. The ministry of the Church must then be seen in relation to the calling of the Church to become a "witness people;" an *avante garde* of a New Humanity in a new Creation.

If ministry resides basically in the laity, what then is the function of the ordained ministry? Ruether refers to the ordained ministry as "enabling" the *laos* to carry out their ministry. Ordained ministry is directed toward the congregation. Its purpose is "to train, equip, inspire and deepen the faith and ability of the people to carry out the ministry of the Church."

This insistence that "ordained ministry" operates only within a congregational setting leads Ruether to draw a conclusion that could not be accepted by many free ministers and quite likely explains why her ideas were not met with much enthusiasm. She says that "the ordained person exercises the ordained ministry only when engaged specifically in enabling ministry for a congregation." She had been associated long enough with SPFM to feel justified in chiding its members for harboring "a residual heritage of the caste concept of sacerdotal priesthood." For Ruether, when ordained persons were engaged in their secular occupations, no matter how much service oriented, they were practicing the "common ministry" of the *laos*, not the "enabling ministry of the ordained."

As if to turn the knife in the wound of those who considered themselves priests, although not serving in a pastoral role with a worshiping congregation, Ruether insists that

> they unwittingly preserved a magical caste-concept of priesthood, as an indelible mark that set them aside forever. A functional concept of ministry would have to criticize the idea that such former priests are priests in this magico-caste sense. Rather what one should say is that they are persons trained to the ordained ministry and seeking to exercise this function again. But they are "ordained" only when they again find a community which elects them as its pastoral or enabling minister.[4]

Undermining further the concept of priesthood to which many of her readers clung, Ruether argues a point now widely made but in 1974 still shocking, namely, that the New Testament does not suggest, let alone mandate, that absolving sins and presiding at the Eucharist is reserved to a special sacerdotal caste. Quite the contrary, it is the members of the community who absolve each other's sins; it is the community that celebrates Eucharist; and it is the community that calls individuals to special enabling ministries. Ruether suggests that the way to break out of the erroneous present practice is to work toward a pool of liturgically equipped people who can alternate in this function, thereby making clear that these functions belong to the life of the community, not the special powers of ordained persons.

Finally, Ruether makes a point that follows logically and inevitably from her argument. "There should be no special 'role' of women in the Church. Women should be free to function in any role of the Church." To achieve this full equality, "the sexist-clericalist model of ordained ministry," which is deeply imprinted in the fabric of the Church, would have to be dismantled.

Aware of the radical character of her vision, Ruether concludes her analysis of ministry by saying that "one is likely to despair of ever getting there by starting from where the Church is now!" The only hope, she believes, is for those who accept her view to develop communities that will begin "to act out of this vision." They in turn will be "teachers and model-builders" for other communities.

Call for the Ordination of Women

Despite the image of free ministry as a movement of and for married male priests, support for the equality of women has long been a plank in its platform. As early as its second convention, held in Berkeley in 1970, SPFM passed a resolution calling on the Church "to eliminate discrimination against women by opening to them all levels of life and office in the church." It was explained that the resolution was "in response to criticism of the Society for its negligence in promoting full rights for women in the church."[5]

After the 1974 convention, the press release was even more specific, calling "for the ordination of women to the Catholic priesthood." The participation of the Episcopal priest, Alla Bozarth-Campbell, was highlighted as evidence of FCM's commitment to the equality of women in ministry as was the fact that several women participated in presiding at the liturgy. The *National Catholic Reporter* article on the meeting quoted FCM president William Manseau as explaining that the selection of women to preside

arose out of the need to give witness that the time has come for women to be publicly ordained as presidents of the eucharist in a formal way. The eucharist is the primary sacrament which reveals the essence of the church, and for men to preside over the sacrament all the time gives a lopsided view of the church.[6]

Nevertheless, the depth of the commitment to the equality of women is open to question. In 1990 Manseau said that, although still favoring the full equality of women, "for political reasons" he felt that it should not be pursued too vigorously. His reasoning was that it would be easier to convince the pope and bishops to authorize a married male priesthood than to accept women. CORPUS, even more than FCM, has a long history of giving lip service to women's equality while actively advancing a married male priesthood. In due time, women would discover that most men in FCM as well as CORPUS were more concerned with their own restoration to ministry than with the broader agenda for reform advocated by Ruether.

More important to Ruether than the ordination of women was the elimination of the male-sexist ethic that permeated all aspects of Church life. She also promoted the emerging personalist philosophy, which saw relationships as central to human development and attributed the decline in religious vocations to a transformation of human self-understanding. She joined her voice to that of Eugene Kennedy and other liberal psychologists when she wrote:

> We are now inclined to believe that we relate to God by relating to our fellow human beings, not by detaching ourselves from them. We are inclined to think that life without love, without warm friendships and deep personal relationships, is less than authentic human life; that, moreover, sexual relationship is a normal dimension of human relationship, and that Christian perfection cannot mean anything if it is contrary to humanization.[7]

Abuses Stemming from Celibacy

In an article on a similar theme, Ruether was even more forceful in her critique of celibacy, comparing it to "the ethic of the totalitarian institution, such as prisons, armies and mental asylums, which demand a similar monolithic and total control that excludes interpersonal dependencies."[8]

Ruether's interest in "the frayed and tattered" institution of celibacy was not strictly academic. In an undated 1972 letter to SPFM President McGoldrick and the organization's board, she drew attention to what she called a widespread and serious problem, namely, that of priests who remain in the structure but had entered into relationships with women, fathered children, and were living lives "of quiet desperation." She urged SPFM to advocate Church policies that would provide "counseling and child support for priests who have fathered children but whose relationship to the Church has not allowed them to make the break to form a responsible marriage."

Prompted by women who had written to her, Ruether argued that hundreds, perhaps thousands, of celibates had adopted "a liberated sexual ethic" while attempting to remain within the "celibate ascetic institution." She said that many of those "have suffered destructive psychic upheavals far deeper than they expected and found no resources for guidance or healing."[9]

There is no evidence that the free ministry movement or the official Church itself paid any heed to this plea. There is evidence, however, that Ruether shifted her attention from the male-dominated free ministers to focus on groups of women who were advocating Church reform.

Women's Ordination Conference

Manseau had worked hard to attract one hundred people to the September 1974 FCM convention in Chicago. Later that same year, a small group of women met at the Catholic Theological Union in Chicago and asked if the time was ripe during the International Women's Year to raise the issue of the ordination of women in the Roman Catholic Church. They answered "Yes" and within the year gathered two thousand people in Detroit for the most impressive women's event to date in the Catholic Church: the first Women's Ordination Conference. One of the speakers was Rosemary Ruether.

Ruether's tone was forceful as she accused the Church of a long history of pervasive discrimination against women:

> Dressed up in the language of God, Christ and the Church, male dominance becomes idolatry, the projection of the vanities of human egoism and unjust power upon the very face of God. For that reason it is truly anathema, and all Christians, male and female, must come to look upon it with the horror and disgust it deserves, rather than continuing to cower before its presumptive authority.[10]

Perhaps they did not "cower," but most of the women attending the conference were loyal to the Church, not ready to take the radical steps that Ruether advocated. Furthermore, the majority of the attendees were women religious with a vow of obedience, conditioned to respect authority. Ruether pointed to this very situation, insisting that the patriarchal system was insidious and had created "an entire symbolic edifice of reality that reflects the social hierarchy of male dominance and female submission."[11]

She proceeded to sound a clarion call for the mobilization of women's religious orders and for all women to change the male-dominated Church, shaking free of "the long conditioning to docility." She saw the women's orders as "a major institutional base" for the push for the ordination of women and was confident that there was enough power as well as discontent to overthrow the established ecclesiastical order. The new vision consisted of a coalition of religious and laywomen just as, a few years before, it had been a coalition of liberal priests and laity.

A second Women's Ordination Conference assembled in 1979 and reflected just how rapidly the consciousness of Catholic women was shifting from one of seeking acceptance by the bishops to one of assuming fuller responsibility for their own spiritual lives. Emboldened by the sense of solidarity that they experienced in their meetings, many women redirected their attention from a desire for ordination to the intoxicating task of exploring the possibility of women themselves redesigning worship and redefining ministry. *Women Church* was being born.

The Women-Church Movement

In what has turned out to be a painfully long effort to reform professional ministry within the Catholic Church, there have been three waves in the assault on the seemingly impenetrable citadel. First, the married priests organized in the late sixties, confident that the rightness of their cause would result in a speedy victory. Their banners proclaimed that they were led by the Holy Spirit. They failed. In the midseventies women religious in even greater numbers asserted their cause, to them so transparently just, that women be afforded equality in the Church to which they had pledged their lives. Their hopes crashed in vain against the Rock of Peter. Finally, in the eighties, it was the turn of laywomen to join with progressive women religious in an assault on the celibate male bastion. As in the first two attempts, Rosemary Ruether was a major strategist.

Over the years, Ruether has written or contributed to dozens of books, published over five hundred articles and reviews, and spoken at hundreds of university campuses and Church conventions.[12] One author referred to her as "perhaps the most prolific and forceful writer of all the feminist theologians" and included her along with

Dr. Martin Luther King, Jr. and Gustavo Gutierrez as "a modern prophet."[13]

Ruether is called upon frequently to articulate the discontents of Catholic women. In 1988, the American bishops solicited feedback on a first draft of a proposed pastoral letter on women. The letter said that women could never be priests. Ruether replied:

> The bishops are unable to rethink the absurd claim that women cannot be ordained because they do not image Christ. That contradicts their own statement that men and women are equal in imaging God.[14]

Two years later, the second draft drew an even more scathing response from Ruether. This time, as the spokesperson for a dozen women's groups, including the National Assembly of Religious Women (formerly the National Assembly of Women Religious), the Women's Ordination Conference, and Women Church, she sent an open letter to all U.S. Catholic bishops. Ruether said that the new draft "reaffirms every aspect of the patriarchal system that is the basis of sexism." The bishops were charged with wanting "to seduce us into helping to rescue your patriarchal ecclesial system while conceding nothing that is essential to that system itself." She claimed that the "male, clerical, patriarchal church" was "disintegrating at its center." Perhaps most threatening of all, she called on women not to support financially an institution that was so demeaning to women. "Not one cent, not one finger lifted, not one knee bent for the church of patriarchy."[15]

Ruether's intellectual interests and organizational involvements have been far-ranging. Although attention here has focused on her role in the Catholic reform movement, she has published and has been active in Christian ecumenism, interreligious affairs, the Third World, the Middle East, and secular social activist causes.

Collaboration with Bianchi

Although Ruether has not been involved directly in free ministry for many years, there remains a link through her collaboration with Eugene Bianchi. Twice they have worked together on books. In 1976, they coauthored a volume of essays on "Sexism and Woman-Man Liberation," an unusual mix of literary styles with Ruether's theological-historical essays alternating with the autobiographical reflections by Bianchi in which he candidly explores his struggle to eradicate his own deeply-rooted "machismo."[16] From their studies of history as well as personal experience, both subscribe to the words that Bianchi wrote in the introduction: "Patriarchy is so deeply entrenched in social institutions, East and West, that we tend to accept it as an immutable axiom of nature and divinity."

In 1992, Bianchi and Ruether collaborated once again, this time as editors of a book on democracy in the Church. The basic argument of the contributors is that neither the Scriptures nor the long history of the Church precludes the emergence of more democratic structures.

Mary Jane Schutzius: From FCM to Women Church

If Rosemary Ruether has been the most significant feminist theoretician, then Mary Jane Schutzius has been the most highly placed woman in a free ministry organization. From 1982 to 1984 she was the first woman editor of FCM's *Diaspora* and then was elected the first woman to serve in her own right as the group's president (1984-88). Her husband, Robert, a former St. Louis priest, has also been active in FCM, succeeding his wife as *Diaspora* editor and in 1988, while relinquishing that position, continuing on as publisher. However, although the Schutziuses are supportive of each other, each has distinct views and affiliations, and Mary Jane functioned throughout the eighties very much as her own person. Her major objective was to increase the presence and influence of women in the movement. An alliance of the two "oppressed" groups—women and married priests—could be a powerful force for change.

Although FCM has attempted on occasion to form an editorial board to work with the editor, the *Diaspora* editor has full control of the content and style of the publication. An examination of the eleven issues that Schutzius edited and the sixteen that were published while she was president and for which she wrote a president's column, reveals consistent attention to the need for women's voices to be heard. Just as evident is her own continuous formation as a Christian feminist and her personal activism in a variety of arenas. Finally, when the Schutzius decade ended, it was very clear that her voice had not been heeded. To a large extent, women and married priests found that their styles and their agendas did not mesh.

Hans Küng on Women

In the Winter 1981–82 issue of *Diaspora*, the first that Schutzius edited, a front page photo shows her with Hans Küng for whom she and her husband had served as hosts when Küng visited St. Louis to deliver a lecture. Just beneath the picture is the question: "What would you suggest that women do in the church here and now?" Küng's answer included the advice that "women have to speak out." He alluded to the forthrightness with which Sister Theresa Kane spoke to Pope John Paul during his 1979 visit to Washington, D.C.[17] Küng said that something similar had occurred when the pope visited Munich. Both times the pope remained silent. Küng commended such action, saying that Church authorities have to be "challenged again and again."

Turning to the issue of women's ordination, Küng said that "more and more women's groups are celebrating the Eucharist," having grown tired of waiting for change. He argued that women's ordination is closely linked with mandatory celibacy and that both issues stem from the same root cause, misunderstanding and mistrust of sexuality, generating a fear of women on the part of the celibate hierarchy.

A Consciousness is Raised

Commissioned, in effect, by Küng's words, Schutzius underwent a process of consciousness-raising to which she alluded in several editor's columns. For example, in the Summer 1983 issue she reported that she was taking a graduate course entitled "Feminine Perspectives on Female Sexuality." She wrote:

> My consciousness has been raised. By the end of the month, when my term paper is due, I expect I will be even more aware of man's inhumanity to 53% of humanity. And particularly institutional religion's.

The new consciousness was enhanced by the strong sense of sisterhood she experienced at the November 1983 Women-Church Speaks Conference in Chicago. Schutzius was deeply moved by how supportive the twelve hundred women were of one another, from lesbians to those involved in relationships with active priests. All revealed the special pain they had suffered because of the Church's views on sexuality. Most revealing were the concluding words in her report on the conference. She wrote that the gathering included rich conversation, stimulating ideas, and a sense of bonding: "Like an FCM Convention, except the women were doing all the talking and listening."[18]

Opportunity for Cooperation Lost

A chance for women to be heard at an FCM convention soon presented itself. Making one of his frequent suggestions, Tom Durkin proposed that FCM link up with Women Church.[19] Since the headquarters of the activist Catholic women was in Chicago and the 1984 FCM convention was to be held at nearby Barat College, the moment was ripe for such a move. As a matter of fact, Paul and Susana Schlesinger, FCM presidents, did invite Maureen Reiff, organizer of the 1983 Women-Church Speaks Conference, to be keynote speaker. However, as has been related, a controversy arose over the proposed acceptance of the Ecumenical Catholic Diocese. Reiff saw the diocese as more of the same sexist, patriarchal, institutional oppression from which women were trying to disentangle themselves and, in protest, refused to participate. So, unwittingly, the ecumenical diocese snuffed out a potential collaboration with FCM, which had always officially promoted the equality of the sexes and the coalition of women's groups.

FCM may not have heard Maureen Reiff, but at that 1984 convention it did elect Mary Jane Schutzius to the presidency. Her apprenticeship as *Diaspora* editor and consequent membership on the FCM board had familiarized her with the organization's limitations and potential. She was confident that she would be able to provide leadership for the revitalization of the group.

Schutzius's commitment to ministry went back to her earliest years. After college, she joined the Papal Volunteers and was assigned to Bolivia. There she met her future husband who was serving with the St. Louis archdiocesan mission in that South American country. Years later, in one of those marvelous, unanticipated life experiences, one of their two college-age daughters on a visit to Bolivia had lunch with the current pastor of the mission and saw her father's picture on the rectory wall.

The president's columns that Schutzius wrote for *Diaspora* reveal the many projects in which she was involved personally such as staffing a booth for the Association for the Rights of Catholics in the Church (ARCC) at a National Catholic Education Association convention and working for the sanctuary movement. However, there is no plan or vision for FCM itself, not even a rationale for women's participation. She urges women to attend the conventions but never gives them reasons why they should.

As her term ended in 1988 Schutzius was deeply discouraged and felt that she had accomplished little. She wrote:

> FCM has been in a holding pattern, it seems to me, these past four years; not really going anywhere .... We are still mostly isolated members, not communities, moving in our own spheres .... Even the members of the National Board are isolated from each other, only coming together twice a year for a few days. ... *Diaspora*, for the most part, reflects the male, theoretical assessment of the world in which we live.[20]

Can a Woman's Voice Be Heard?
There are several reasons why Mary Jane Schutzius failed to make an impact on FCM. For one thing, as will be seen in the next chapter, she became president just as CORPUS was entering a phase of vigorous leadership for a married male priesthood and siphoned off a number of people who had once looked to FCM as their organizational base.

Other factors internal to the group itself also contributed to the failure of what was a courageous experiment by free ministry in witnessing to the equality of women by selecting one as president. First, as has been implied, Schutzius was not an effective leader. She has an impressive record of participation in a variety of organizations, in particular the St. Louis chapter of Church Women United of which she served as president for a year. She continues to host a weekly call-in show on a local radio station, providing her with a forum for ideas on women, religion, peace and justice, and other components of the liberal agenda. However, the minutes of FCM board meetings and the dearth of correspondence with other organizational leaders attest to her inability to inspire the group, promote development, or work in collaborative fashion with her peers in the Church reform movement.

Another reason for the failure to have an impact on FCM is that the core members were aging and beyond the time in life when they were likely to take any dynamic action. Schutzius's successor, Joseph Ruane, has had no more success than she in stimulating activity. In a 1990 interview, he said that he saw himself as simply holding the fort. Ten years of board minutes are striking in their lack of new ideas and the seeming contentment of the members with going through the familiar motions of certifying members and planning the annual convention. Just as in the seventies, Rosemary Radford Ruether was usually the only woman at SPFM meetings, so in the eighties, Mary Jane Schutzius looked around a table and saw mainly married priests, now some fifteen years older.

Finally, and, perhaps most importantly, there was a pervasive deafness when it came to hearing a woman's voice. One of the most theoretical articles ever to appear in *Diaspora* compared the work of the psychologist Lawrence Kohlberg with that of his protégé, Carol Gilligan. Gilligan compared the male and female perspectives on moral behavior and on life in general.[21] For example, her research found that women tend to be "oriented toward relationships and interdependence, while men define themselves in opposition to, rather than in relation to, others." Gilligan helped Ruether, Schutzius, and many other women understand more clearly the root of their difficulty in being accepted as moral equals in the Church and in FCM. It was not simply a question of domination by men but also domination by the male way of thinking. Once this was realized, many women decided that they must work alone, developing their own "culture" in which their voice could be heard, a voice that would express the femaleness of God and bring to Gospel ministry the full range of women's gifts.

Part V

The Emergence of CORPUS and Prospects for the Future

13

Second Spring:
The Flowering of CORPUS

We have history, time, people, and the Holy Spirit on our side.
We're going to win.
Terry Dosh, *Minneapolis Star and Tribune*, August 10, 1985

A social movement needs three basic ingredients if it is to thrive: a clear and compelling cause, inspirational leadership, and skillful administration. In the late eighties these elements coalesced for the first time in the twenty-year history of the free ministry crusade.

When, in 1974, a small group of Chicago priests established CORPUS, their cause was set in clear relief: a married priesthood. However, for a decade CORPUS remained a quiet, respectful voice for change with neither an inspirational spokesman nor a hands-on organizer. Frank Bonnike provided minimal visibility for the group by occasional public appearances and letters to bishops and supporters, but he lacked the drive or the vision to make CORPUS a significant force in the American Catholic Church.

An alternative explanation is that the time was not propitious for a more highly organized and assertive move and that Bonnike's low-profile approach for CORPUS was appropriate. SPFM had undertaken a high intensity campaign in the late sixties and early seventies. The troops were tired and disheartened. The movement needed a period

of rest. Perhaps there was a parallel period in the women's movement. The traditional view is that the movement died after women
gained the vote in 1920 and was reborn in the sixties. Verta Taylor in
the *American Sociological Review* argues that the movement did not
die but continued through "social movement abeyance structures."
She says that such structures provide "organizational and ideological
bridges between different upsurges of activism by the same challenging group." Abeyance is "a holding process by which movements
sustain themselves in nonreceptive political environments and
provide continuity from one stage of mobilization to another."[1] For
the first ten years of its existence, CORPUS might be viewed as such
an "abeyance structure" for free ministry.

Whichever explanation may be valid, the fact is that a new mobilization began late in 1984 and was in full vigor by the end of the
decade.

Two men have been central figures in this second stage of the
development of CORPUS and in this concerted effort to reform
Catholic ministry. One is Anthony Padovano, a respected theologian,
whose writings and addresses have long held a prominent place in
the post-Vatican II movement to shape a modern spirituality and a
revitalised Church. Chapter 14 will relate his inspirational leadership. The other is Terence Dosh, a former Benedictine monk, whose
organizational skills, unflagging optimism, and seemingly bound-
less energy shaped CORPUS into an extensive network that has
attracted considerable media attention, sponsored several national
meetings, and revived once again hopes for a return to the priesthood
in the hearts of many.

Both men brought impressive free ministry credentials to their
work with CORPUS, having been key players in SPFM/FCM as that
group groped its way toward a viable position, vis-à-vis the institutional Church, and eventually spun off on its own, losing momentum and support. As FCM settled into the role of certifying
people for ministry, CORPUS emerged on to the center stage of the
movement. However, it was the lessons that Padovano and Dosh
learned through FCM that made possible their success with CORPUS.
The main lesson was that the real hunger of married priests is for
priesthood, *not* some amorphous freelance "ministry" that they share
with the nonordained.

In the years since 1985, Padovano has been the heart and Dosh the
arms of the body of men, whom they believe are awakening from a
Rip Van Winkle-like sleep to face the light of the new day that is

dawning and that requires one last push to bring about change. Padovano is the new Eugene Bianchi, bringing to the movement a national reputation, stimulating insights, calm strength, and a convincing spirituality. Dosh is the new Thomas Durkin, an indefatigable letter writer, traveler, and media magnet, amassing a wealth of files, clippings, and lists that for six years made his house the motherlode of free ministry information.

Early in his tenure as paid staff person for CORPUS, Dosh spoke of having "time" on his side. But how much time? The clock keeps ticking. Obituary notices appear in *Corpus Reports*, which Dosh edited from 1985 thru 1990. Men who once left the priesthood through resignation are now leaving their secular careers through retirement. Most have loving wives with whom they have raised children, proving themselves to be the sort of mature family men whom St. Paul said should be selected as priests and bishops (1 Tim. 3). The lives of most of these men have been very good. What more could they want?

Just one more thing: their priesthood back.

Patrick F. Kelly: Priestly Ministries/USA

One of those with a passion for priesthood was Patrick Kelly, a married priest from the Crookston, Minnesota, diocese. In association with Dosh, Kelly undertook a project that willy-nilly was to lay the groundwork for the expansion of CORPUS. His idea was to develop a "research and information service" on the married Roman Catholic priesthood. In June 1976, Kelly, then age forty-six and recently married to Christin Lore, a lay campus minister, met in Chicago with Frank Bonnike, CORPUS facilitator, Bill Manseau, president of FCM, and two other married priests, Dave Corcoran and Bill McMahon. Kelly presented his plan:[2]

1. To identify and locate all resigned American priests;
2. To publish a national directory of resigned priests;
3. To establish frequent communication with resigned priests and other parties and organizations interested in ministry;
4. To promote theoretical and practical development of new models of ministry;
5. To identify those resigned priests willing to resume some form of ministry.

Bonnike was supportive and agreed to turn over to Kelly the several hundred names that CORPUS had gathered in its two years of existence. Manseau went further. He agreed to allow Kelly to use FCM as "the corporate base" for registering Priestly Ministries/USA in the state of Minnesota and invited Kelly to present the plan at the August convention of FCM in Washington, D.C. Manseau then sent the proposal to the FCM board, alerting them to the project. At the convention, Priestly Ministries/USA was accepted as an FCM "program division."

The grand plan was for this research and development to be sponsored not just by the two groups of married priests but also by the National Federation of Priests Councils, which represented the active priests of the country. In October, Rev. James Ratigan, president of NFPC, wrote a letter to Kelly stating:

> On September 2, 1976, the executive board of the National Federation of Priests' Councils agreed to endorse the goals of Priestly Ministries/USA, as presented to the board in your proposal of August 1976.[3]

Although not the long-dreamed of coalition, Priestly Ministries did offer the first formal collaboration of the three groups. Certainly there could be no objection to supporting someone eager to gather information rather than to make demands.

Fund-raising Difficulties

Armed with this backing, Kelly proceeded to put together a grant proposal that projected a three-year $108,000 budget. The proposal was sent to sixty foundations, requesting $53,000 with the balance to be obtained by the fund-raising efforts of Priestly Ministries itself. Included in the budget was a $15,000 salary for Kelly, whose hope was to raise enough money so that he could work full time on the new project.

Eager to get going, Kelly designed a logo, had stationery and business cards printed, a rubber stamp made, and opened a bank account. With the first money he received, he rented an office and hired a part-time secretary. However, the optimism of the first batch of letters he sent to Manseau soon changed to concern about finances. The projected budget for the first year had been $35,000, including Kelly's salary. The financial report for the year, August 1, 1976, to July 31, 1977, showed total receipts of $10,000 and expenditures of $9,000.

Kelly had taken nothing for himself. In June 1977 he had notified Manseau that because of the lack of funds he would have to let the secretary go and move from the office back into his own home. His one last hope was the FCM convention that he, the Dees, and the Doshes were hosting at St. Catherine's College in St. Paul. As Kelly wrote to Manseau, "Hopefully, I can keep things going until convention time and we can decide on the future then."

There was to be no future. It was clear that grant money would not be forthcoming and that FCM was in no position to provide any assistance. Priestly Ministries/USA had been like a comet that flashed across the sky of free ministry only to disappear into the darkness within a year.

In June 1977, both Pat and Christin Kelly had undertaken doctor of ministry studies at United Theological Seminary and in correspondence regularly commented on how satisfying it was. Although he would not complete the program, in a somewhat eerie forecast of things to come, Kelly's dissertation topic was "The Evolution of the Christology of Anthony T. Padovano."

After the collapse of Priestly Ministries, Kelly never found a steady job and experienced long and painful periods of unemployment. In May 1985 he was diagnosed as having cancer. A month later, after an operation related to the cancer, he died. With characteristic hyperbole, John Dee observed that Kelly was really a martyr of the free ministry movement, that he gave his life in service to the Church that had rejected his ministry.

Kelly and Dosh: Friends and Collaborators

Where Kelly failed, his friend Terry Dosh would succeed. In fact, the achievements of Dosh with CORPUS would be almost a point-for-point fulfillment of the agenda of Kelly. A close collaboration had existed between the two men, not just during the brief history of Priestly Ministries but up to the time of Kelly's death. Dosh says that Kelly died at peace, knowing that Dosh had just been hired by CORPUS to develop the movement for a married priesthood.

Dosh refers to Kelly as his best friend and says that during the Priestly Ministries venture, they were on the telephone with each other nearly every day. A major reason for the extensive communication was that *Diaspora*, which Dosh was then editing, became the joint publication of FCM and Priestly Ministries. As Kelly acquired names, they were added to the *Diaspora* mailing list. During 1977, the struggling publication increased its distribution from a few hundred to two thousand, even though few of the people added had expressed any interest in FCM. Each issue included the "Broken Cross" logo of Priestly Ministries and an explanation of the project as well as a brief survey questionnaire aimed at expanding the list of married priests interested in ministry. Some of the funds collected by Priestly Ministries were used for printing and mailing *Diaspora*.

The accomplishments of Dosh in some real sense stand as a tribute to the vision of Kelly. A list of thousands of married priests would be compiled, a national network established, a directory published, and, yes, at last substantial funds raised. Dosh himself would be the world's first paid, full-time free ministry staff person, serving as executive secretary and then as national coordinator of CORPUS from 1984 to 1990.

The Transformation of a Monk

Born in 1930, Dosh was ordained a Benedictine priest at St. John's Abbey in Collegeville, Minnesota, in 1957. He earned a Ph.D. and taught European history at St. John's University until 1969. In 1971 he resigned from the canonical priesthood and married Millicent Adams. The Doshes have two sons, whose names suggest the causes that inspired their parents at the time. Martin Luther King Chaves Dosh was born in 1972 and Paul Gandhi Joseph Dosh in 1974.

Dosh obtained a position as associate professor of history at California State College in Dominguez Hills. Despite gaining tenure there, he returned to Minnesota in the summer of 1974 and bought a house in Minneapolis where he and his family have lived ever since. In 1984, it would become the national headquarters of CORPUS.

During the intervening years, Dosh had taught part time and given lectures on Church history but had been unable to obtain a full-time position. It may also be that, like Kelly, the preoccupation with resuming a priestly ministry impeded a vigorous pursuit of a secular career. Just as the employment of Kelly's wife, Christin, facilitated the free ministry activities of her husband, Millie Dosh's work as a Montessori teacher gave Terry the freedom to do the reading, thinking, and corresponding that prepared him for the role he would assume and that would catapult him to national prominence in free ministry.

Apprenticeship in SPFM/FCM

For his eventual leadership of CORPUS, Dosh had a lengthy and varied association with SPFM/FCM. While living in California, he became regional vice president and organized the 1972 Los Angeles convention at which his fellow Minnesotan and future collaborator in ministry, John Dee, was married to Louise Tacheny.

Earlier, with Charles Ara, a psychotherapist, Dosh joined a group of married priests that met for lunch every month at the Green Frog restaurant in Long Beach. The meetings were opportunities for socializing and networking for job opportunities. During the same period, Joe Burns was holding similar monthly lunches at a German restaurant on the East Side of Manhattan. On both coasts, the organizers, highly committed to SPFM, found that few of the other resigned priests were interested in much more than the good feelings generated by a sandwich, a beer, and a few old seminary stories. Nevertheless, Dosh, Burns, and their counterparts in other cities were engaging in an important ministry to their fellow resigned priests who were embarking on their own uncertain journey to the "lay state."

In December 1972, Dosh and several other married priests and their spouses met with five members of the Los Angeles priests senate. Dosh reported that it went well as an opening meeting, exploring ways that married priests might be utilized by the Church. Such meetings between resigned priests and active priests occurred in numerous dioceses in the late sixties and early seventies, invariably ending with little concrete action.[4]

Two developments in 1972 directly foreshadowed Dosh's subsequent work with CORPUS. First, he made all the arrangements for the SPFM convention that included responding to the crisis of being informed by the Los Angeles archdiocesan chancery two days before the event that it could not be held at the Newman Center at the University of Southern California campus as had been scheduled. Dosh hastily moved the one hundred delegates to the Hillel Center. When it came time in the late eighties to arrange CORPUS conventions, Dosh made sure that they were held in non-Catholic settings. Eventually, after similar awkward experiences, FCM also would eschew Catholic facilities.

Second, Dosh, who had edited a mission publication while a Benedictine, made a number of recommendations about the fledgling SPFM publication, *Diaspora*. In particular, he clarified the roles of publisher, editor, and editorial board. After serving for a time on the editorial board, he became *Diaspora* editor in 1976. One of his major responsibilities with CORPUS was editing *Corpus Reports* (*CR*), which eventually became the major organ for the dissemination of information on the issue of a married priesthood.

Free Ministers at Call to Action

From the point of view of reform-minded Catholics, one of the most promising events in the post-Vatican II American Church was the Bishops' Bicentennial Conference's Call to Action, held in Detroit in October 1976. The conference was called by and controlled by the bishops in the sense that they selected the delegates who would represent their dioceses. It was a grand occasion, with lay people, religious, priests, and bishops coming together in a spirit of participatory democracy. However, it proved to be an embarrassment to the hierarchy. The conference, something like Vatican II itself, voted for proposals that were more radical than anticipated. In fact, despite the way that most delegates were selected, Archbishop Joseph Bernardin, then of Cincinnati, complained that they did not adequately represent the Catholic people of America.

He may have been correct if he was thinking of the small band of married priests who attended and successfully lobbied the credentials committee to have Frank Bonnike approved as a voting delegate. Besides Bonnike, the conference was attended by Terry Dosh and Patrick Kelly, representing FCM and Priestly Ministries/USA, respectively. Spearheaded by these three men, several free ministry proposals were presented, debated, and approved. How it all happened was both a vivid example of democracy at work in the Church and a chilling warning to the bishops of how easily such participatory government could undermine their power.

Democratic Process in a Catholic Setting

Dosh's lengthy report of the conference records the complex process by which the proposals supporting a married priesthood were maneuvered through the various layers of committees to eventual acceptance.[5] What follows is a summary of a political event unique in Catholic history, one in which bishops, priests, and lay persons debated and voted as equals on issues central to the life of the Church.

Two years of regional consultations in preparation for Call to Action had generated eight working papers. The more than thirteen hundred delegates divided up the work on each paper. The committee on Justice in the Church attracted three hundred people, including a number of bishops. This sectional group was further divided into three working bodies: Justice in the Church, Women in the Church, and Education for Justice. The Justice in the Church subgroup had about one hundred delegates and observers and included about fifteen bishops.

This subgroup in turn divided into seven groups of fifteen each to analyze line by line the seven paragraphs under the recommendations for Justice in the Church. The small group that discussed the paragraph in which the words "married clergy" were included decided to remove the phrase from its original context and treat the question of married priests, women priests, and resigned priests in newly created, separate paragraphs in order to reflect more clearly the importance of these issues.

According to Dosh, the people most instrumental in advancing these paragraphs were Bishop Charles Buswell of Pueblo, Colorado; Rev. Richard Sinner, FCM member from Kent, Minnesota; Rev. James Ratigan, president of NFPC; and Rev. Martin Geraghty of Brooklyn, New York.

When the new paragraphs were brought to the full Justice in the Church section, there was a discussion in which Bonnike and Cardinal John Krol of Philadelphia "had a polite but sharp debate over the role and status of resigned priests." The final vote was 28–21 in support of the paragraphs. Dosh noted that "only two non-black-sleeved arms voted against the proposal." At this point several bishops left the room.

The next day when the work of the smaller groups was brought to the full Justice in the Church section, there was once again animated discussion on the controversial proposals. It looked like the paragraph dealing with resigned priests would be voted down, but Rev. William Callahan of Priests for Equality "made a beautiful intervention" that turned the tide.

Effective Lobbying

There remained one last hurdle—acceptance by the plenary session on the final day of the conference. Because of the tension over the question of resigned priests, the phrase *or resume* had been omitted from the final draft of the resolution on a married priesthood. The phrase, of course, had particular importance for men like Bonnike, Kelly, and Dosh, who did not just want the Church to approve a married priesthood but to allow *them* to "resume" their ministry.

Dosh reported that Pat Kelly "went to work in the corridors to have these words officially inserted as an amendment the next day." When the time came, Rev. Roberto Peña, president of Padres, the organization of Hispanic priests, spoke of the plight of his people and of how they were ready to receive the ministrations of resigned priests. Dosh concluded: "Remembering that for every amendment that passed, six were shot down, we were thrilled when 90% voted Yes to these words 'or resume.'"

The dynamics of what happened at Detroit was explained in *Commonweal* as a "snowballing" effect. "On each day and during every level of discussion, the recommendations grew longer and stronger." Despite the numerous consultations around the country attempting to identify areas of discontent, it was not until Detroit that the delegates realized how many others "harbored similar thoughts and feelings that radical change within the church is required."[6]

In a letter to Manseau, Kelly was excited about what he called the "historic event." He said that the overwhelming approval of the free ministry causes would not have happened "if we had not been enabled to be there." Kelly saw the outcome of Call to Action as a positive fruit of his Priestly Ministries project. However, the bishops simply ignored the recommendations and never again summoned such a representative assembly.

Reincarnation of Call to Action

It would not, however, be the end of the phrase *call to action*. In an effort to maintain the spirit of the 1976 meeting, Dan and Sheila Daley of Chicago—long-time Catholic activists—began to issue a *Call to Action* newsletter. In 1989, the informal Call to Action group drafted a statement titled "A Call for Reform in the Catholic Church" that contained a long list of desired reforms. The following year, they hit upon a novel, communications-age technique for promoting Church renewal. They collected money from 4,500 people, bought a full-page in *The New York Times* on Ash Wednesday 1990, and printed their "pastoral letter" that, among other things, called upon the Church

> to discard the medieval discipline of mandatory priestly celibacy, and to open the priesthood to women and married men, including resigned priests, so that the Eucharist may continue to be the center of the spiritual life of all Catholics.[7]

Then in 1991, on the fifteenth anniversary of the Detroit meeting, the Chicago group sponsored a national conference with the daring title: "We Are the Church: What If We Meant What We Said?" A broad spectrum of Catholics gathered to hear such veteran reform leaders as Bernard Cooke, Rosemary Radford Ruether, and Terry Dosh. More significant than listening to speakers exhort the true believers to keep up their spirits was a Caucus of National Organizations that attempted to find a basis for cooperative action among such disparate groups as CORPUS, FCM, the Women's Ordination Conference, and several organizations of gay and lesbian Catholics. A council of groups was formed that resolved to meet twice a year. The representatives of both CORPUS and FCM supported the plan, recognizing that married priests were but one small segment of the disaffected Catholic population and that the reform of the Church must be a unified effort. It remains to be seen if Call to Action can coordinate the coalition and if any common initiatives can be undertaken. It also remains to be seen if married priests will be able to meet as equals with other segments of the Church, listen sympathetically to their grievances, and perhaps minister to them without pressing the free ministry agenda.[8]

Dosh's Developing Relationship with Bonnike

At the 1991 Call to Action meeting Dosh might have recalled that original gathering fifteen years before and reflected on all that had happened in the intervening years. Although they had met in 1972 and talked on the telephone and corresponded, it was at the 1976 conference that he and Frank Bonnike had the opportunity to become better acquainted. Dosh, still active in FCM, was becoming increasingly uncomfortable with that organization's agenda and found himself drawn to the "single issue" focus of CORPUS. Bonnike, for his part, became aware of the commitment and talents of Dosh.

What would become the second generation of CORPUS leadership took further form at the FCM convention in St. Paul in 1977 when Dosh invited Anthony Padovano to give the keynote address. The stature of Padovano was such that he drew 275 people to his opening night address titled, "The Spirituality of Ministry." This audience was the largest ever to attend an FCM-sponsored event and brought together the two men destined to become closely associated a decade later in what would be the most significant campaign for reform ever mounted by the free ministry movement.

Dosh's relationship with Bonnike was further developed when in 1980 the Chicago-based CORPUS facilitators brought together thirty-five people from around the country and invited Dosh to make a formal presentation. This assembly of "national coordinators" was the first time any consultation or planning had taken place other than among the small Chicago group. For the first six years of its existence, CORPUS had maintained the idea that it was not an organization at all but simply a list of people who subscribed to a statement supporting the acceptance by the Church of a married priesthood. In 1980, the process of transforming CORPUS into a bona fide organization began.

Dosh and others believed that the time had arrived for a more formal structure, that the Church would not change the requirement of celibacy unless more direct action were undertaken. Bonnike was sympathetic to the suggestion that CORPUS hire a full-time executive secretary to work on fund-raising and organization. However, both Dosh and William Pfeiffer, who had worked with Bonnike in organizing the meeting, say that Frank McGrath was opposed and that William Nemmers, the third facilitator, went along with McGrath, who apparently was reluctant to relinquish any control over the destiny of CORPUS. The two-to-one vote resulted in no action being taken.

Several more years passed. Then in 1984 McGrath wrote a letter asking those on the mailing list what they felt CORPUS should do. Membership and fund-raising had stabilized. Nothing was happening. McGrath received about sixty letters urging that an executive secretary be hired. Yielding to the pressure, McGrath capitulated and late in 1984 Bonnike called Dosh and asked if he were available. Over the next six years, Dosh would transform a list of names into the world's largest organization of married priests.

Organizing CORPUS

Dosh had learned several lessons from the failure of his friend Pat Kelly's Priestly Ministries/USA, such as working from the bottom up, not from the top down; that is, he learned to enlist the support of grass roots people before attempting to do anything on a national scale or with the hierarchy. He made sure that the base was strong.

Further, the experiences of Kelly, Durkin, and Manseau taught Dosh that seeking money from foundations was futile. Fortunately, Dosh did have some seed money. For the ten years of its existence, CORPUS had collected about $5,000 a year. Of this, it had spent $4,000, mostly on mailings, and saved $1,000. The facilitators said to

Dosh, "We have $10,000 and are willing to take a chance on you. See what you can do."

What Dosh did was begin a development campaign that generated striking results. (See Table I.)

Table I

Year	Total Money Raised
1985	$27,000
1986	34,000
1987	40,000
1988	50,000
1989	54,000
1990	65,000

Dosh attributes his achievement to suggestions given to him by two prominent Catholic writers. Michael Novak, who himself had produced a newsletter, advised Dosh to be patient and generous and not to demand too much of people. He even recommended, in the initial stages, distributing free literature. Tim Unsworth, a columnist with whom Dosh would maintain contact over the years, said that the way to gain support is to give people "privileged information," that is, information that they could acquire nowhere else. So, Dosh expanded the number of "area representatives" and sent to this inner circle four or five times a year a lengthy letter that contained a wide range of information gathered through his extensive networking by telephone, letter, and travel. It was the recipients of this "insiders information" who would feel special responsibility toward CORPUS and be its most generous supporters. In his first annual report, he said that "the number of CORPUS area representatives had risen from 37 to 94."[9] By the middle of 1990, there would be 235 representatives.

While this personally typed, informal letter went out to the core group, a more polished, professionally printed newsletter, *Corpus Reports*, was mailed six times a year to a much wider audience. Heeding Novak's suggestion, Dosh put on the list anyone who expressed interest in CORPUS—and many who did not, including all three hundred American bishops and over three hundred secular newspapers. At the time Dosh became editor of *CR* in 1985, there were 3,500 people on the mailing list. When he left in 1990, there were 11,000—including 5,500 married priests.

During Dosh's editorship, *CR* was similar to the early issues of SPFM's *Diaspora*, containing a collection of news items, letters, reports, and media reprints chronicling the progress of the movement and communicating a sense that momentum for change was building.

On the Road for CORPUS

Beginning in 1986, Dosh began to travel extensively, eventually visiting over two hundred of the area representatives, deepening their commitment and providing them with advice and encouragement. Typically, he would fly into a city such as San Antonio, have two or three media interviews, eat lunch with a small group of married priests, and in the evening meet with a larger group of men and their wives. He would spend the night with the area representative, getting to know him and his family as well as capturing something of the feel of the diocese. The next day Dosh would fly to another city and repeat the pattern.

With the local people, Dosh stressed that CORPUS was a loose network of autonomous groups, that the national office was not trying to impose a standard mold but rather to serve as a resource for whatever initiatives the local members might undertake. It is clear that Dosh relished the excitement of his travels and the celebrity that his position afforded him within the free ministry community.

However, it was not to last. For four years, CORPUS *was* Dosh. He was answerable only to Bonnike, who gave him free rein. With the formation of a national board in 1988, and, more particularly, with the board's adoption of the constitution in 1990, Dosh found that his role was changing. The board president, Anthony Padovano, and the constitution that Padovano had commissioned called for greater central control. Dosh saw his position converted into that of a functionary whose job was to carry out board policy, not to take initiatives. Dosh had worked with virtual independence too long to adjust to this closer accountability. He knew that the time to leave had arrived. After the 1990 convention in San Jose, he announced his resignation, effective at the end of the year.

Extensive Media Attention

Dosh understood well that media coverage is critical to the success of a movement; in fact, it is its life blood. People have to read about the issue, hear the leaders being interviewed on television, and see their names mentioned in magazines. In its initial years, in the late sixties, the free ministry movement had received substantial media attention. Then the novelty of married priests wanting to change the Church wore off, and the media lost interest. Dosh was able to recapture their attention. He proudly and regularly reported on media coverage. At the end of the first year, he wrote:

> . . . at least 60 articles or news reports in the U.S. secular press in the past 3 months; 12 TV or radio shows since Sept. 1. I have received 3–4 calls a week from the media in Sept. and Oct.[10]

By the time he would leave his post, Dosh would boast that the organization had "reaped the harvest of more than 1000 media presentations."[11]

Several events in particular drew attention to CORPUS. One was the September 1987 visit of Pope John Paul II to the United States. Dosh sent a press release with the heading "We are ready to serve!" to the American bishops and to hundreds of secular newspapers. As well as recounting the now familiar facts on the declining number of priests and seminarians and the thousands of CORPUS members ready to resume their ministry, the release made a direct appeal to the pope:

> We ask our brother John Paul II to be more sensitive to his brother priests who have married. After a long period of prayer and reflection and after many years of service to the Church, these priests have responded in conscience to add the charism of marriage to their charism of priesthood. Their commitment to Christ and the Reign of God is enhanced, not diminished, by this deeply felt choice.[12]

As if to reinforce the CORPUS message, Rev. Frank McNulty, the priest selected to address the pope on behalf of the rank-and-file American clergy, spoke respectfully but directly to the issue of celibacy and the effect it was having not only on vocations but on those who continued to serve the Church as celibate priests. He said:

> Morale suffers when we see so few young men follow in our footsteps. Morale suffers when we see parishes without priests. . . . But even as we promote vocations,

the celibacy question—as you well know—continues to surface. Its value has eroded and continues to erode in the minds of many.[13]

Without directly calling for their ordination, McNulty also addressed the pope on the issue of women in ministry, saying that "the movement of women toward practical equality is a major dynamic of our time." The press reported these remarks extensively as well as the silence with which they were greeted by the Pontiff.

Sexual Behavior and Orientation of Priests

Another series of developments that drew extensive media attention to priesthood and to CORPUS were revelations of illicit sexual behavior by prominent clerics as well as a spate of books and articles on homosexuality and pedophilia among priests.

The encounters that Fr. Bruce Ritter of New York's Covenant House reportedly had with some of his young male charges were front page news for weeks in 1990 to be followed shortly thereafter by revelations that Archbishop Eugene Marino of Atlanta had been having an affair with a woman. In dioceses all over the country, priests were being sued for pederasty, and the Church slapped with court awards amounting to millions of dollars for the illegal behavior of its personnel.

Dosh, Bonnike, and Padovano were called upon frequently to respond to these occurrences on behalf of CORPUS. They argued that a married priesthood would add health to a profession so obviously sick because of the sexual repression demanded by celibacy. *Time* concluded its article on scandals in the priesthood with the suggestion that fidelity to priestly celibacy would be more likely to be achieved "when celibacy is a choice, not a demand."[14]

A more damaging argument was that perhaps the rule of celibacy tended to attract to the priesthood "certain people precisely because it excludes marriage." University of Notre Dame theology professor, Richard McBrien, suggested that the priesthood offers gay men "an esteemed and rewarding profession in which their 'unmarried and uninterested' status is self-explanatory and excites neither curiosity nor suspicion." McBrien added that the very increase in the proportion of gay clerics may serve to decrease sympathy for a married priesthood on the part of the clergy.[15]

> It is a matter of simple logic that the more gays we have in
> the priesthood and in our seminaries, the less pressure
> there will be, from within the body of Catholic clergy it-
> self, for a fundamental change in the present discipline of
> obligatory celibacy.[16]

McBrien, whose syndicated column appears in many diocesan
newspapers, has continued to address the issue of the crisis in the
clergy. For example, in 1989, he cited two studies. One reported that
the priesthood no longer attracts "the best and the brightest of
Catholic high school students" and that "the top tenth intellectually
has been lost." The other study, commissioned by the National
Conference of Catholic Bishops, reported that the serious morale
problem within the ranks of the priesthood has resulted in priests no
longer encouraging young men to follow in their footsteps.[17]

When the first CORPUS national conference was held in 1988 one
of the principal speakers was Richard Sipe, a married priest, who
presented gripping data on the sexual distress of the Catholic clergy.
The book that resulted from Sipe's twenty-five years of clinical work
with priests appeared just as the Ritter and Marino scandals were
breaking and attracted widespread attention.[18] Sipe argued that Ritter
and Marino were not exceptions, but symptoms. He charged: "At
any one time no more than 50 percent of American priests practice
celibacy."

All over the country newspapers ran feature articles that combined
all these developments and more. For example, Long Island's *Newsday*
ran a three-page article that said that "more than 200 priests nationwide
are believed to have contracted AIDS, almost all through gay sex."[19]
Further, it cited Sipe's estimate that almost one-fourth of all priests
are gay, and half of those are sexually active. The scientific validity
of Sipe's data has been challenged, but the impact on the public
perception of the priesthood could not help but be damaging.

CORPUS's Irresolute Position on Women

One of the most serious challenges that CORPUS has faced is the
claim that it is sexist, championing only the acceptance of a married
male priesthood and not the ordination of women. Dosh claims that
he personally has always supported full ministerial equality for
women but that his job was to carry out the policies of the organization, not to promote his own views.

The issue was brought to the surface in dramatic fashion at the 1988 CORPUS conference in Washington. Some women hung a makeshift poster on the speakers' platform that read: MEN OF QUALITY RESPECT WOMEN'S EQUALITY. Many women at the conference were insisting that the root problem was sexism, not marriage. In fact, Sister Theresa Kane in her address catalogued in no uncertain terms the long history of "patriarchy" that continued to be deeply ingrained in Catholic culture and in Church hierarchy.

This situation was dramatized to the three hundred fifty assembled men and women when Dosh announced the members of the committee charged with drawing up conference resolutions. All members were male. When a woman in the audience drew Dosh's attention to the absence of women on the committee, his response was, "You have heard the names of the committee members."[20]

In a 1991 interview, Dosh explained his behavior by saying that CORPUS was just in the process of creating a board but that Bonnike was still in charge. Dosh was the secretary. Immediately after the session at which the incident about the absence of women on the committee had occurred, Dosh went to the back of the hall, sat down next to Bonnike and said, "Frank, we've got to change." Two women were added to the committee.

However, this still did not mean that CORPUS would actively promote full ministerial equality for women. Of the twenty resolutions issued at the 1988 conference, two were under the heading "Gender Issues." Their wording skillfully dodged full commitment to the cause of the ordination of women. The resolutions were:

1. CORPUS affirms its intention to be a model in respecting women by promulgating women's concerns and perspectives in the continuing dialogue for married priests' ministry.
2. Genesis and the Gospel of Jesus proclaim the radical equality of woman and man. In baptism all Christians, male and female, are called to witness their faith. Hence the continued exclusion of women from the priesthood on the basis of gender alone is contrary to justice and the Spirit of Christ. CORPUS therefore affirms the right and aspiration of women to full participation in all ministries of the church and asserts solidarity with those who are moving to open these ministries to women.[21]

Dosh clarified the CORPUS policy, citing a survey had found that

> a slight majority of CORPUS priests favored the ordination
> of women. Others were opposed, but all agreed it was not
> our cause. Our position was clear. CORPUS had but a
> single purpose. While we respect (and in many cases
> agree) with those concerned about other causes, they are
> not the issue of CORPUS. To confuse these organizations
> with CORPUS is to do a disservice to both.

The initial twelve-member CORPUS board included no women. However, in June 1989, two women, Ann O'Brien and Linda Pinto, were added. Both are the wives of priests long associated with CORPUS. By 1991 CORPUS had revised its self-understanding substantially, defining its mission as the promotion of "an expanded and enriched priesthood of married and single men and women in the Catholic Church."[22]

Dosh's Continuing Ministry

In what in this media age might be considered the highest affirmation of his contributions to the free ministry movement, Terry Dosh's picture appeared on the front page of *The New York Times*, accompanying a report on the June 1990 CORPUS conference in San Jose, the third and last that he would organize before his resignation.[23] Dosh left behind an organization that had grown dramatically in size and was widely respected as the premier voice of the movement for the reform of the priesthood.

Only time will tell if he left just as the movement crested. Financial support had become a serious concern. During 1990, President Padovano sent two "begging letters." The first, directed to the 240 area representatives, generated 31 responses, only half of which included the requested commitment to raise $500 from supporters.

Further, each of the first three national conferences attracted fewer attendees than the one before. (See Table II.)

Table II: CORPUS National Conferences

Year	Location	Attendance
1988	Washington, D.C.	350
1989	Columbus, Ohio	220
1990	San Jose, Calif.	215

Ironically, the 1991 conference in New York City that drew an unprecedented seven hundred fifty people produced a controversy that may have been a setback to the cause. That conference and *Commonweal* editor Margaret O'Brien Steinfels's sharp criticism of CORPUS will be discussed in chapter 15 in the context of the contributions of Thomas McCabe, the prime mover of the New York gathering.

Most importantly, from the point of view of the free ministry movement, the institutional Church shows few signs of change and the Catholic laity in general are yet to rally to the cause.

Pope John Paul II, well into the second decade of his papacy, continues to insist on mandatory celibacy, going so far as to exclude discussion of the subject from the 1990 Synod of Bishops. Despite the dire need of priests in many parts of the world, no conference of bishops or even an individual bishop has broken rank and publicly ordained married men or permitted married priests to function. There are the "pastoral provisions" that have allowed the ordination of a number of married Anglican priests and two cases of married men in Brazil being ordained (on condition that they live a brother/sister relationship with their wives).[24] In the spring of 1992, it was confirmed by the Vatican that a number of married men as well as several women had functioned as priests during the communist control of Czechoslovakia.[25] Prompted by the expulsion of these priests from their ministry, Dosh traveled to Czechoslovakia and met with some of these married priests and even a married bishop. He hoped to dramatize the plight of men and women, whose services were welcomed during the period of Church persecution but cast aside when the crisis ended.

It is obvious that Dosh is not retiring from the movement. On the contrary, since leaving the CORPUS position he has begun publication of a newsletter titled *Bread Rising*. Encouraged once again by writer Tim Unsworth, he is convinced that he has access to information that people need and that they cannot obtain elsewhere. As with his letters to the CORPUS area representatives, he promises that *Bread Rising* will contain "privileged information" on Church reform issues.[26] By the summer of 1992, there were eight hundred subscribers to the publication.

The Importance of Dreams
Dosh says that the idea for a newsletter came to him in a dream. Many men have had dreams. Dr. Martin Luther King, Jr., as leader of the

civil rights movement, had a dream for a more just society. All movements are based on dreams. There is the world as it exists, and there
is the world as it might be. There are those who maintain or tolerate
the status quo, be it ever so oppressive, and there are those who in
their dreams create a new order. Their task is a simple one: To share
that dream with all who will listen, trusting that it will activate a
similar dream within the hearts of others. When many people join
dreams, a movement comes to life. The dreams of men like Dosh are
the best hope for the eventual success of the free ministry movement.

14

A Voice of Encouragement
for an Aging Movement

The call for a married priesthood challenges the idolatry and
absoluteness of the Church, the authoritarianism and vengeful
spirit which are unworthy of it. The more happy we are as
married priests, the more public we are about our vocation, the
less bitter and angry we are, the less we become victims of guilt
or insecurity, the more able we are to see our role as prophetic and
charismatic, then the more thoroughly we become a sign of that
future Church God's people yearn for with an intensity which
is painful in its ardor and in its need.

Anthony T. Padovano, CORPUS conference, 1988

On what basis Padovano concludes that people are yearning for a
renewed Church "with an intensity which is painful" is not clear.
What is clear is that he and hundreds of other married priests seek to
be readmitted to the official priesthood. They see a harmony between
the sacrament of Orders and the sacrament of Matrimony and
believe that the Church would be enriched were it to enable all
pastoral ministers to unite in their lives the blessings of these two
signs of Christ's life-affirming love.

Few voices in the post-Vatican II American Church have spoken
more consistently and persuasively to the dream of making the

ancient Catholic tradition more fully meaningful to modern people than Padovano. In 1966, in the first of over twenty books he has authored, he asked how God should be presented today. His answer was that two qualities had to characterize those who would hope to communicate to others the wonderful reality of God: love and freedom.

> We must approach modern man in love. . . . As an individual I never reach reality unless I love. I never know who my fellow-men are or who I am unless I love. Love is the supreme value on earth and in heaven. . . . We must approach modern man in freedom as well. Freedom must become so identified with Christianity that men will not be able to think of one without the other.[1]

The book was based on the course "On the One God" that Padovano was teaching at the Seminary of the Immaculate Conception in Darlington, New Jersey. He called the book and the course "an experiment in what dogmatic theology can do and might be today" and employed an existential and pastoral approach. The principal authors he cited were the philosophers Sartre, Heidegger, and Kierkegaard and the fiction writers Dostoevsky, Salinger, and Orwell. He was searching for a way into his own Catholic heritage by reflecting on the insights of men who were not Catholic. Centuries before, another seminary professor, Thomas Aquinas, had found a way to explain Christianity in his day through the genius of the pagan Aristotle and the Moslem Averroes.

Who is qualified to bring to the world the message of God? For Padovano, the answer was clear: people who know love and people who are free. Eventually, he felt that the priesthood as he knew it was not the context within which he could most effectively bring the Good News to others. He needed human love and he needed greater freedom. He found both. And having found them, he set out on the seemingly impossible task of bringing to the Church an understanding of what he had discovered.

Long before he left the canonical priesthood, Padovano had been in communication with the free ministry movement. His involvement has been continuous and intensive. He sees it as the hope for an urgently needed renewal of Christian ministry. In 1988, after many years of inspirational leadership, he ventured into the turbulent waters of organizational leadership, accepting the position of first president of CORPUS. It remains to be seen whether he will be able to translate his talents as preacher and teacher into the diplomatic, managerial, and fund-raising skills needed to hold together the nebulous free ministry network.

Laying a Foundation; Building a Reputation

Born in Harrison, New Jersey, in 1934, Anthony Padovano holds an S.T.D. from the Gregorian University in Rome where he was ordained in 1959. He also has a Ph.D. in literature from Fordham University in New York and a Ph.L. in philosophy from the Angelicum in Rome. From 1960 to 1974 he was a professor of systematic theology at the Newark archdiocesan seminary. He resigned from the canonical priesthood in 1974 and married Theresa Lackamp, a former Sister of Charity. They have four children.

Besides holding a professorship in literature and religious studies at Ramapo College in New Jersey, Padovano teaches theology across the country, writes extensively, and serves as a vice president of the International Federation of Married Priests as well as president of CORPUS.

In 1990, as he reflected on his life, Padovano said that Vatican II "changed everything. I'd never be a married priest or reformer without it." This is Padovano's self-definition: married priest and reformer. He maintains that today he does everything he did as a canonical priest, "except for the public celebration of Eucharist." He is a certified member of FCM and responds to requests for pastoral service, including ministering in an ecumenical setting with a congregation near his home in New Jersey.

Early Association with SPFM

In 1970, the Senate of Priests of the Newark archdiocese established a committee to dialogue with priests who had left the active ministry. Although Padovano himself was four years from leaving, it was evident that he was sympathetic to those who had taken such a step. At the October meeting of the group, he said that "men who leave ought to be considered laity in good standing and the idea of admitting them to the diaconate ought to be explored."[2]

Formal involvement with SPFM would begin a year later when, after the 1971 convention in New York, Roméo DiBenedetto, living in New Mexico but originally from New Jersey, telephoned his former seminary professor to ask him for his ideas on SPFM and priestly ministry. Padovano indicated that he was supportive of the objectives of the group, welcomed his name being added to the mailing list, and offered his help. Perhaps reflecting his own growing discontent, Padovano told his former student that there was a "general malaise" among the clergy, especially those ordained for less than ten years. With his typical analytical style, he said that there were three categories of priests: "1) those who definitely will leave; 2) those who will leave if. . . and . . .; 3) those who will stay at all costs."[3]

It would seem that at the time Padovano was in the second category and that one of his "if . . . ands . . . " was the outcome of the fall 1971 International Synod of Bishops in Rome, where he urged DiBenedetto to have SPFM wait for the synod before determining its goals. When the synod proved to be disappointing, Padovano and many others moved into the first category.

As a respected theologian, Padovano had been called upon to serve on the Bishops Subcommittee on the Systematic Theology of the Priesthood. The committee, chaired by the Jesuit Carl Armbruster (who also subsequently married), issued a report in 1971 that made a negative reference to "free ministry."[4] Afterward, Padovano telephoned SPFM vice president Tom Durkin "to apologize for any slight to SPFM in the paragraph on free ministry in the Theology Report." Durkin reported that Padovano said that "although he had no clear idea of the theology of free ministry," he felt "the movement was vital psychologically to American priests at this time."[5]

Hans Küng's Why Priests?

By happy coincidence, within months of saying that he did not have a "clear idea of the theology of free ministry," Padovano was provided with precisely that by none other than Hans Küng, whose 1972 book, *Why Priests? A Proposal for a New Church Ministry*, Padovano reviewed.[6] Reacting favorably to Küng's idea that the Church was unjustly monopolizing ministry by attempting to restrict it to those whom it ordained, Padovano argued that

> the essence of ministry resides in its unofficial character rather than in its official structure. Official recognition of ministry is only the matrix or framework in which ministry is conducted. In the final analysis, how a man responds to his own ministry is more important than how the church officially regards his ministry.

Küng's book was a response to the synod of 1971, which he, as had Padovano, found disappointing. In fact, Küng said, in terms sure to intensify the Vatican's determination to silence him,

> the third ineffectual bishops' synod in Rome since Vatican II has confirmed our worst fears that there is little reason to hope the bishops will reach the decisions needed to deal with the emergency.[7]

The emergency, of course, was the startling increase in departures from the priesthood and decline in vocations. Küng spoke of the crisis as "taking on catastrophic proportions."

If then the Church was in a state of crisis, and the bishops could not be counted on to act, who would? Free ministers felt that it was incumbent on *them* to assume responsibility to save the priesthood.

The first section of Küng's revolutionary book, which was to have far-reaching impact on the movement, was titled "Democratization of the Church?" It suggested that priests who had been educated with a democratic mentality found it very difficult to serve as functionaries in an authoritarian institution. In other words, the problem was much deeper than priesthood, certainly much deeper than celibacy. It was a matter of freedom. The Gospel calls us to freedom, and the Church has rescinded much of that freedom.

The radical nature of Küng's analysis was accentuated by his rejection of the very term *priest* as a serious misunderstanding of the intention of Christ. Certainly there was a need for ministry, for service, for leadership. But a separate, priestly caste set apart from the laity was an unbiblical historical development. Better to speak of people who "preside" or who are "pastors" than of "priests." There is but one priest, Jesus Christ, who shares his self-sacrificing, priestly character with all the baptized.

The Küng book did not go unnoticed by SPFM, much in need of the legitimacy provided by someone of Küng's stature. The editor of *Diaspora* suggested that the bishops should read *Why Priests?* in order to understand that essentially priests should provide "a service of leadership" and not just be ecclesiastical "office holders."[8] A subsequent review of the book claimed, in effect, that Küng had articulated the fundamental theological basis for free ministry:

> Küng's proposal to remedy the crisis among priests is simple—less concern with the office the priest or bishop holds, and more concern with the purpose for which they

have been called—that of being free ministers of service. . . . Küng points out that such a ministry does not have to be full-time or for life or based on academic standing or encased in celibacy or exclusively for males. . . . Priesthood is, as Küng states, "a free calling to a free ministry in the Church."[9]

Though not often cited, *Why Priests?* contained all the elements that would give rise to FCM and the other efforts to transform the Church and her ministry.

Becoming Active in the Movement

Although Padovano's introduction to SPFM was through DiBenedetto, it was Gerald Grudzen who cultivated the relationship. In December 1971, while he was regional vice president for New York, Grudzen invited Padovano to speak at an evening of reflection at Mercy College in Dobbs Ferry, New York. Padovano's topic was "The Question of Doctrinal and Moral Dissent," a pivotal issue for the movement and one that would be addressed frequently.[10] Grudzen sponsored several such days of reflection in an effort to provide married priests with the best of theological resources. For example, in November 1972, the speakers included Rev. Thomas Stransky, C.S.P., president of the Paulist Fathers and Rev. Avery Dulles, S.J., who with Padovano had been a member of the bishop's committee that prepared the theological study of the priesthood.[11]

After his resignation from the priesthood in 1974, Padovano devoted several years to establishing a family and a secular career. But by 1977 he was ready once again to participate in the movement and accepted an invitation to give the keynote address at the FCM convention in St. Paul. Not only did he renew his connection with Grudzen, now president of FCM, but he met Terry Dosh, convention coordinator, with whom he would work ten years later in CORPUS. Padovano's address not only drew a record crowd, it also was featured on the front page of the *National Catholic Reporter*, published in full in *Diaspora*, and reprinted in Grudzen's 1979 book.[12]

Defining the Christian Minister

The address examined the concept of ministry and gave ten characteristics of a minister. Written in the lyrical style that had become

Padovano's trademark, it embodied his existential orientation and pastoral concern. He wrote:

> Ministry derives from the fact that we are born with a need to be cared for. This need is most intense in its demand for someone to see our worth. We are not able to accept our worth unless someone declares this to us by revealing to us who we are. This is the most basic notion of ministry.

For Padovano "the spirituality of all ministry begins with the sensitivity and compassion of the human heart." He insists that no discussion of ministry should neglect this fact. No concern with denominational ministry should obscure the reality that loving service to others is the essential element and that God always raises up people to minister, even if denominations falter. To be a minister then is to open oneself to the power of God, continuously healing and saving the world.

The ten characteristics of a minister are striking, as is the essay as a whole, in that no mention is made of priesthood or of Catholicism. What Padovano did was present a generic formula for the kind of person who best could minister. The word *asceticism* appears numerous times. The authentic minister must stop complaining, stop grasping for power, stop avoiding pain, be truly available to others, and when it seems as though one has no strength left—when it seems as though there is only death and no resurrection—continue to hope.

There is no mention of celibacy or bishops or Rome and no tone of anger—only of pain and yearning. Padovano concluded his 1977 paper with words that would be echoed in his 1988 CORPUS conference address, "Broken Promises," cited at the beginning of this chapter and to be discussed more fully later. He urged his listeners to dedicate themselves to a life of unflinching and unwavering fidelity to their calling. He challenged married priests to

> trust the human family we belong to and the respective communities we have served to choose us again for their love, trusting that even if the communities we loved could desert us, we would follow them forever with the memories of the life and the love we once had there and with hope for the day when each of these communities would bear words of forgiveness not only for us but also for themselves.

A Ministry of Writing

To many people, Padovano is best known for the inspirational books that he has written over the years for Paulist Press. While still a canonical priest, one such book was titled *Free to be Faithful*. It contains a mystical and perhaps prophetic reflection on the prodigal son:

> The faithful man is the prodigal son who breaks his father's heart because he knows he has a heart to break. He is the one unfaithful enough to have run away.[13]

Not many months later, Padovano himself would be the faithful prodigal, who would prove his fidelity by running away. When the Grudzens moved to San Jose in 1978, they invited Padovano to visit them, which he did several times. On one such occasion, he was writing a book on Thomas Merton.[14] Jerry Grudzen said that Padovano would rise each morning at six, write until ten, and then come down for breakfast. Both Marita and Jerry Grudzen cherish the memory of the visits of Padovano as special blessings in their lives.

St. Sebastian's Community, New York

On Palm Sunday 1980, in conjunction with its semiannual board meeting, FCM sponsored an open session at Christ Lutheran Church in Manhattan. Rocco Caporale, the first vice president of SPFM, welcomed the group of sixty people, introducing himself as the liturgical leader of St. Sebastian's community, a long-established assembly of Catholics housed under the roof of the Lutheran Church. The Lutheran pastor expressed support for the objectives of FCM, commending it for the capacity to generate small communities.

FCM president Grudzen introduced Padovano, who gave a Palm Sunday homily in which he stressed the need for a ministry modeled after that of Jesus, one that sought to serve rather than win admiration. Padovano exhorted his listeners to pursue love and renewal and to rid themselves of "the pretensions of ministry."[15]

Stirred by Padovano's words, and impressed with the model of community St. Sebastian's seemed to provide, the New York area members decided to reorganize the moribund region. They envisioned free ministry communal worship, mutual support groups, Scripture study, discussion of political and religious issues, and the sharing of ministerial experiences. Caporale offered St. Sebastian's as a centrally located base of operation for the groups that would be formed in Manhattan, Westchester, Long Island, and New Jersey. Representatives were elected for each of these four areas.

St. Sebastian's has continued as an FCM-affiliated community, but it never became the hub of free ministry in New York as envisioned in 1980. The New York regional vice president, Louis Gioia, pastor of St. Sebastian's, made numerous efforts throughout the eighties to stimulate activity. For a brief time he published a newsletter, *Diaspora Junior*, as an organ of regional communication.

Well aware of the organization's difficulties, Padovano refused to accept offices in FCM, preferring to advance the movement through his words. In this manner, he could avoid the frustrations of failure while continuing to urge free ministers to be faithful to their freedom: "The person who is most free is the person who finds a commitment so deep and real that alternatives to it are not attractive."[16]

A Less Denominational Ministry

In a 1981 article in *National Catholic Reporter*, Padovano reiterated many of the themes already presented in the unfolding process of reconceptualizing ministry.[17] To them he added two ideas that were key elements of the theology of free ministry, namely, that ministry must break out of denominational narrowness and that marriage is a logical concomitant to ministry.

On the first point, echoing Hans Küng, Padovano insisted that valid ministry is "global." It must serve a truth that is outside and beyond the denominational system. To have an orientation that limits itself to the needs of the denomination alone is to "create a clique rather than a church." Those whose activities "make sense only in church terms are not involved in ministry. They merely maintain a private club."

The second point, that of the compatibility of ministry and marriage, was one to which Padovano would return many times. Here he argued:

> Both marriage and ministry have love as their central focus; in both, care for the other is of the essence of the commitment; in both, fidelity is crucial, a faithfulness which makes the person reliable and dependable. . . . In both ministry and marriage, the community one serves brings life to the minister or spouse and identifies them in

a radical manner. In both, community is formed, not from ties of blood but from ties of shared faith. There is no necessity between ministry and marriage, but a compatibility profound enough for the New Testament to expect ministers to be married. God's first intention in creation is not a church but a marriage. . . .[18]

Frequent Convention Keynoter

It was moving ideas such as these that resulted in Padovano being invited time and again to speak at free ministry gatherings. In 1982 and 1984 he was the principal speaker at the FCM conventions, just as he had been in 1977. In 1982, the liturgy took place on August 15, the Feast of the Assumption of Mary. In his homily, Padovano recalled that it was on that date in 1974 that he had celebrated the Eucharist for the last time as a canonical priest. His love for priesthood was evident in his reflections on this unusual anniversary:

> The church, at least officially, has tried to take something away from me, tried to make it difficult for me, for us, to function legally, publicly, canonically. To some extent it succeeds and there is a sense of loss because of that, to you, to me, to us, to the community at large. But the official church cannot take away the word of God pregnant in us. It cannot make our hearts unmindful of the word that makes us priests or ministers, faithful people, Christ-consecrated, made holy by the word spoken deep into the inner recesses of our very being. We are a federation of Christian ministers to the extent that we allow God's word to take on life in us.[19]

By the time that the 1984 FCM convention arrived, it had become clear to Padovano that the walls of Rome would not come tumbling down. What to do then in a period marked by a mixture of turmoil and inertia? In answer, he proposed three elements for the survival of the movement as a force for Church renewal: 1) base community; 2) contemplation; and 3) dreams.[20]

Base community. Every minister needs a small community for survival, that is, a group of people who come together for social, culinary, educational, liturgical, and biblical reasons. Traditional parishes are too large; they are public gatherings, not the kind of settings in which essential human hunger can be fed. In each base community, leadership will emerge naturally. There are always a variety of charisms available. "What that group should be for everyone is an area of safety, a base, a home for something that is truly basic for human survival," Padovano insisted.

Contemplation. Drawing from his study of Thomas Merton, Padovano argued that contemplation is not some rare and rarefied activity but the way in which one gets insight into the wholeness of life. Contemplation is "enormously energizing" and rescues one from "frantic pursuit," helping people to concentrate on creativity and to avoid the superficiality that occupies so much time and energy. In words that describe his own ministerial style, Padovano said that contemplation

> enables me to speak and act from greater strength, to heal and forgive rather than hold grudges, to be capable of magnanimity at the petty moments of life, with people who seem small when greatness is called for, and enables me to be lost for a moment against a greater background than that of my own fear, to merely be still and to know that God is God.

Dreams. If we are to be effective as ministers, notes Padovano, we must have dreams for the Church. We must not, in other words, become cynical or defeatist. On the contrary, we must dream that there will be women priests; that there will be a married priesthood; that there will be a papacy more accountable to the other structures in the Church.

It is perhaps here, with dreams, that the free ministry movement provides its greatest service to the Church. Free ministers are living witnesses to the dream of alternative ministerial life-styles and to a renewed Christianity.

Moving from FCM to CORPUS

As Padovano was speaking at the FCM convention in Chicago in the summer of 1984, Frank Bonnike and his associates were moving toward a dramatic transformation of CORPUS. They were about to hire Terry Dosh and give him a mandate to organize CORPUS into a national force for a married priesthood. Dosh soon enlisted Padovano to the cause and together with Bonnike chose a CORPUS board in

1988, with Padovano as its president. His message would now be found not in FCM's *Diaspora* but in *Corpus Reports.*

Through his involvement with CORPUS, Padovano has made five major contributions to the movement:

1. The " Broken Promises" talk at the 1988 conference.
2. His 1989 "Theological and Canonical Reflection."
3. His presence on an international level.
4. His role as national spokesman.
5. The constitution that he commissioned for CORPUS.

Broken Promises

In the July–August 1987 *Corpus Reports,* Dosh announced that CORPUS would hold its first national conference in June 1988 at the American University in Washington, D.C. As if history were repeating itself, CORPUS would call together "Catholics of all stripes who share our vision of optional celibacy" in the same city where in 1969 SPFM had assembled similar people for its first national meeting. Continuity over those nineteen years would be provided by several people who had remained active in the movement from its inception.

The most striking link across the years was the presence of Carl and Pat Hemmer. Carl, in 1966, as a young Jesuit priest, had helped to organize NAPR as the pioneering agent for optional celibacy. Then, with his wife, he had coordinated the first SPFM convention. Through the years he had been a member of both FCM and CORPUS.

Also in attendance was William Manseau who, with Mary, his wife of only a few weeks, had attended the meeting back in 1969. Along the way, he would serve as president of FCM, attend countless meetings, write hundreds of letters, attempt to raise money for the cause, talk with bishops, and form free ministry communities in New England, Chicago, and Washington, D.C.

Also at both gatherings was Mary Lou Zehfuss. In 1969 she was a single laywoman. In 1988 she was accompanied by her husband, an active priest. Although the marriage was a secret, it was a secret she shared with all she met. During the years, Zehfuss had been recording secretary of SPFM and, years later, treasurer of FCM.

Others at the 1988 meeting included John Dee, who had been married at the 1972 SPFM convention, Bernard McGoldrick, a former SPFM president, and Joseph Ruane, current president of FCM.

In 1969, only fifty-six people attended the convention. In 1988, there were three hundred fifty, and the speakers were confident, knowledgeable, and convincing. Perhaps at last the moment was at hand.

Dosh had experience with conventions, having organized two for FCM—in Los Angeles in 1972 and St. Paul in 1977. But this time he had over three years to develop a national reputation for CORPUS as well as the financial resources to plan and publicize a major event. The high point would be the address by Padovano.

The conference was titled "Shaping the Future Priesthood." What Padovano did was dispel any lingering doubts that resigned priests might harbor about the rightness of the step they had taken. His address, "Broken Promises," confronted directly the issue of fidelity. Using the story of Jephthah from the Book of Judges (11:29–40), Padovano argued that there is a higher fidelity than the promise of lifelong celibacy, namely, fidelity to life and to the evolving truth that so many priests had discovered about themselves. Jephthah had made a promise also, but it became clear that a higher good super-seded that earlier promise. Sometimes promises should be broken.

Like a compassionate priest in the confessional, Padovano in effect granted absolution to men who may have doubted their own goodness and the loving understanding of their heavenly Father. New categories of thought were needed, he counseled, new ways of understanding the mysterious transformations occurring within individual lives and within the Church.

Speaking very softly, and looking out over the stilled audience, Padovano concluded:

> In any case, we are here, my brothers. And we are here, in many cases, with our wives and children. We have given ourselves to a new fidelity, one which assumes and ab-sorbs all our priesthood and the substance of our life in the arms of our wives and in the hearts of our children. We are still faithful but to a different Church, a new Church, one which all God's People need us to help them build. We are the bridge between the old and the new since we have lived in both Churches; between clerical and lay life, since we have known both profoundly; between celibacy and marriage, since we have been given both gifts.[21]

Theological and Canonical Reflection

The Code of Canon Law embodies the rules by which the Catholic Church governs itself. A new code was issued in 1983, substantially reformulating many of the laws, including those that pertain to priests. In 1989, Padovano analyzed the New Code and had his monograph critiqued by several canon lawyers and published by CORPUS.[22] The New Code contains what Padovano claims are significant opportunities for married priests to function in a ministerial fashion. First, it abrogated penalties that earlier had been incurred by priests who left and married without a dispensation. Specifically, "a married priest, dispensed or not, is not the subject of penalties or censures in the 1983 Code nor of excommunication, even if he marries civilly."

Furthermore, the code supports the legitimacy of a "full lay ministry for dispensed priests including diocesan curia appointments, pastoral care, sacramental ministry, preaching, wedding and funeral services."

Also, the code says that "the Christian faithful have the right to receive . . . the word of God and the sacraments." Padovano analyzes the wording of the code in detail, noting, for example, that Canon 976 says that "any priest validly and licitly absolves any penitent in danger of death, even if an approved priest is present." Further, Canon 976 adds that when confronted with the danger of death any priest is *obliged* to hear the confessions of the Christian faithful. Padovano stresses that the canons use the phrase *danger of death* and not *in articulo mortis*. He explains that "danger of death" can include hospital patients who are about to undergo serious operations, people who are seriously sick, and those who are about to take a perilous trip.

The entire treatment serves to provide a legal basis for resigned priests to minister to the faithful. Copies of the paper were sent to all three hundred twenty American bishops, "hoping that they will seek legitimate and healthy ways to utilize the talents and gifts of their brother priests, now married."

An International Role

As has been noted, several efforts had been made by SPFM leaders to forge links with their counterparts in other countries. Rocco Caporale attended a meeting in Rome in 1969 but reported to the first SPFM convention that the Europeans were not on the same wavelength with Americans. In 1972, SPFM president Bernard McGoldrick made an abortive effort to summon an international meeting in Switzerland. FCM leader Gerald Grudzen attempted in the late seventies to join forces with married priests in Latin America.

However, it was not until the eighties, and with the Europeans taking the initiative, that such international cooperation was realized. Groups similar to CORPUS had been formed in several countries. In 1985 a "married priests' synod" was convened in Ariccia, near Rome, attracting priests and their wives from sixteen countries of Europe and North and South America. Anthony Padovano, one of the participants from North America, was elected a vice president by the group, which called itself the International Federation of Married Priests.

A second meeting was held in Ariccia in 1987. Once again, Padovano attended and, in a *National Catholic Reporter* article, compared the two Ariccia meetings:

> The 1985 synod was somewhat defensive and concentrated on the need for the law of obligatory celibacy to be changed. The 1987 congress emphasized, instead, not what the church might do to solve the problem, but rather the experience of married priests as a lived reality. The 1987 congress asked for nothing. It witnessed, rather, to the enrichment of life that occurs when marriage and priesthood, sexuality and prayer, work and children, personal freedom and lay concerns are fused into a whole.[23]

This change in perspective would be reflected in CORPUS, under Padovano's guidance, as it strove to position itself for the years ahead.

The Third International Federation of Married Priests was held in Utrecht, Holland, in August 1990 and drew over 200 participants, in contrast to the 150 and 120, respectively, at the two Ariccia meetings. More than thirty Americans attended, including Padovano and Dosh. By now, dozens of countries all over the world had organizations of married priests. The hope continued that a worldwide demand for change eventually would be effective. As a follow-up to the August congress, the International Federation sent two of its leaders to hold a press conference in Rome on October 1, 1990, the opening day of the Bishops' Synod. Their position was carried widely by the world press.

It is interesting to note that just as the affluent American Catholic Church had long provided financial support to poorer areas of the world, so now the American married priests, through CORPUS, contributed funds that enabled a European representative of the

International Federation of Married Priests to attend the first Latin American Congress of Married Priests, which was held in Brazil in January 1990. CORPUS itself was represented by board member Michael Breslin, formerly a Brooklyn diocesan priest and now, with his wife, the owner of a pottery shop in New York.[24] The meeting drew four hundred people and was addressed by two Brazilian bishops who spoke to the group in very supportive terms. One of them said:

> You have so much to add to the Church as a symbolic and prophetic image. You may not see the fruit of your efforts right away, but you will soon. People will be asking, "What difference does it make whether a priest is married or not?"[25]

A National Spokesman

In his "Broken Promises" talk at the 1988 CORPUS conference, Padovano had reassured married priests that they had not betrayed their vows. At the 1989 conference in Columbus, Ohio, he took a step further and urged his listeners to action, saying:

> We all know that we are priests. We have been called by God and must act. Every time we find a pastoral need, we are responding to it. We're not interested in creating schism. None of us is doing anything wrong with our ministry: The call is from God, and the church cannot make us powerless to act.[26]

The reference to schism recalled a charge directed at FCM sixteen years before when it had counseled members to "act." FCM supporters had grown weary of waiting for acceptance by Rome or the American bishops and decided that the call to ministry was from God and that Church officials had no right to stifle their desire to be of service. In a 1990 interview, Padovano said that CORPUS had indeed reached the place where FCM had arrived so many years before. Although it would maintain its determination to change the Church law that mandated clerical celibacy, it would also encourage disobedience to Church law in response to a "higher law."

The question now arose: How would the hierarchy react to the CORPUS declaration of independence? Perhaps the answer came in the aftermath of the 1990 CORPUS conference in San Jose, California.

By coincidence, the American Catholic bishops were holding their annual retreat at nearby Santa Clara University. About one hundred married priests and their families held a prayer service outside the church where the bishops had celebrated Mass. In a show of friendship and empathy, four bishops joined the married priests at prayer.

Later the same day, Bishop Donald W. Wuerl of Pittsburgh, head of the NCCB Committee on Priestly Life and Ministry, together with several other bishops, met for an hour with Padovano and other CORPUS board members after which they exchanged cordial words. Although many bishops had met in their dioceses with married priests, this was the first meeting in a decade between bishops and married priests that at least might seem to be "official." It was publicized by CORPUS as a sign of hope.[27]

On June 29, 1990, six days after the meeting, Padovano wrote a lengthy "Dear Don" letter to Wuerl, thanking the bishop for meeting with CORPUS and reviewing what had occurred at the meeting. Padovano wrote "Feast of Peter (married Apostle) and Paul (celibate Apostle)," implying the obvious point that married and celibate priests could serve the Church together.

It is clear from the letter and from Padovano's reference to "dialogue with the NCCB" that he considered the meeting official.[28] In fact, at the meeting he asked the bishops for "a permanent married priest liaison with the Priestly Life and Ministry Committee," suggesting that this "would enable dialogue to be ongoing and orderly."

However, Rome did not want bishops to lend legitimacy to groups such as CORPUS. Bishop Wuerl received a letter from Antonio Cardinal Innocenti, the head of the Vatican Congregation for the Clergy, asking for an explanation of the meeting.[29] Wuerl defended his action, saying that the bishops had met as individuals and not as representatives of the NCCB. Padovano's reaction to the letter from Rome was that it was likely to have "a chilling effect on other bishops who might consider meeting with married priests."[30]

This may be precisely what Cardinal Innocenti had intended.

Once Padovano assumed the title of president of CORPUS in 1988, he became the principal spokesman for the married priests of the country, eclipsing Dosh. During the last half of 1990 alone he was involved in more than twenty media interviews, providing him with a national forum for publicizing the CORPUS message.

It was clear that he believed that conditions were ripe for change. In an August 1990 letter to the 244 area representatives, echoing words used by SPFM twenty years before, Padovano said, "Never before have we had a climate so responsive to our message." And in a December 1991 letter to the ten thousand people on the CORPUS mailing list he urged everyone to attend the 1991 conference in New York "and to give a signal to the country that Church reform has started in earnest in the U.S.A." For many who had been working on reform for a generation such words must have evoked a feeling of *déjà vu*.

The CORPUS Constitution

Whereas SPFM and its successor FCM has had a constitution since 1969, CORPUS operated on an informal basis from its inception in 1974 until 1990, when a constitution was prepared by John O'Brien of Baltimore under Padovano's direction. The constitution went through eight drafts and wide consultation before its unanimous adoption by the board. The constitution makes clear that the primary goal of CORPUS is not to promote a married priesthood but a much narrower objective, namely, "to reinstate to active canonical minis-try in the Latin Rite of the Roman Catholic Church those non-clerical priests who are qualified and ready to serve." It might be asked whether CORPUS has the welfare of the Church as its main concern or simply the self-interest of the married priests. However, other statements by CORPUS make clear that although it must respond to its major constituency's concerns, it does support a much broader agenda for ministerial reform.

A comparison of the 1969 constitution and statement of purpose of SPFM with the corresponding 1990 documents of CORPUS shows striking continuity over time. To a large extent, the CORPUS of today is a reincarnation of the SPFM of more than twenty years ago. That coming full circle of the struggle for a married priesthood is perhaps most touchingly symbolized by the fact that Thomas Durkin, one of the original SPFM board members, asked CORPUS members in 1991 to nominate him for one of the first member-elected positions on the CORPUS board.

Opportunities and Dangers

As is characteristic of social movements, both sets of documents insist that change is urgently needed and that the group has a mission to provide leadership. Although few CORPUS members are aware of the history they share with SPFM, they are beating the same "drum," using much of the same language and expressing the same firm conviction that change is imminent. Although the average age of married priests, as celibate priests, is rising, several of the members of the CORPUS board are men ordained after Vatican II. They are replacing in the leadership ranks of the movement those formed in the preconciliar Church. It is not just a new generation of priests who are emerging but a "new breed," men perhaps not as patient as their elders.

This sense of urgency is reflected in the 1990 CORPUS "Strategies for the Future," which boldly presents a timetable for change, forecasting that by 1995 nonclerical priests will be restored to a sacramental ministry and by the year 2000 the Church will ordain both men and women, whether married or celibate. However, it might be recalled that in 1970, the Jesuit, John Haughey, confident that he was reading accurately the signs of the times, had predicted that by the midseventies there would be a married priesthood.[31]

In terms of the rhythm of a social movement, it is clear that after a lull of nearly two decades there is a resurgence of enthusiasm on the part of married priests for Church reform. The last hurrah of older men and the youthful optimism of their juniors seem to have coalesced to fashion what may well be the final push against the fortress gate.

Although Padovano is committed personally to a more ecumenical Christianity and a more democratic Church structure, he is wise enough to avoid Eugene Bianchi's mistake of leading people more quickly than they are prepared to follow. Most free ministers are neither sophisticated theologians nor daring revolutionaries. They are men who want to be priests. Padovano, ever the good teacher, knows that the best way to reach one's goal is by taking one step at a time. Therefore, several items included in the mission statement are not emphasized, including a call for experimentation, a restructuring of the Church, and a leadership more responsive to the people. It is possible that these issues will have to be left to the next century, perhaps to be taken up by the children of the present free ministers.

There are other challenges facing the CORPUS leadership. The periodic board meetings must not focus on planning the annual conference at the expense of promoting local initiatives and identifying new leaders. As the experience of FCM, countless small worship communities, and religious orders of men and women attests, to neglect the recruitment and formation of new members is to consign the group to stagnation and decline.

A related challenge is for a leadership scattered throughout the country to be able to work together effectively. The constitution calls for the national coordinator to be responsible for the day-to-day operation of the national office "under the direction of the President," whose duties include acting as "spokesperson and representative to the public." It remains to be seen how a president in New Jersey can work with a coordinator in California, let alone how volunteer board members, with demanding career and family responsibilities, will be able to provide the direction and energy for what are likely to be the many years of effort that lie ahead.

A Hymn to Marriage

Padovano's writing has focused on ministry. However, in 1987 he published a book on marriage in which he who yearns for priesthood sings of married love.[32] He dedicated the book to his wife, Theresa, "who has made her world a sacrament so that all who enter it receive grace."

The book returns to a theme from his earliest analysis of ministry, namely, that all ministry must affirm the worth of the individual. He says that marriage partners minister to one another, caring for one another, and nourishing the joy that one should take in one's own lovableness. Marriage is the framework within which God's loving work can take place.

Although Padovano can write in careful scientific fashion he can also express himself poetically. It may be this dreamer side of him that is most appealing and most likely to touch the hearts of Church officials, who may remember that, in the Scriptures, God was often revealed in dreams as in the cases of Isaac's son, Joseph, and Joseph, the husband of Mary.

Padovano concludes his short book on marriage with words that reverberate with liturgical images and reflect the source of his hope and strength:

> In another land, in an everlasting home, the lovers will break bread and share words. They will touch each other's bodies and see, as the disciples did, that the wounds of death have been healed. . . . The marriage will make them happy forever.[33]

15

Free Priests in the Church Today

It is a very serious mistake to think about the number of men who have resigned from the active ministerial clergy as separate individuals, the meaning of whose experiences can only be the sum of isolated psychological histories. These resignations—and the continuation of the lives of faith of these men—are a complex event in the life of the priesthood in the western Church . . . . We must come to a useful and thoughtful recognition that the decisions, changes and life experiences of these men are a significant dimension of the life of the ministerial priesthood.
Rev. Robert S. Smith, *Diaspora*, Spring 1980

A movement is not just dreamers as if somehow dreams take flesh and dwell among us without the labors of the many who greet each dawn with a wide awake "Yes!" Free ministry is not just organizations and meetings and newsletters. It is men who consider themselves free priests and are busy doing the tasks of their ministry. They must not be sought in churches or in chanceries but in the workplaces of the world and the neighborhoods of the needy. It is possible to miss the men who embody the new priesthood just as once it was easy to miss One who ate with sinners, rejected titles, and gathered around him an unpromising band of followers.

Free priests are convinced that a world is ending and a world is being born; that the priestly caste of the monarchical Roman Church is an obsolete structure, crumbling before our very eyes. Young people know this and stand back lest they be crushed beneath its weight. But as it falls, shards of light shoot here and there through the darkness—nothing impressive, nothing newsworthy—yet just possibly the first promise of spring in the chill of a long winter.

This final chapter will spotlight four free priests, two of whom are engaged in full-time ministry and two of whom are engaged in secular employment but giving much of their free time to priestly ministry. Two have wives who are their partners in service, and two have wives who are supportive although not directly collaborating with their husbands in the work of ministry.

The men featured here are but a few of the scores who might have been selected. Just as no one outside of a local community knows most of the canonical priests who serve them, so most free priests labor in obscurity, known only to those to whom they minister and to Him to whom they have pledged their lives.

The men live in different states and have no contact with one another. None are officers of FCM or CORPUS, although all are members and feel a need to be connected to the brotherhood of those who work on the margins of ministry. If they are not recognized by bishops, they hope that they are recognized by Christ. The apostle John once complained that a man was driving out demons in Christ's name who did not belong to their group. Jesus replied, "Do not try to stop him . . . . For whoever is not against us is for us" (Mark 9:38–40).

John and Louise Dee in Minnesota and Bill and Cindy Pfeiffer in Connecticut are engaged in full-time ministry. Pascal Baute is a psychotherapist in Kentucky and Tom McCabe is an educator in New York. They are very diverse in personality and background but alike in a determination to live today what may be models of priesthood for tomorrow.

John and Louise Dee

"You're nothing but trouble. Nobody wants you. I'm not going to reassign you. Find your own job." This is how John "Dee" Csaplweski recalls the frustration of Bishop Fitzgerald of the Winona, Minnesota, diocese. Dee had worked in one parish until, as he says, "the pastor ran me off." He was then assigned to an alcoholic pastor. After that "chaotic" situation, Dee was in effect given permission to become a free minister.

The bishop of the diocese where he had been ordained in 1964 considered him a "troublemaker" because of the unorthodox views he espoused on ecclesiastical and world issues as well as the free-wheeling life-style he had developed. He did not conform to the prevailing image of a priest.

Dee had become "The Singing Priest," teaming up with children to present revival-style, multimedia programs. He traveled throughout Minnesota conducting retreats and workshops and was not at all hesitant to proclaim his views on the war in Vietnam, birth control, and priestly celibacy.

Once released by the bishop he ranged more extensively, presenting his programs to Protestant and Catholic congregations. Suspicious of this wandering cleric, some Catholic clergy would call his bishop for verification of Dee's legitimacy. Perhaps continuing to be grateful that Dee was someplace other than Winona, the bishop always affirmed the good standing of the radical priest.

In October 1971, Dee went to Vietnam and, with four other priests, chained himself to the U.S. embassy gate in Saigon. The priests then carried to the Vatican a petition that asked Pope Paul VI to condemn American intervention in Southeast Asia.

The notoriety of this behavior preceded Dee back to the United States, where he found it more and more difficult to get bookings. At the invitation of Mary Lou Zehfuss, the local SPFM coordinator, Dee was invited to speak at two Catholic churches in Pittsburgh. At the last minute, his appearance at one church was canceled and at the other he was permitted to preach at a folk mass on condition that he not discuss Vietnam, birth control, or celibacy.[1]

Itinerant Team Ministry

For most of the past twenty years, Dee has composed a lengthy Christmas letter chronicling his adventures and promoting his ideas. The one written in January 1972 announced two developments of significance for his personal life as well as for his ministry. First, although he was still working with children, he was attempting to form an adult team. He had already recruited "a former nun with an M.A. in Communications, a good musician too. We're hoping for some extensive tours this summer and next year." The former nun was Louise Tacheny, who had been a School Sister of Notre Dame for fifteen years. Dee also announced that the tours would be possible because of the acquisition of a camper "for our travelling church, office and home."

That camper would serve all those functions for John and Louise for three years as they crisscrossed the country before ultimately settling down. However, John still owns the ancient vehicle and uses it occasionally in his work.

The first long trip the couple took brought them, after many perils—including a wheel breaking loose and coming up through the floor of their camper—to the SPFM convention in Los Angeles in the summer of 1972. Having decided to marry, they felt that there was no more appropriate place for the exchange of vows than at the gathering of free ministers. What they were doing, and intended to continue to do, was to travel the country, singing their religious songs and proclaiming their joy at being Christians. For them, it was not essential to have approval from the official Church. It would be enough to be commissioned by their peers in the movement. As it turned out, they went forth from the convention, not only as husband and wife, but as ambassadors-at-large for SPFM.

Compatibility in the vision of the idealistic couple was revealed in the way that Louise explained to a Minnesota reporter the life she was undertaking with John. She said:

> I consider my move out of the convent and into the married ministry as part of the same original call that led me to the convent when I was 17. The call is one of total life dedication to the service of God's people. For a time I lived that dedication in a celibate community lifestyle. . . . Now I live that dedication as a married woman whose husband is also living a lifelong commitment of service to God's people through Word and sacrament. Our lifestyle seems especially relevant in today's world.[2]

John and Louise Dee were metaphors for the unrest, coupled with optimism, that characterized countless priests and religious after Vatican II. Although the Dees were in their thirties, their rootlessness was similar to that of the hippies who hitchhiked across the country, lived in communes, and rejected the values and institutions of their elders. There were no maps for the journeys that such people undertook.

The Dees embarked on what would be a two-year continuation of their itinerant ministry, similar to the two years of travel undertaken several years before by Charles Sullivan and Pauline Fox. Correspondence with SPFM officers attests to the high hopes with which both couples embraced their missionary ventures. It also reveals that they received painfully little support from SPFM, either moral or financial, as the organization stumbled along short on money, members, and morale. To a large extent, credit for the survival of free ministry must be attributed to these "ambassadors," who carried the torch of the movement to the large cities and the small towns of America, gaining media attention and recruiting those who would embrace the cause.

There is no doubt about the intensity of Dee's enthusiasm for SPFM in the early seventies. Impassioned letters in the summer of 1973 reflect his apprehension that the organization was about to be destroyed by people like Eugene Bianchi and Thomas Durkin, who were arguing that it was no longer needed. To strengthen the wavering commitment of the SPFM officers, Dee wrote:

> We would appeal to all the Genes and Toms of SPFM that they please move on to wherever they have to go and do what they must do with SPFM's blessing and support. Maybe we should have a document of laicization from SPFM for those who wish that freedom. But please, don't burn the bridges that so many of us still need.

The statistics that Dee provided offered convincing testimony that his strong words were backed up by impressive deeds. Through the first eight months of 1974 the Dees conducted eighty-one programs in twenty-seven towns, traveling from Minnesota to New York to Florida and back. Much of this trip was a repeat of what they had done the previous year. In particular, they wished to visit once again the Florida community that had been so helpful to them when their daughter, Christie Beth, was born there prematurely while they were conducting a program.

Putting Down Roots

In the midseventies a new phase began in the Dees' lives. Christie's birth contributed to their decision to settle down, but it wasn't just the child. After nearly three years on the road, there was a weariness with traveling and a disappointment with the movement. FCM had not made a commitment to the charismatic spirituality that the Dees espoused nor had their reception by the people been as positive as they anticipated. John wrote on one occasion that Catholics liked what they were doing but were hesitant to support them because they were not approved by the hierarchy. So, in the fall of 1974, with money borrowed from their families, the Dees purchased from the federal government a large Dutch colonial in a Minneapolis neighborhood scarred by the race riots of the late sixties. Their home became the hub of a wide range of services to a depressed community. They called themselves Mission OK: Ecumenical Ministry, a name under which they had incorporated their work in 1972.

Music ministry remains central to the Dees. Louise conducts a music school in their home, generating much of the family's meager income over the years. Christie, their only child, has learned to play ten instruments and conducts violin concerts on a regular basis throughout Minnesota. Her father boasts that whereas he used to be the performer he has been reduced to chauffeuring Louise and Christie to their engagements, during which Louise provides piano accompaniment to the young prodigy.

For several years, in affiliation with the home school movement, Louise conducted a school in their home, providing an education to ten neighborhood children as well as to Christie.

Besides sponsoring the school, Mission OK has been a house of hospitality for numerous people in need. Every Saturday evening, the Dees conduct a liturgy attended by a fluid congregation of worshipers.

Other than handyman jobs, John has never held paid employment. His letters relate the extensive volunteer contributions he has made to an ever more deprived neighborhood, including a food pantry, the distribution of used clothing, and advocacy for people evicted or for whom landlords did not provide services. But John's greatest satisfaction is reserved for his work on a telephone crisis hotline of which he is the only Catholic priest among the two hundred volunteers. Several years ago, he was given an award as the volunteer with the longest period of service.

Traditionally, Catholic priesthood was symbolized by the Roman collar. Dee, like many others, discontinued wearing the collar in the early seventies. However, after attending the 1988 CORPUS conference, where it was suggested that free ministers should use the title "Reverend" and wear the collar in order to make socially visible their priestly identity, Dee began to wear it again. He claims that his decision to reclaim his membership in "the uniformed clergy" has afforded him many opportunities for ministry. For example, in the summer of 1990, he attended the International Federation of Married Priests in Holland wearing the collar. A man approached him on the street and asked if he were a priest. It turned out that the man was terribly troubled and wanted to go to confession. The two sat on the steps of a closed church for an hour. Dee heard his confession and gave him advice on how to avoid sin. "It made the whole trip worthwhile," Dee concluded, "and it would not have happened were I not wearing the collar."

Although they may seem to work alone and to be disconnected from the Church, the Dees are a conscious part of the free ministry world. While Dee disavows the direction that FCM has taken, he serves as a CORPUS representative and attends local as well as national meetings. He has over seven hundred names on the Mission OK mailing list. Aware that a movement is not isolated individuals, but a network of people attempting to bring about change, he keeps before the consciousness of many the witness of the unique twenty-year ministry of Louise and himself. They have been music makers for the movement, unconcerned that some might consider that they are singing off-key.

William and Cynthia Pfeiffer

Far to the east, in Hebron, Connecticut, another couple is singing, not literally, but in the sense of the well-being they experience in their full-time ministry and in their confidence, as Bill Pfeiffer says, that "the Lord has called us to be prophetic voices to the institution." Like the Dees, the Pfeiffers speak with the language of charismatic Christians and practice what is largely a family-focused ministry, with their home as the base for a variety of services to the community.

Bill Pfeiffer was ordained in 1963 for the diocese of Allentown, Pennsylvania, and worked in parishes for five years before being assigned to teach religion in a high school. Eventually, he became the principal of a Catholic high school.

For nine years Pfeiffer had a "brother-sister" relationship with his future wife, Cindy, who was fifteen when they met in the parish to which he was assigned. Later, she was a student in his religion class. Then in 1976, at separate prayer meetings, they received the message from God that they were to marry. As Cindy explained it, "The Lord told Bill that He was going to make him a married priest and that He was going to raise up the married priesthood again."

The newlyweds moved to Chicago in search of work. For a year Bill applied to Catholic institutions, but to no avail. In desperation he took a job as a delivery man, working at $3.50 an hour. This he did for several years, barely able to support Cindy and the first of their six children.

Despite his precarious economic situation, Pfeiffer worked on a volunteer basis with Frank Bonnike in developing the CORPUS area representatives network and organizing in 1980 the first national gathering of CORPUS members.

Mary's Field

With the promise of a position in a publishing firm, the Pfeiffers moved to Connecticut in 1981. On arrival they found that the job had evaporated. Within weeks, living in motels, they were down to their last twenty dollars. Aided by the generosity of friends, they struggled along for three more months, until Bill obtained a job selling replacement windows and siding. However, as misfortune would have it, the company was cheating its customers, and he resigned.

In the midst of all this change, the call to ministry reasserted itself, and Bill and Cindy began to respond to local needs on a part-time basis. Soon after, with no regular position materializing, they decided to undertake a full-time ministry. They took as their own the words of the pioneer settlers of the area and now inscribed on the Connecticut state seal: "He who uprooted us, will sustain us."

Their earliest ministry was to unwed pregnant girls, offering counseling on alternatives to abortion, clothing for the babies, assistance in dealing with public agencies, and even, at times, temporary lodging in their home. Although radical in some respects, the Pfeiffers are traditional in their devotion to the Mother of Jesus and call their ministry Mary's Field. A picture of Mary cradling the Holy Infant in her arms is the symbol of their concern for life.

As the community became aware of their presence, calls for help increased and their work diversified. Referrals came from local pastors and government agency social workers. Like the Dees in Minneapolis, the Pfeiffers made themselves available to those in need and found that they had no trouble keeping busy.

A board of directors was formed in order to provide some policy guidance for their work as well as a base for legal status and fundraising. Bill began publishing a newsletter, *Of Seeds and Flowers*, a blend of accounts of their work and inspirational short essays.

A More Spiritual Focus

In 1990, after prayer and consultation, the Pfeiffers instituted a major reorientation of their ministry. As Bill related in an interview the following year, he had become more clearly convinced that he was a priest, not a social worker; that he wanted to do those things that were more directly priestly as he understood the term. He knew that such a change in the work of Mary's Field might cost him the support of the local Catholic Church, which readily accepted him as long as he remained in the religiously nonthreatening role of social worker. As Bill said:

> Everyone loves people who help unwed mothers. It's not clear whether financial support and institutional favor will continue now that we are evolving into a more spiritual type of ministry, one that, in effect, more directly challenges the Church's monopoly on worship and the spiritual life. We feel that what is happening is a process guided by the spirit, but the risks are considerable.

Not the least significant risk is financial. The 1990 annual report shows donations of $30,479 and expenses of $32,992. Bill's salary for the year was $16,923 and Cindy's, $2,100. An April 1991 letter to supporters from the Mary's Field Finance Committee said that, in light of the Pfeiffers' responsibility for their children, the board wanted to increase donations so as to provide Bill with long-term disability insurance and a pension plan. The only other income the Pfeiffers have is derived from Bill's part-time teaching of Latin at a public high school. Cindy is busy as mother and homemaker and has no educational or work experience to fall back on should Bill become disabled.

When the Pfeiffers refer to the institutional Church, it is with frustration and sadness. Like many other free ministers, they are becoming more assertive in their impatience. Cindy says that she sees the Mother Church as an alcoholic parent. Out of embarrass-ment, everyone has been hiding the sick mother. It is time to realize that it is not healthy to shield her. The whole family is at risk. It's more important to take care of the other family members.

As if echoing his wife's impatience, Bill adds, "Let's start doing it!"—that is, offer spiritual ministry to people, including performing the Eucharist.

Pfeiffer is FCM-certified "to do legally the things I have to do." However, he finds the theology of the organization too vague. He insists that he is no "Lone Ranger" practicing a ministry discon-nected from the Church. Although the hierarchy may not recognize his ministry, he feels that all that he does is within the Body of Jesus, "even if the Body doesn't know it." With reference to FCM's ignoring the Church, he argues:

> Be prophetic to the institution. It's not going to go away. It will last; you won't. If you are going to do something significant, do something about the Body of which you are a member. History will show that free ministry detached from the institution did not have the wisdom to understand what really makes things happen.

Becoming an Ex

Bill Pfeiffer and John Dee have reached a similar point in their self-understanding. By wearing the Roman collar once again, Dee is proclaiming to all that he is a Catholic priest. Similarly, Pfeiffer's new direction is aimed at clarifying his identity: He is not a social worker, but a priest. Although he had never hidden the fact, he is convinced that he must be more direct in witnessing unequivocally to the Church's need for married priests.

Viewed sociologically, both men may be examples of the difficulty that many priests experience in "exiting" the role of priest. One sociologist, Helen Rose Fuchs Ebaugh, an ex-nun herself, describes what she calls the process of *role exit* and the complementary process of assuming the *ex-role*.[3] Although Ebaugh does not refer to ex-priests, leaving the priesthood bears similarities to that of a divorcée leaving a marriage, a physician retiring from practice, or a convict returning to society. All leave a role that was a major part of their social identity. All maintain some residual or shadow dimension of the previously held position. Their new social identity remains influenced by the former status.

Ebaugh says that usually there is considerable socialization for assuming a significant role, what she terms *role entry*, but often little preparation for exiting that role. So, a priest spends many years in a seminary, preparing for the day when he will be ordained and assume his place in the ranks of the clergy. Men like Dee and Pfeiffer had never experienced themselves as anything other than a priest or someone preparing to become a priest. However, when the decision to leave the priesthood is made, the transition is likely to be rapid and unprepared.

Furthermore, whereas exiting most roles is socially accepted, even expected, priesthood has been defined as permanent, a role that one cannot really exit. Finding appropriate terminology is difficult. Some resigned priests reject the label "ex-priest" and live in a murky land of role ambiguity, with no one, least of all themselves, knowing precisely how to relate to them.[4]

Pascal Bernard Baute

Some men are what has been referred to as *hyphenated priests*, having a dual professional identity. When they relinquish the priesthood, they retain the other dimension of their status. So, Eugene Bianchi, Bernard McGoldrick, and Anthony Padovano were priest-professors and experienced no interruption in the academic dimension of their lives. Pfeiffer had attempted to maintain his status as educator but was unable to do so. Dee, like most parish priests, had no socially recognized occupational identity other than that of clergyman. Pascal Baute of Lexington, Kentucky, was a priest-psychologist. When he resigned from the ministry, he continued his practice as a psychologist.

Since 1984, Baute has had more than twenty articles, letters, and poems published in *Diaspora*. In his initial communication with the FCM publication, he reported a history not unlike that of many others. He said that for thirteen years after leaving the priesthood he had been busy "establishing a family, building a marriage and making a living."[5] Then in 1982, he made a Cursillo—an intensive, highly emotional three-day course in Christianity—resumed the study of theology, and became caught up once again in the excitement of the ministry he had put aside in 1968.

Although born and raised in Kentucky, Baute traveled and studied widely. After serving in the Army, he attended the University of Notre Dame and then at age twenty-three entered the Benedictine community in Florida. He was ordained in 1959 but continued his studies, first at St. Louis University and then at Loyola University in Chicago, where he conducted research on the training of priests in pastoral counseling and received a masters degree. Awarded a fellowship, he moved to the University of Pennsylvania, where in 1965 he earned a doctorate in psychology. His dissertation research was on intimacy in the lives of Catholic couples.

Feeling the need for more intimacy in his own life, the priest-psychologist resigned from the Benedictines and at age thirty-nine married Janette Osborne Mobley, a widow with a young child. Janette, a psychiatric nurse, does not share Pascal's religious heritage, having been raised as a Baptist. Baute says that although his wife does not participate in his religious activities, she is supportive and works with him in their Institute for Human Responsiveness, Inc., the in-home setting for their private practice of psychotherapy. The Bautes have two college-age children.

Free Ministry Lay Initiative

Baute has two major free ministry projects, both of which are the outgrowth of many years of groundwork in the Lexington, Kentucky, area and of his intensifying conviction that he has a calling to ministry. One is Vocare, a CORPUS-like lay group committed to work for "an expanded priesthood." The other is the Spiritual Growth Network, designed to provide opportunities for spiritual growth outside traditional ecclesiastical structures.

Vocare emerged from the group of married priests that Baute had been able to gather for monthly meetings. For years he had sent letters to resigned priests in Kentucky, getting minimal response. Finally, in 1989, perhaps as a result of the increasing visibility of CORPUS, of which he is an area representative, Baute was able to bring together in brotherhood men who had shared the Catholic priesthood and who were willing to explore what that meant to them today.

The group has hosted the local bishop at a meeting and also sponsored a social evening with a number of canonical priests. Baute feels the ground has been broken for establishing warmer relationships, where previously there had been awkwardness and rejection.

From the married priests' group emerged the idea to organize laypeople to lobby for a married priesthood. Accordingly, a petition was drawn up and lay supporters enlisted. Baute reports that laymen and laywomen have responded and are now carrying the project themselves with him as consultant. They have been able to include flyers about their ideas in parish bulletins and to meet with groups of Catholics in order to explain to them the history of celibacy and the Church's ideas on human sexuality. The bishop, while not approving the project, has allowed his pastors to decide for themselves whether or not to cooperate. Baute is hopeful that after Vocare is well established locally, it will spread to other areas.

The second project, the nonprofit and nondenominational Spiritual Growth Network, conducts monthly days of recollection, weekend retreats, and a Twelve Step group for the spiritual journey. Since several of Baute's *Diaspora* articles have decried the superficiality of churchgoers, he hopes that he will be able to contribute to a deeper spirituality.

Effort to Revitalize FCM

Concerned that FCM has drifted aimlessly, Baute made a bold move in 1991 in an effort to help it find a direction. He offered to facilitate at the annual meeting in St. Louis a process for discerning just what the members felt the organization should be and how they might go about putting it on course. Only twenty-four people attended the meeting, but many participants reported that the small group made possible a very reflective experience. Baute's process was for groups of eight people to enumerate on Friday evening what they valued about FCM. On Saturday night the groups prioritized what they believed should be the agenda for FCM in the years ahead.

It is instructive to assess the lists that were generated by the groups. Recalling that FCM grew out of SPFM, it is striking to note that there is no reference to priesthood or to efforts to change the Church. And a group that initially was all male has proposed that its number one priority for the future should be "more affirmation and recognition of women." The lists also dutifully repeat many of the buzzwords and ideas that have long been staple elements of the free ministry agenda such as small faith communities, empowerment, and certification.[6]

At the end of October, Baute followed up on the meeting with a letter to some two dozen FCM members, soliciting their ideas and hoping to advance the process begun at the St. Louis meeting. By late December 1991, he had received two replies "and they were not in any great depth." Nevertheless, Baute maintains that he is not losing interest and intends to continue to challenge the members to come up with a viable formula for reviving FCM, one-third of whose 1990 members did not renew for 1991.

Thomas A. McCabe

Over the years, a number of married priests have attempted to organize their colleagues. Often such efforts have failed. It took considerable perseverance and skill by Baute to form such a group and to motivate it to undertake free ministry projects. Perhaps the most striking success of all has been attained by Tom McCabe of New York, who has been able to fashion a small group of friends into the most effective local force the free ministry has ever witnessed.

Early in 1988, McCabe invited to his house near New York City several of his former priest associates from the diocese of Brooklyn. The purpose of the meeting was to explore the possibility of holding a convocation of resigned priests in the New York area. McCabe explained to his friends that it was important for married priests to be updated on questions of ministry, to remain visible, and to issue a public statement in support of optional celibacy.

Although not a young man, having been ordained in 1960, McCabe was a new leader in the movement. He had never heard of FCM and had no affiliation with CORPUS until he began to explore the possibility of sponsoring a meeting. Although listed in the 1990 CORPUS directory, McCabe has maintained his independence of the national organization, convinced that his role is to concentrate on New York. He is an example of what Dosh felt was the key to the success of the movement: local initiatives.

The small group of married priests called itself the Renewal Coordinating Committee, subsequently changing the name to the Renewal Coordinating Community (RCC), to reflect the growing sense of what the group had become. Eventually, the RCC decided to hold a one-day convocation at Hofstra University on Long Island in the fall of 1989, trusting that a substantial number of people would make a commitment to a conference on Church renewal. As it turned out, this local meeting attracted a larger attendance than did the national CORPUS conference held that year in Columbus, Ohio. Among the speakers on Long Island were Dosh and Padovano, who took note of the RCC's skill in attracting an audience that included scores of active priests as well as religious women sympathetic to the cause of a married priesthood. Careful not to offend anyone, the RCC invited a canonical priest to preside at the Eucharist.

Heartened by the experience, the RCC went ahead and sponsored a second convocation in 1990. Once again, it drew more people than did the CORPUS conference in San Jose.

Unable to ignore the impressive organizing capabilities of the RCC, the CORPUS board invited the RCC to coordinate the 1991 CORPUS weekend in New York.[7] The group agreed and from the outset McCabe and his close collaborator, Joseph Dougherty, predicted that theirs would be the largest gathering of married priests ever assembled. They were correct. However, rather than generating the hoped for positive momentum, the gathering of seven hundred fifty people was the scene of a divisive controversy.

Margaret O'Brien Steinfels's Bombshell

The RCC's strategy for attracting a large registration was to feature a variety of presenters who would address a range of Church renewal topics, not just the issue of a married priesthood. As usual, Padovano was to be a principal speaker, but also scheduled were appearances by theologian Harvey Cox and *Commonweal* editor Margaret O'Brien Steinfels.

To dramatize the call for a married priesthood, two actions were planned. One was a liturgy celebrated by three married priests dressed in liturgical vestments. The other was a peaceful demonstration on the street across from St. Patrick's Cathedral. The New York media was contacted, and it was anticipated that the two actions would elicit widespread attention.

There was attention all right, not however to the two events but rather to the sharp *opposition* to the events by none other than Steinfels, one of the conference speakers.

The organizers knew in advance that Steinfels was opposed to the illicit liturgy and to the demonstration. She told them that when she agreed to speak she did not know that these acts of direct defiance of the hierarchy were on the schedule. By hindsight, some CORPUS leaders felt that as soon as her position was known, her participation should have been canceled. As it was, they expected her to issue a press statement disassociating herself from the actions. However, in addition to the written statement, her presentation at the conference itself was a sustained, carefully argued attack on the CORPUS actions.

Steinfels objected to what she considered the use of the Eucharist as a political tool. She chided CORPUS, saying that their behavior was "more apt to postpone than hasten the acceptance of a married priesthood." She labeled Padovano's arguments justifying the actions "filigreed rationalizations" and claimed that she was speaking "as one of the Christian faithful on whose behalf you claim to be acting."[8]

In an editorial titled "A Prophetic Challenge," the Brooklyn diocesan paper commended Steinfels's courage and her insistence that efforts at Church reform be limited to actions that did not violate Church law.[9] Follow-up letters criticizing the editorial and supporting CORPUS included one from veteran free minister Joseph Burns, who twenty years before had organized the SPFM convention in New York that also had called for a married priesthood and that also had sought dialogue on the issue with Church officials.[10] Obviously unaware of the long history of the movement, Steinfels had charged that the married priests were impatient and wanted "instant gratification."

A Deep Love for Priesthood

McCabe had chaired the session at which Steinfels spoke and had been the one to introduce her and then had tried to mollify the audience when she finished and would not remain for questions. Perhaps as a sign of evenhandedness, Steinfels offered to publish in *Commonweal* an article by McCabe in which he offered his personal story as an example of how a married priest might feel about himself, priesthood, and the Church. McCabe wrote:

> I have never loved a "job" as much as I loved the "job" of being a priest. I have been a teacher and a special education administrator for years. It is good work but it does not give me the same satisfaction I found as a priest. This is my loss but it is also a loss for the church and for the parish that I could have served for the past twenty years.[11]

McCabe had served in the Brooklyn inner city for nine years, earning a reputation as a gentle, sensitive man, with a heart easily touched by the plight of the poor. He had studied Spanish in Puerto Rico and had fallen in love with the warm Spanish-speaking men and women whose poverty did not dampen their faith and whose affection sustained a young priest struggling to speak their language and respond to their needs.

Close priest friends in the inner city formed supportive bonds. Although outsiders to the privations of the minority group people they served, these young priests wanted to bring to their troubled neighborhoods the message of the Gospel. They were deeply distressed by the dilapidated housing, the crowded schools, the crime, and the drugs that the people they served confronted daily. As they sought to fashion a priesthood for the ghetto, many of them, McCabe included, looked into their own hearts and knew that they themselves were deprived; that the hunger of their people for bread was more than matched by their own hunger for love and their own thirst for an updated priesthood. There was an impatience during the sixties, an impatience with the war in Vietnam, an impatience with the pace of the War on Poverty, and an impatience with the pace of Church reform. The priests of the inner cities of America had been stripped naked of the consciousness in which they had been formed in the pre-Vatican II seminary, and they hurried into a future shrouded in uncertainty.

In 1969 McCabe resigned from the priesthood, married Eileen Dowd, a former Sister of St. Joseph, and became certified to teach in the New York City public schools. He and Eileen, who is principal of a Catholic elementary school, have four children.

Dissent in the Church

In her explosive CORPUS talk, Margaret O'Brien Steinfels raised the question of dissent against Church laws. The issue is critical to the direction that free ministry has taken. Steinfels might applaud Dr. Martin Luther King, Jr., for his civil disobedience in the struggle for racial justice, but she urged free ministers not to use that model in their quest for change in the Church. She spoke of disobedience as divisive and said that she was "profoundly saddened that I will not be with you at the Eucharist" to be celebrated by married priests. She urged her listeners "not to fracture the unity of the Church" by their rebelliousness. She was "heartsick" because the men she was addressing were planning to violate Church laws and demonstrate against the hierarchy. She counseled them to use only legal means to promote their cause.

Realizing that her talk had attracted widespread attention to the issue of dissent in the Church, Steinfels published the text in *Commonweal* and invited McCabe to write a response. Thus, within three months, McCabe was to have two articles published in *Commonweal*. The second would be more important. In effect, it bore the responsibility of justifying the free ministry movement itself.[12]

McCabe argued that breaking laws goes back to Jesus himself, who enraged the scribes and Pharisees by numerous violations of Jewish law. Pointing to a distinction between just and unjust laws, McCabe insisted that the behavior of the married priests was justified because the law mandating priestly celibacy is unjust in that it injured the common good of the Church. McCabe concluded his defense of married priests celebrating the Eucharist and of the free ministry movement in general by quoting the words of Gamaliel, "If this plan or action should be of men, it will be overthrown; but if it is of God, you will not be able to overthrow it; or else you may even be found fighting against God" (Acts 5:38–39).

Perhaps there is a cycle to social movements, and the arguments of those advocating change have to be repeated every generation until at last they are heeded or proven to be unfounded. The issue of dissent had been addressed in 1969 by Eugene Bianchi as first president of SPFM. He did so in the pages of *Commonweal*.[13] He argued that the task of changing long entrenched institutions requires the use of "organized pressure." In a *National Catholic Reporter* letter that same year, he said that "obedience and dissent are not mortal enemies, but rather two poles of a creative tension leading to the progress and health of the whole body."[14] Bianchi placed free ministry squarely within the "movement in contemporary society for maximizing man's development through freer options in human community." Sometimes, for human freedom to be obtained, laws must be broken and authority defied.

What Bianchi argued in 1969 and McCabe argued once again in 1991 was that dissent is not the enemy of truth, but its lifeblood; that dissent does not mean a rejection of the Church, but a desire to make it better. Institutions, like individual persons, need to be pruned and shaped if they are to remain fruitful. The knife of dissent may seem cruel, but it is the source of next season's harvest.

By their very nature, all social movements are voices of dissent. An institution can attempt to suppress dissent, but to do so is to risk stagnation, to risk the withering of freedom, and to risk the stifling of creativity and initiative. Free ministers continue to insist that their dissent springs from their love for the Church, not from any desire to harm it. Of course, they might be misguided. Sincerity is no protection from error. But what they ask is a hearing for the insight they have gained from what is now a generation of struggle. The ranks of the clergy in the United States continue to thin and to age. Free ministers wonder what the bishops can lose by sitting down with them as brothers and exploring the possibilities for rethinking priesthood.

In the article quoted at the beginning of this chapter, Rev. Robert Smith, a Long Island theologian, refers to the massive exodus of men from the priesthood as the "most extraordinary series of events in the life of the ministerial priesthood since the Sixteenth Century."[15] He maintains that this hemorrhaging from the priesthood is converging with the issue of the status of women and the idea of a baptismal priesthood of all Christians to offer the contemporary Church a rich challenge and a promising opportunity. It is precisely these three themes that underlie the free ministry movement and suggest that it serves a positive function in the never-ending search for the Incarnate and Risen Lord.

Heirs of Vatican II

For most free ministers, the day grows late. The shadows of evening gather. If the work is to be done, it must be done soon. Despite being ignored by the hierarchy and criticized by sincere people like Margaret O'Brien Steinfels, it is clear that men like Manseau, Dosh, Grudzen, Dee, Pfeiffer, Baute, and McCabe are not about to give up. They and hundreds of others believe that a renewed ministry is possible and that the movement must be sustained.

There is a feeling that the nineties is the decade of decision. Certainly it is the last during which most of those who have led the movement for the past twenty-five years can hope to participate personally in anything other than an emeritus status. What seems to be happening is that all over the country, and perhaps the world, men are making one last effort at reform before the sunset of the century, of their lives, and possibly of the Church itself.

In a letter inviting people to the 1991 conference, CORPUS President Anthony Padovano showed no loss of hope or of energy when he wrote words intended to rally the forces for the final struggle of their beloved cause:

> Every person who attends will be part of the collective witness that the time for a reformed ministry for men and women has come. We are the heirs of the Second Vatican Council who will not extinguish the spirit or let the dream die.

Appendix A

A Chronology of the Society of Priests for a Free Ministry/ Federation of Christian Ministries

President	Convention site	Diaspora editor
1969 Eugene Bianchi	Washington, D. C.	Rocco Caporale
1970	Berkeley, Calif.	
1971 Bernard McGoldrick	New York City	William King
1972	Los Angeles, Calif.	

At 1973 convention, SPFM is transformed into FCM

President	Convention site	Diaspora editor
1973 William Manseau	Staten Island, N. Y.	
1974	Naperville, Ill.	Gilbert Romero
1975	Ypsilanti, Mich.	
1976 Gerald/Marita Grudzen	Washington, D. C.	Terence Dosh
1977	St. Paul, Minn.	
1978	Scottsdale, Ariz.	Gaston Cadieux
1979	Cazenovia, N. Y.	

President	Convention site	Diaspora editor
1980 Paul/Susana Schlesinger	Monterey, Calif.	William Powers
1981	St. Louis, Mo.	
1982	Convent Station, N. J.	Mary Jane Schutzius
1983	Berkeley, Calif.	
1984 Mary Jane Schutzius	Lake Forest, Ill.	Robert Schutzius
1985	Long Island, N. Y.	
1986	Berkeley, Calif.	
1987	St. Charles, Mo.	
1988 Joseph Ruane	Philadelphia, Pa.	
1989	Charleston, S. C.	Judy Clarence
1990	San Jose, Calif.	
1991	St. Louis, Mo.	
1992	Baltimore, Md.	

Appendix B

Chronology of the Corps of Reserve Priests United for Service (CORPUS)

Founders and facilitators: 1974–1988
(The association was headquartered in Chicago.)

Frank Bonnike
Frank McGrath
James Wilbur
William Nemmers
Charles Hund
Joseph Marto

Salaried National Coordinators and Location of National Office

Terence Dosh 1984–1990; Minneapolis, Minn.
Leonard "Skip" Sikora 1991–present; Mill Valley, Calif.

Collegial Board 1988–1991

Anthony T. Padovano, President, Morris Plains, N.J.
Robert Charpentier, Vice President, Kensington, Calif.
Thomas Abel, Secretary, Baton Rouge, La.
Patrick Callahan, Treasurer, Seattle, Wash.
Thomas Bice-Allen, Green Bay, Wis.
Frank Bonnike, Chicago, Ill.
Michael Breslin, Brooklyn, N.Y.
Bernard Henry, Chicago, Ill.
Anthony Kowalski, Arlington, Va.
Frank McGrath, Chicago, Ill.
Ann O'Brien, Severna Park, Md.
Linda Pinto, Milford, Pa.

National Conferences

1988 Washington, D. C.
1989 Columbus, Ohio
1990 San Jose, Calif.
1991 New York, N.Y.
1992 Chicago, Ill.

Notes

Introduction

[1] There is extensive sociological literature on social movements, generated in large measure by the propensity of American society to produce them. Neil J. Smelser in *Theory of Collective Behavior* (New York: The Free Press, 1962) relates this to the encouragement of individual autonomy in the American political system. He uses the term *conduciveness* to describe the tendency for the cultural emphasis on individual rights to lead various segments of the population to feel "oppressed" and to organize themselves to achieve fuller freedom. Blacks, women, homosexuals, the handicapped, and, in the present study, Catholic priests are examples.

Although the author believes that the free ministry movement has passed through stages such as those enumerated by Malcolm Spector and and John I. Kitsuse in 1973 and by Armand L. Mauss in 1975, sociological references are kept to a minimum and every effort is made to permit the data to flow where it will. All stage theorists caution that to specify stages is to risk oversimplification and distortion.

[2] For example, in January 1991, Archbishop Rembert G. Weakland of Milwaukee announced that when a priestless Catholic community met certain conditions of faith and vitality he would be willing to present to Rome a married male candidate for the priesthood.

However, in November of the same year, Weakland reported that the Vatican Secretariat of State had informed him that the proposal was "out of place" ("Archbishop's request to ordain married men rejected," *The Long Island Catholic*, November 13, 1991).

[3] There is no accurate figure. Dean Hoge in *Future of Catholic Leadership* (1987, p. 10) says that dioceses underreport priests who leave. Fewer priests may be leaving in recent years in large measure because ordinations are down and will continue to decline, since seminary enrollment declined more than 43 percent between 1979 and 1990. See "Seminary numbers down for sixth straight year," *The Long Island Catholic*, January 2, 1991. On the other hand, the majority of priests want the right to marry, predisposing them to leave. See "Poll Shows Most Priests Want the Right to Marry," *The New York Times*, September 11, 1987.

Chapter 1

[1] Charles Davis, *A Question of Conscience* (New York: Harper and Row, 1967). *National Catholic Reporter (NCR)* further extended Davis's audience by publishing "The Loneliness of Conscience" (March 5, 1969), in which Davis described in very personal terms his decision to leave the Catholic Church and to marry a former student, Florence Henderson.

Frequent references to *NCR* reflect the fact that this independent Catholic newspaper is the foremost source of information about reform efforts in the Church. It is widely read by free ministers who through its letters page and news items have sought to promote their cause.

[2] Betty Friedan, *The Feminine Mystique* (New York: Norton, 1963).

[3] Davis, *A Question of Conscience*, 14.

[4] Charles Davis, *A Spirituality for the Vulnerable* (Kansas City: Sheed and Ward, 1990).

[5] Bernard Cooke, *The Challenge of Vatican II* (Chicago: Argus Communications, 1966), 8.

[6] Ibid., 15.

[7] *The Brooklyn Tablet*, December 4, 1969, quoting a statement Cooke had given *NCR*.

8 Letter to Tom Durkin, December 21, 1970.

9 Bernard Cooke, *Ministry to Word and Sacraments* (Philadelphia: Fortress Press, 1976).

10 "Critical Look at Catholic Church," *San Francisco Examiner*, May 8, 1971.

11 Edward Schillebeeckx, *Ministry: Leadership in the Community of Jesus Christ* (New York: Crossroad, 1981).

12 Edward Schillebeeckx, *The Church with a Human Face* (New York: Crossroad, 1985). Schillebeeckx has continued to provide free ministers and other reformers with a theological basis for their positions. See *Church: The Human Story of God* (New York: Crossroad, 1990), which offers a detailed justification for a democratic Church government.

13 *The New York Times* (January 28, 1980, A17) published an essay by Küng, "Why I Remain a Catholic," in which the recently censured theologian decried the oppressive conditions in the Church but pledged himself to continue to work for reform, urging that the Catholic Church "must not become confused simply with the Catholic hierarchy, still less with the Roman bureaucracy." As early as 1961, in *The Council, Reform and Reunion* (New York: Sheed and Ward), a book that for many Catholics set the tone for the upcoming Vatican II, Küng had emerged as an influential spokesman for reform. In February 28, 1969, *Time* reported on Küng's speaking tour of the United States and referred to him as "the most impatient and influential advocate of greater freedom in the Catholic Church." His monumental study, *The Church* (New York: Sheed and Ward, 1967), purported to explain to educated Catholics what the council had taught. It would take the Vatican many years to disassociate itself from Küng, by which time the damage had been done in the sense that many, including free ministers, had embraced Küng's vision of the Church as their own.

14 National Federation of Priests' Councils, "Reconciliation: Pastoral Priorities," 1975.

15 Cf. Hans Küng, *Theology for the Third Millenium* (New York: Crossroad, 1988) and *Reforming the Church Today* (New York: Crossroad, 1990).

16 *Journal of Ecumenical Studies*, 8 (1971): 344–9.

[17] *Concilium* (April 1972).

[18] Peter Kelly, *Searching for Truth: A Personal View of Roman Catholicism* (London: Collins, 1978).

[19] James Kavanaugh, *A Modern Priest Looks at His Outdated Church* (New York: Trident Press, 1967).

[20] Ibid., 23.

[21] Charles W. Freible, S.J., "Teilhard, Sexual Love and Celibacy," *Review For Religious* (March 1967).

[22] Quoted in Paul Chauchard, *Teilhard de Chardin on Love and Suffering* (New York: Paulist Press, 1966), 44.

[23] Pierre Teilhard de Chardin, *The Divine Milieu* (New York: Harper Torchbooks, 1957), 66.

[24] Gerald Vann, *To Heaven with Diana* (Chicago: Henry Regnery, 1965).

[25] Ibid., 134, 136, 138.

[26] Ibid., 49.

[27] Eugene C. Kennedy, "A Quiet Catholic Question," *America* (January 28, 1967).

[28] Eugene C. Kennedy, "The Psychology of Religious Suppression," *The Critic* (February–March, 1969).

[29] Eugene C. Kennedy and Victor J. Heckler, *The Catholic Priest in the United States: Psychological Investigations* (Washington, D.C.: U.S. Catholic Conference, 1972). Some of the findings are reported in David Rice, *Shattered Vows* (New York: William Morrow and Co., 1990), which relates the experiences of priests who have left, including some free ministers. However, Rice pays scant attention to the movement for ministerial reform, focusing instead on married priests as isolated individuals.

[30] "Priests Who Date: The Third Way," *Newsweek* (December 3, 1973): 107f.

[31] Ibid., 108.

Chapter 2

[1] Much of the material in this chapter is derived from the private correspondence and NAPR records of Carl Hemmer.

² Privately printed preliminary overview. No one has studied the Catholic Church and the priesthood more exhaustively than Joseph Fichter, who by 1965 had published fourteen books on the sociology of religion. However, it is startling to note that in *Priest and People* (New York: Sheed and Ward, 1965), which is based on a survey of over two thousand Catholic priests and two thousand lay Catholics, no mention is made of Vatican II nor is there the slightest hint of the impending massive resignations from the priesthood. It was as if Fichter approached a sample of parish priests during a lull before the hurricane of change crashed across the Catholic landscape.

³ George Gallup, Jr. and Jim Castelli, *The American Catholic People* (Garden City, N.Y.: Doubleday, 1987), 56.

⁴ Rund J. Bunnik, "A Question of Married Priests" (*Cross Currents*: Fall 1965 and Winter 1966). See also *Priests for Tomorrow* (New York: Holt, Rinehart and Winston, 1969).

⁵ John Cogley, "Discussion of Celibacy Rolls on Unchecked," *The Voice*, October 15, 1967.

⁶ Ibid., 11.

⁷ John A. O'Brien, *Why Priests Leave* (New York: Hawthorne Press, 1969).

⁸ Letter dated December 17, 1971.

⁹ Years later, a biographer who had access to Merton's private papers, revealed that Merton had fallen in love with a nurse while in the hospital, putting to the test his commitment to celibacy. Michael Mott, *The Seven Mountains of Thomas Merton* (Boston: Houghton Mifflin, 1984).

Chapter 3

¹ Unless otherwise indicated, quotations in this chapter are from unpublished documents in the SPFM file.

² Joseph Fichter, *The Pastoral Provisions* (Kansas City: Sheed and Ward, 1989). Since 1982 about fifty Episcopal priests and a few Lutheran and Methodist ministers have been ordained. One explanation of why this is permitted while married Catholic men cannot become priests is that people raised as Catholics are

presumed to know and accept the Catholic discipline that married men are not ordained to the priesthood. Converts, on the other hand, were not raised with the same understanding. ("Policies regarding married priests from other faiths still being formed," *Catholic Standard*, October 11, 1991.)

[3] "An Ex-priest Proposes That They Organize Too," *National Catholic Reporter*, March 13, 1968.

[4] "Free Priests' Bag: Love and Be Honest," *Detroit Free Press*, October 7, 1968.

[5] Ibid.

[6] Dagenais's wife, Francoise, had been the only woman present at the St. Louis meeting where SPFM was founded.

Chapter 4

[1] *National Catholic Reporter*, May 25, 1969, Letters.

[2] Eugene C. Bianchi, *Reconciliation* (New York: Sheed and Ward, 1969).

[3] Eugene C. Bianchi, "Resistance in the Church," *Commonweal* (May 16, 1969): 257–60.

[4] Ibid., 258.

[5] Eugene C. Bianchi, *The Religious Experience of Revolutionaries* (Garden City, N.Y.: Doubleday, 1972).

[6] Bianchi, *National Catholic Reporter*, May 25, 1969.

[7] "Proceedings of the First Annual Conference of the Society of Priests for a Free Ministry," November 7–9, 1969. Proceedings were printed also for the 1970 conference (now called convention). Thereafter, no separate proceedings were prepared. Some addresses have been published in *Diaspora*.

[8] Eugene C. Bianchi, "The Free Ministry," *Commonweal* (January 23, 1970).

[9] "A National Petition," *National Catholic Reporter*, August 21, 1970.

[10] "Dissident Priests Seek Lay Support," *The New York Times*, August 10, 1970.

[11] *Catholic Voice*, August 13, 1970.

[12] *Oakland Tribune*, August 3, 1970.

[13] Eugene C. Bianchi, "Man to Man on Women's Liberation," *National Catholic Reporter*, May 26, 1972, 11.

[14] Eugene C. Bianchi and Rosemary Ruether, *From Machismo to Mutuality* (New York: Paulist Press, 1976).

[15] In a study of 460 resigned priests and their wives, Maureen Hendricks-Rauch concluded: "In a time of so much pathology and lack of healthy marriages, the great majority of those involving resigned priests are very good marriages." Of the married priest couples, 83.9 percent reported that their marriages were "very happy" compared with 68 percent of couples in the general population as found in previous studies. Also, whereas the general divorce rate was 40 percent, that of resigned priests was 2 percent. "High Stability Found in Marriages of Ex-Priests," *Los Angeles Times*, February 9, 1980, 32.

[16] *Diaspora*, Fall 1983.

[17] Eugene C. Bianchi, *Aging as a Spiritual Journey* (New York: Crossroad, 1983).

[18] Donald J. Moore, book review, *America* (vol. 148, no. 12): 242, March 26, 1983.

[19] Bianchi has continued to write and speak on Church reform. Most recently, with Rosemary Radford Ruether, he edited *A Democratic Catholic Church* (New York: Crossroad, 1992).

[20] Bianchi, *From Machismo to Mutuality*.

[21] "Catholic Underground Churches Grow," *The New York Times*, April 22, 1968, 1.

[22] John A. Coleman, *Evolution of Dutch Catholicism: 1958–1974* (Berkeley, Calif.: University of California Press, 1978).

[23] Rocco Caporale, "We've Moved from a Temple Religion to the People of God," *Diaspora*, May–June 1977. Yet another Caporale paper, "An Ecumenical Catholic Diocese," sparked a major conflict within FCM in 1984.

Chapter 5

1 *San Francisco Examiner*, October 6, 1969.

2 Letter of Joseph Burns to SPFM board, February 12, 1972.

3 "'Free Ministry' Idea Scored," *The Advocate*, November 5, 1970. See also *National Catholic Reporter*, October 23, 1970.

4 "To Exit or Disperse?," *Diaspora*, August 1973. See also *National Catholic Reporter*, August 12, 1969.

Chapter 6

1 "Underground Church Seen Surfacing," *Catholic Bulletin Reporter*, January 9, 1970.

2 "Clarification of Society of Priests for a Free Ministry," *The Catholic Week*, April 12, 1970.

3 "New Order of Married Priests Urged," *Chicago Today*, March 24, 1970.

4 *Diaspora*, March–April 1971.

5 *Diaspora*, May–June 1974.

6 James H. McCown, S.J., "From Parish to Prison: Seeking to Serve," *America* (June 17, 1978): 481–83. An adulatory account of Sullivan's life through the early years of CURE.

7 It was in response to this remark by Cardinal Dearden that Carl Hemmer had reacted in the letter discussed in chapter 2.

8 *Diaspora*, August–October 1971. Ruether's address is discussed in chapter 12.

9 "Dissident Priests Seek Union of Six Organizations," *The New York Times*, September 5, 1971, 1. Burns had been featured also in "The Exodus Goes On," *New York Daily News*, October 20, 1970, 44, which referred to him as "one of the more vocal members of the Society of Priests for a Free Ministry."

10 "U.S. Seminarians Form Federation," *National Catholic Reporter*, April 21, 1972, 1. Article said that they had been meeting for five years but never formed an organization or drew up a constitution. A SMR brochure from the period began with the

words, "Why do men leave the ordained ministry day after day after day after day . . . ?"

11 "Demise of NAL," *National Catholic Reporter*, July 7, 1972. Article quoted a lay leader as saying that by 1972 NAL "couldn't muster enough energy to officially disband." See also David J. O'Brien, *The Renewal of American Catholicism* (New York: Oxford University Press, 1972). O'Brien experienced NAL in 1968 when its convention was attended by one thousand people whereas the founding meeting in 1967 had drawn only two hundred. O'Brien predicted that these "new laymen" were going to be difficult for the hierarchy to control and that "the days of the monolithic church bent upon harnessing and channeling lay energies were over." (p. 12)

12 Twenty years later, Rosemary Ruether was still attempting to rally Catholic reform groups to assume a more participatory role in Church government. See Call to Action's *Church Watch*, October 1991.

Chapter 7

1 "French Students Demonstrate for Change," *The New York Times*, November 13, 1990, 3.

2 "The Church: An Underdeveloped Political System," *National Catholic Reporter*, March 10, 1972, 7.

3 *Diaspora*, July–August 1972.

4 "'Free' Priests Back International Congress," *National Catholic Reporter*, September 5, 1972, 5.

5 *Diaspora*, September–October 1972.

6 "The Changing Priesthood in a Changing World" (Rome: International Documentation on the Contemporary Church, August 1972).

7 Letter from Paul N. Halvonik to Bernard McGoldrick, April 6, 1972.

8 "Married Priests Suspect Job Bias," *The New York Times*, September 2, 1973, 46.

9 Joseph Girzone, *Joshua* (New York: Macmillan, 1987), 73.

10 Letter from Robert Duryea to SPFM executive board, March 31, 1973.

[11] Letter from Bernard McGoldrick to SPFM, January 15, 1973.

[12] Letter from Robert Duryea to William Jerman, April 5, 1973.

[13] Undated letter from Robert Duryea to FCM board, Summer 1974.

[14] Letter from Robert Duryea to author, January 2, 1991.

Chapter 8

[1] "Priests' Society Votes to Change Direction," *National Catholic Reporter*, September 14, 1973, 2.

[2] "Married Priests Hope to Reform Church," *Boston Globe*, September 12, 1973.

[3] "Married Priests Change Directions," *Oakland Tribune*, September 4, 1973.

[4] William Manseau. The Chicago Generating Community unpublished proposal, Spring 1973; and unpublished paper submitted to the Chicago Theological Seminary, June 10, 1974.

[5] "Eucharist Service Held as Protest," *Chicago Tribune*, September 2, 1974, 3. See also "40 Married Priests Concelebrate Mass," *Chicago Sun-Times*, September 2, 1974.

[6] James F. Colaianni, ed. *Married Priests and Married Nuns* (New York: McGraw-Hill, 1968).

Chapter 9

[1] *Corpus Research I*, 1988. Much of the material in this chapter is derived from literature published by CORPUS and NFPC over the years. NFPC publishes a newspaper *Priests USA*. CORPUS publishes a newsletter, which in recent years has been called *Corpus Reports* (CR).

[2] Unpublished report to NFPC Philadelphia province.

[3] John C. Haughey, S.J., "The Priesthood," *America* (January 10, 1970): 18–20.

[4] Proceedings from NFPC convention, March 1971.

[5] "Synod Celibacy Stand Irks U.S. Spokesman," *Boston Globe*, October 17, 1971.

[6] Frank Bonnike, "A Role/Function/Content Approach to Ministry," *Connector* newsletter, Catholic Committee on Urban Ministry, Notre Dame, Ind., 1975.

[7] "Vote Listing for Laicized Priests," *National Catholic Reporter*, March 30, 1973.

[8] F.J. McGrath, "Married Priests in the Church: Preparedness in America," *Clergy Review*, February 1978, 73–74.

[9] Ned Reidy, "The CORPUS Movement," unpublished paper for Institute on Culture and Creative Spirituality, California, 1990.

[10] "Who Speaks for the Resigned Priest?," *Diaspora*, March–April 1975.

[11] "Update of CORPUS Statement," CORPUS newsletter, January–February 1976.

[12] McGrath, "Married Priests in the Church," 74.

[13] CORPUS research pamphlet, vol. 1, 1988.

Chapter 10

[1] Letter from Dan Duffy, *Diaspora*, Fall 1985.

[2] "Chaplain's Dismissal Challenged," *Sacramento Bee*, May 5, 1985. The case was followed throughout by California papers. See "Flap over Firing of a Prison Chaplain," *San Francisco Chronicle*, January 6, 1988, and "No Decision Reached on Prison Chaplain," *Sacramento Union*, January 6, 1988.

[3] Duffy v. California state personnel board et al., 283 Cal. Rptr. 622 (3rd Dist. 1991). Summarized in Thayer Brown & Platt newsletter, September 1991.

[4] Duffy letter, *Diaspora*, Fall 1985.

[5] "Married Priest Awaits Word on Reinstatement as Chaplain," *Sacramento Bee*, January 5, 1988.

[6] "Fellowship of Christian Ministries Certifies Five," *National Catholic Reporter*, November 8, 1974, 6.

[7] Gerald Grudzen, "Women Priests and Professional Certification," *Diaspora*, September–October 1974. See also, "Clergy Group will support 'disestablished,'" *National Catholic Reporter*, September 13, 1974.

8 Robert C. Scharf, "Certification," *Diaspora*, Winter 1982–83, quoting Schillebeeckx, *Ministry: Leadership in the Community of Jesus Christ* (New York: Crossroad, 1981), 76.

9 Schillebeeckx, op. cit, 41, 47.

10 In a November 1991 letter to the author, Joseph Ruane, FCM president, wrote: "The board has been on my back for at least two years to get the 'volunteer exclusionary indemnity' clause placed in our charter. It is presently in the hands of a Philadelphia lawyer."

11 "Test Case of FCM Certification," *Diaspora*, September–October 1977.

12 *Catholikon*, vol. 1, no. 1, January 1985. Mimeographed two-page newsletter authored by Brennan. It was the only issue produced.

13 Rocco Caporale, "For An Ecumenical Catholic Diocese of America," *Diaspora*, Spring 1984.

14 "Reform Catholics Consider New Sect," *Chicago Tribune*, August 18, 1984, 7. The Associated Press also reported the rejection of the ECDA proposal: "Catholics Rebuff Separate Diocese," *Chicago Tribune*, August 21, 1984.

Chapter 11

1 "Base communities see world in a different way," *National Catholic Reporter*, August 16, 1991, 10.

2 Gerald Grudzen, *Genesis of the Christian Experience* (White Plains, N.Y.: Diakonia Press, 1975).

3 Gerald Grudzen, *New Age Catholicism: A Life of Service in the World* (San Jose, Calif.: Privately published, 1979).

4 Gerald Grudzen, "Spirituality and Ministry in Diaspora," *Diaspora*, July–August 1978.

5 Edward Schillebeeckx, *Church: The Human Story of God* (New York: Crossroad, 1990).

6 Joseph Fichter, "Heirs to the Kingdom," *Commonweal* (July 12, 1991): 432–34.

[7] Antonio Soto, "Women Seize the Moment," *Diaspora*, September–October 1978.

[8] "'Careers, ministry not separate,' group told," *National Catholic Reporter*, October 20, 1978, 3.

[9] "Beards, pinstripes mix at central java house," *San Jose Business Journal*, November 25, 1985. Article includes a picture of the phoenix statue and announces the opening of the Phoenix bookstore as a "project of FCM Publishing." The bookstore failed.

[10] "Former Maryknoll Priest Evolves a New 'Ministry,'" *The New York Times*, April 9, 1978, Westchester, N.Y., edition.

[11] "Now it's Maryknoll-in-Diaspora," *Diaspora*, November–December 1977. See also "Former Maryknoll Priests, Many Married, Joining in New Ministry," *The New York Times*, August 10, 1977.

[12] Gerald Grudzen, "The Exodus Experience Within Maryknoll: Assessment and Implications for Community and Mission," *Diaspora*, Summer 1983.

[13] "Los Sacerdotes Casados Buscan Cambio Necesario en La Iglesia," *El Espectador*, January 7, 1973. Article in Bogotá, Colombia, newspaper, "Married Priests Seek Needed Changes in the Church," reported meeting of the Grudzens and a Colombian couple, Carlos and Clemencia Rodriguez. A picture of the two couples identified Carlos Rodriguez as president of the "International Association of Married Priests" and Grudzen, incorrectly, as president of SPFM.

[14] "SPFM representatives in South America," *Diaspora*, April–May 1973.

[15] Bernard Cooke, "Does Liberation Theology Have Something to Say to U.S. Catholics?" *Diaspora*, Spring 1983.

[16] The story of Anthony and Phyllis Soto could be a chapter of its own in the history of free ministry. Anthony, born in 1921, was ordained a Franciscan priest in 1947. For twenty-five years he held a series of positions within the Church in California. In 1972 he left Church work and in 1974 married Phyllis Armas. Since that time, the two have been active in a wide variety of ministries among Mexican-Americans and have been close associates of the Grudzens.

[17] Letter from a base community in Nicaragua, *Diaspora*, Fall 1988.

[18] Walt Melfi, "The Challenge of the Base Ecclesial Communities to the Affluent Church," *Diaspora*, Fall 1986.

[19] Joseph P. Ruane, "Basic Ecclesial Community and Home Church Consultation," *Diaspora*, Spring 1990.

[20] In November 1991, Call to Action compiled a list of small Christian communities. Forty-six were identified, ranging from parish-affiliated to gay and lesbian to Women-Church groups. Only one, Reaching Out in St. Louis, had been established by married priests. Interest in home religious gatherings may be spreading to Jews. See "Conversations with God and Friends at Home," *The New York Times*, December 1, 1991.

Chapter 12

[1] Rosemary Ruether, "Organizing for Survival," *Diaspora*, August–October 1971.

[2] Ibid.

[3] Rosemary Radford Ruether, "The Relation of the Ministry of the People and the Ordained Ministry, with Special Reference to the Question of Women," *Diaspora*, March–April and May–June 1974.

[4] What Ruether was saying to FCM in 1974 was similar to what she had written seven years earlier as the only woman contributor to a collection of essays on the priesthood. An excerpt from that essay appears at the beginning of this chapter. Rosemary Ruether, "Ministry in the Church of the Future," in *Secular Priest in the New Church*, edited by Gerald S. Sloyan (New York: Herder and Herder, 1967), 246.

[5] "Woman Power," *Diaspora*, July–August 1970.

[6] "Clergy group will support 'disestablished,'" *National Catholic Reporter*, September 13, 1974.

[7] Rosemary Ruether, "The Vanishing Religious Order and the New Human Community," *The Christian Century* (April 7, 1971): 427.

[8] Rosemary Ruether, "The Ethic of Celibacy," *Commonweal* (February 2, 1974): 391.

[9] Ibid.

10 Anne Marie Gardiner, ed., *Women and Catholic Priesthood: Proceedings of the Detroit Ordination Conference* (New York: Paulist Press, 1976), 31. The proceedings identified Ruether as a member of the SPFM board of advisors even though the organization had changed its name to FCM in 1973.

11 Ibid.

12 Ruether's writings on women are voluminous. See especially *Women Church: Theology and Practice of Feminist Liturgical Communities* (San Francisco: Harper and Row, 1985).

13 William M. Ramsay, *Four Modern Prophets* (Atlanta, Ga.: John Knox Press, 1986).

14 "Conference Celebrates Women-Church Movement," *Sojourners* (January 1989): 12.

15 Rosemary Radford Ruether, "Dear U.S. bishops, you insult our intelligence," *National Catholic Reporter*, May 18, 1990. After years of controversy, the proposed pastoral on women is scheduled to be voted on by the bishops at their November 1992 meeting in Washington, D.C. They appear to be in a no-win situation. If the pastoral is approved, it will be roundly condemned by critics such as Ruether. If it is not approved, the bishops will be ridiculed by those same critics as being unable to speak convincingly to American Catholic women.

16 Eugene C. Bianchi and Rosemary Ruether, *From Machismo to Mutuality* (New York: Paulist Press, 1976).

17 Kane was keynote speaker at the 1989 FCM convention in Charleston and made a forceful indictment of patriarchy in the Church. In 1991 at a convocation sponsored by married priests on Long Island, New York, her address, titled "The Living Church: Building Community," was an effort to find a basis for cooperation among conflicting elements in the Church.

18 M.J. Schutzius, "Womanchurch Spoke," *Diaspora*, Winter 1983–84.

19 Letter from Tom Durkin, *Diaspora*, Spring 1984.

20 Mary Jane Schutzius, "And from our outgoing president . . . ," *Diaspora*, Fall 1988. This attitude had been expressed more than a year before when in her president's report to the FCM board she

said, "We provide service to certified members. Do we hear from them? Is FCM only for certified members and thereby dying out? Reports note base communities may be dying out also . . . . What is the importance of FCM?" (board minutes, August 7, 1987).

21 Kathleen Krekeler, "Moral Development Theory: Implications for Organizational Church Hierarchies," *Diaspora*, Spring 1985. See also Carol Gilligan, *In A Different Voice* (Cambridge, Mass.: Harvard University Press, 1982).

Chapter 13

1 Verta Taylor, "Social Movement Continuity: The Woman's Movement in Abeyance," *American Sociological Review*, 54: (October 1989): 761–75.

2 Priestly Ministries/USA brochure, 1976.

3 Despite the minimal impact on the bishops and questionable support from rank-and-file clergy, NFPC had continued to promote a married priesthood and the more sensitive issue of restoring married priests to active ministry. See "Clergy unit: Reconcile ex-priests, remarrieds," *National Catholic Reporter*, March 21, 1975, 1.

4 Efforts to establish local support groups have not ceased. In 1986, for example, married priests in Seattle organized. With the support of Archbishops Hunthausen and Murphy, they invited over two hundred active priests to join them for a fraternal dinner. Only seven attended. *CR*, September–October 1991.

5 Terry Dosh, "A Report on Resigned Priests and the Role of Ministry in Detroit," *Diaspora*, September–October 1976.

6 Thomas C. Fox, "Made in Detroit," *Commonweal* (November 19, 1976). Auxiliary Bishop James Shannon, who resigned and married, subsequently wrote a column, "The Pilgrim Church," for the *Minneapolis Tribune*. Following the Call to Action conference, he wrote that his former episcopal colleagues "will face the delicate task of reconciling their dual allegiance to formal Catholic doctrine and to the mature judgment of a blue-ribbon Catholic assembly which differs radically from many venerable Catholic teachings." October 31, 1976, 29.

7 In an article following the Call to Action ad, *Times* religion editor Peter Steinfels suggested that the proposals offered "nothing

new" and "have been in the air ever since the Second Vatican Council closed." *The New York Times,* March 3, 1990.

8 See Tim Unsworth, "Call to Action weary but still feisty after 15 years," *National Catholic Reporter,* November 22, 1991, 18. Unsworth noted that "most delegates were over 50" and cited a curial bishop who said that the Church could wait out "fringe groups" that try to change it.

9 "Upbeat account signals hope," *CR,* November–December 1985.

10 Ibid.

11 *CR,* July–August 1990.

12 "We are ready to serve," *CR,* July–August 1987.

13 "U.S. Priest Urges Pope to 'Explore' Issue of Celibacy," *The New York Times,* September 11, 1987, 16.

14 "What to Do When Priests Stray," *Time* (September 24, 1990).

15 Richard McBrien, "Homosexuality and the Priesthood," *Commonweal* (June 19, 1987).

16 See also James G. Wolf, ed., *Gay Priests* (New York: Harper, 1990); Jeannine Gramick, ed., *Homosexuality in the Priesthood and the Religious Life* (New York: Crossroad, 1990); and Andrew Greeley, "Bishops paralyzed over heavily gay priesthood," *National Catholic Reporter,* November 10, 1989, 13.

17 Richard McBrien, "The Priesthood at the Crossroads," *Brooklyn Tablet,* August 18, 1989. See also William Wells, "If I Had a Son, I Wouldn't Want Him to Be a Priest," *St. Anthony's Messenger,* August 1986; and Paul Wilkes, "The Hands That Would Shape Our Souls," *The Atlantic* (December 1990): 55ff.

18 Richard Sipe, *A Secret World: Sexuality and the Search for Celibacy* (New York: Brunner/Mazel, 1990.)

19 "Celibacy and the Church," *Newsday,* December 6, 1990.

20 "FCM and Corpus 1988," *Diaspora,* Summer 1988.

21 "Corpus Directions," *CR,* July–August 1988.

22 Mission Statement, *CR,* September–October 1991.

23 "Growing Pressures for a Married Priesthood," *The New York Times,* July 10, 1990, 1.

[24] "A Married Man's Road to Priesthood," *The New York Times*, October 24, 1990.

[25] "Vatican Rejects Secret Priests Ordained in Czechoslovakia," *The New York Times*, April 12, 1992.

[26] The first issue of *Bread Rising* (November 1991) said that its goal was "to inspire and empower people concerned with Church reform."

Chapter 14

[1] Anthony Padovano, *The Estranged God* (New York: Sheed and Ward, 1966)

[2] *The Advocate* (Newark, N.J., diocesan paper), November 5, 1970; cited in *Diaspora*, September–October 1970.

[3] September 22, 1972, letter of Roméo DiBenedetto to SPFM board.

[4] "Report on Priesthood," *National Catholic Reporter*, October 8, 1971.

[5] October 19, 1971, letter of Tom Durkin to Bernard McGoldrick.

[6] Hans Küng, *Why Priests? A Proposal for a New Church Ministry* (Garden City, N.Y.: Doubleday, 1972). Review of book by Anthony Padovano, *National Catholic Reporter*, September 29, 1972.

[7] Hans Küng, *Why Priests?*, op. cit., 13.

[8] "Priests/USA: Looking at Two Issues," *Diaspora*, May–June 1972.

[9] William King, Review of *Why Priests?*, *Diaspora*, September–October 1972.

[10] "SPFM: New York," *Diaspora*, November–December 1971.

[11] "SPFM: New York," *Diaspora*, December 1972–January 1973.

[12] "Ex-priests reach for universal priesthood," *National Catholic Reporter*, September 2, 1977; "Ministry and Meaning," *Diaspora*, November–December 1977; and Gerald Grudzen, *New Age Catholicism: A Life of Service in the World* (San Jose, Calif.: Privately published, 1979).

[13] Anthony Padovano, *Free to be Faithful* (New York: Paulist Press, 1972).

[14] Anthony Podovano, *The Human Journey: Thomas Merton, Symbol of a Century* (New York: Paulist Press, 1982).

[15] "Special Report," *Diaspora*, Spring 1980.

[16] *Diaspora*, January–February 1980.

[17] Anthony Padovano, "Our Vulnerability Needs Ministry," *National Catholic Reporter*, October 23, 1981.

[18] Ibid.

[19] Anthony Padovano, "We Cannot Abolish the Word of the Lord," *Diaspora*, Fall 1982.

[20] Anthony Padovano, "The Ministerial Crisis in Today's Church," *Diaspora*, Winter 1985.

[21] Anthony Padovano, *Reform and Renewal* (Kansas City: Sheed and Ward, 1990), 42.

[22] Anthony Padovano, "Pastoral Ministry and the Non-Clerical Priesthood: A Theological and Canonical Reflection," CORPUS, 1989. See also *Reform and Renewal*.

[23] Anthony Padovano, "Married Priests Locked Out, but Still Changing Church," *National Catholic Reporter*, October 9, 1987. See also, "Married Priests Tilt Bravely at Unyielding Vatican," *The New York Times*, September 4, 1985.

[24] "Spiritual Pain: Ex-Priests Seek Return to Church," *The New York Times*, August 25, 1987, B20.

[25] "Brazilian Bishops affirm married priesthood," *CR*, March–April 1990.

[26] "CORPUS members assert: 'We're still priests'," *National Catholic Reporter*, July 14, 1989.

[27] "Prayer v. Prayer at Bishops Retreat," *The New York Times*, June 25, 1990, 13. See also, "National Conference: Eucharist, Women, Bishops," CR, July–August 1990.

[28] Anthony Padovano, "State of the Association," *CR*, July–August 1990.

[29] "Vatican Critical of a U.S. Bishop," *The New York Times*, October 24, 1990.

³⁰ "National Coordinator Notes," *CR*, November–December 1990.

³¹ John C. Haughey, S.J., "The Priesthood," *America* (January 10, 1970): 18–20.

³² Anthony Padovano, *Love and Destiny* (New York: Paulist Press, 1987).

³³ Ibid., 88.

Chapter 15

¹ "Area Church Kills Priest's Talk—Nearly," *Pittsburgh Post-Gazette*, December 5, 1971.

² "Married priest, wife: We're Still Priests," *Winona Daily News*, September 20, 1972.

³ Helen Rose Fuchs Ebaugh, *Becoming an Ex* (Chicago: University of Chicago Press, 1988).

⁴ In an article on Catholic higher education, "Bland Secularism?," *Commonweal* (June 1, 1991), Raymond A. Schroth, S.J., said that "the last generation of the broadly educated humanists may be the priests and ex-priests in their fifties, trained in philosophy and the classics." Tom Durkin, perennial free ministry gadfly, wrote to *Commonweal*, protesting the use of the term "ex-priest," calling it a "redundancy." His letter was not published.

⁵ Letter, *Diaspora*, Winter 1983–1984.

⁶ "What Did We Do at FCM—St. Louis?," *Diaspora*, Summer 1991.

⁷ As well as hosting the CORPUS conference in June, 1991, the RCC conducted the third of its own convocations at Hofstra University in October. Richard McBrien and Theresa Kane addressed about two hundred participants.

⁸ "Keynoter Tells 'Married priests': You're Hurting Your Own Cause," *Brooklyn Tablet*, June 29, 1991; Margaret O'Brien Steinfels, "Ecclesia Semper Reformanda," *Commonweal* (October 11, 1991).

⁹ *Brooklyn Tablet*, July 6, 1991.

¹⁰ Joseph J. Burns, "Report on Married Priests Meeting Was Incomplete," *Brooklyn Tablet*, July 13, 1991. In a letter in *National Catholic Reporter* (August 16, 1991), Carl Hemmer criticized that paper's

coverage of the CORPUS conference and added: "CORPUS may have been denied an episcopal presence at the conference, but Steinfels provided the missing pontifical statement."

[11] Thomas A. McCabe, "A Married Priest," *Commonweal* (July 12, 1991): 434.

[12] Thomas A. McCabe, "An Exchange of Views," *Commonweal* (October 11, 1991).

[13] Eugene C. Bianchi, "Resistance in the Church," *Commonweal* (May 16, 1969).

[14] Eugene C. Bianchi, Letter, *National Catholic Reporter*, May 25, 1969. On dissent in the Church, see also Philip S. Kaufman, *Why You Can Disagree* (New York: Crossroad, 1989).

[15] Robert S. Smith, "Priesthood in Crisis," *Diaspora*, Spring 1980.

Further Reading

Bianchi, Eugene C. "The Free Ministry." *Commonweal* (January 23, 1970).

———. Letter to the editor on free ministry. *National Catholic Reporter* (May 25, 1969).

———. *Reconciliation*. New York: Sheed and Ward, 1969.

———. *The Religious Experience of Revolutionaries*. Garden City, N.Y.: Doubleday, 1972.

———. "Resistance in the Church." *Commonweal* (May 16, 1969): 257–260.

Bianchi, Eugene C., and Rosemary Ruether. *From Machismo to Mutuality*. New York: Paulist Press, 1976.

Bunnik, Rund J. *Priests for Tomorrow*. New York: Holt, Rinehart, and Winston, 1969.

———. "A Question of Married Priests." *Cross Currents* (Fall 1965 and Winter 1966).

Chautard, Paul. *Teilhard de Chardin on Love and Suffering*. New York: Paulist Press, 1966.

Colaianni, James F. ed. *Married Priests and Married Nuns*. New York: McGraw-Hill, 1968.

Cooke, Bernard. *The Challenge of Vatican II*. Chicago: Argus Communications, 1968.

———. "The Eucharist: A Threatened Species." *National Catholic Reporter* (May 11, May 18, May 25, 1990).

———. *Ministry to Word and Sacraments*. Philadelphia: Fortress Press, 1976.

Davis, Charles. "The Loneliness of Conscience." *National Catholic Reporter* (March 5, 1969): 5.

———. *A Question of Conscience*. New York: Harper and Row, 1967.

———. *Sacraments of Initiation: Baptism and Confirmation*. New York: Sheed and Ward, 1964.

———. *A Spirituality for the Vulnerable*. Kansas City, Mo.: Sheed and Ward, 1990.

———. *Theology for Today*. New York: Sheed and Ward, 1962.

Ebaugh, Helen Rose Fuchs. *Becoming an Ex*. Chicago: University of Chicago Press, 1988.

Fichter, Joseph H. "Heirs to the Kingdom." *Commonweal* (July 12, 1991): 432–34.

———. *The Pastoral Provisions*. Kansas City, Mo.: Sheed and Ward, 1989.

———. *Priests and People*. New York: Sheed and Ward, 1965.

Fox, Thomas C. "Made in Detroit." *Commonweal* (November 19, 1976).

Freible, Charles W., S.J. "Teilhard, Sexual Love and Celibacy." *Review for Religious* (March 1967).

Gallup, George Jr., and Jim Castelli. *The American Catholic People*. Garden City, N.Y.: Doubleday, 1987.

Gardiner, Anne Marie. ed. *Women and Catholic Priesthood: Proceedings of the Detroit Ordination Conference*. New York: Paulist Press, 1976.

Gramick, Jeannine. ed. *Homosexuality in the Priesthood and Religious Life*. New York: Crossroad, 1989.

Greeley, Andrew. "Bishops Paralyzed Over Heavily Gay Priesthood." *National Catholic Reporter* (November 10, 1989): 13.

Haughey, John C., S.J. "The Priesthood." *America* (January 10, 1970): 18–20.

Hoge, Dean. *Future of Catholic Leadership*. Kansas City, Mo.: Sheed and Ward, 1987.

Kaufman, Philip S. *Why You Can Disagree*. New York: Crossroad, 1989.

Kavanaugh, James. *A Modern Priest Looks at His Outdated Church*. New York: Trident Press, 1967.

Kelly, Peter. *Searching for Truth: A Personal View of Roman Catholicism*. Cleveland: Collins, 1978.

Kennedy, Eugene C. "The Psychology of Religious Suppression." *The Critic* (February–March 1969).

———. "A Quiet Catholic Question." *America* (January 28, 1967).

Kennedy, Eugene C., and Victor J. Heckler. *The Catholic Priest in the United States: Psychological Investigations*. Washington, D.C.: U.S. Catholic Conference, 1972.

Küng, Hans. *The Church*. New York: Sheed and Ward, 1967.

———. *The Council, Reform and Reunion*. New York: Sheed & Ward, 1961.

———. *Reforming the Church Today*. New York: Crossroad, 1990.

———. *Theology for the Third Millenium*. New York: Crossroad, 1988.

———. "Why I Remain a Catholic." *The New York Times* (January 28, 1990): A7.

———. *Why Priests? A Proposal for a New Church Ministry*. Garden City, N.Y.: Doubleday, 1972.

Leahy, John. "An Ex-Priest Proposes That They Organize Too." *National Catholic Reporter* (March 13, 1968).

McBrien, Richard. "Homosexuality and the Priesthood." *Commonweal* (June 19, 1987).

McCabe, Thomas A. "An Exchange of Views." *Commonweal* (October 11, 1991).

——. "A Married Priest." *Commonweal* (July 12, 1991): 434.

McCown, James H., S.J. "From Parish to Prison: Seeking to Serve." *America* (June 17, 1978): 481–83.

McGoldrick, Bernard. "The Church: An Underdeveloped Political System." *National Catholic Reporter* (March 10, 1972): 7.

McGrath, F.J. "Married Priests in the Church: Preparedness in America." *Clergy Review* (February 1978): 73–74.

Mauss, Armand L. *Social Problems as Social Movements.* Philadelphia: J.P. Lippincott, 1975.

Mott, Michael. *The Seven Mountains of Thomas Merton.* Boston: Houghton Mifflin, 1984.

O'Brien, John A. *Why Priests Leave.* New York: Hawthorne Press, 1969.

Padovano, Anthony T. *The Estranged God.* New York: Sheed and Ward, 1966.

——. *Free to Be Faithful.* New York: Paulist Press, 1972.

——. "Married Priests Locked Out, but Still Changing Church." *National Catholic Reporter* (October 9, 1987).

——. "Our Vulnerability Needs Ministry." *National Catholic Reporter* (October 23, 1981).

——. *Reform and Renewal.* Kansas City, Mo.: Sheed and Ward, 1990.

Rice, David. *Shattered Vows.* New York: William Morrow, 1990.

Ruether, Rosemary Radford. "Dear U.S. Bishops, You Insult Our Intelligence." *National Catholic Reporter* (May 18, 1990).

——. "The Ethic of Celibacy." *Commonweal* (February 2, 1974): 391.

——. "Ministry in the Church of the Future." In *Secular Priest in the New Church.* Edited by Gerald S. Sloyan. New York: Herder and Herder, 1967.

————. *Women Church: Theology and Practice of Feminist Liturgical Communities*. San Francisco: Harper and Row, 1985.

Schillebeeckx, Edward. *Church: The Human Story of God*. New York: Crossroad, 1990.

————. *The Church with a Human Face*. New York: Crossroad, 1985.

————. *Ministry: Leadership in the Community of Jesus Christ*. New York: Crossroad, 1981.

Sipe, Richard. *A Secret World: Sexuality and the Search for Celibacy*. New York: Brunner/Mazel, 1990.

Smelser, Neil J. *Theory of Collective Behavior*. New York: The Free Press, 1962.

Spector, Malcolm, and John I. Kitsuse. "Social Problems: A Re-Formulation." *Social Problems* 21 (1973): 145–59.

Steinfels, Margaret O'Brien. "Ecclesia Semper Reformanda." *Commonweal* (October 11, 1991).

Swindler, Leonard, and Herbert O'Brien. *A Catholic Bill of Rights*. Kansas City, Mo.: Sheed and Ward, 1989.

Taylor, Verta. "Social Movement Continuity: The Woman's Movement in Abeyance." *American Sociological Review* 54 (October 1989): 761–75.

Teilhard de Chardin, Pierre. *The Divine Milieu*. New York: Harper Torch Books, 1957.

Wilkes, Paul. "The Hands That Would Shape Our Souls." *The Atlantic* (December 1990): 55ff.

Index

O'Rourke, Joseph, 194
Optional celibacy, *xvi*, 5, 21, 23,
29–31, 170–71, 276, 298. *See also*
Celibacy.
Ordinariate, 20
Ordination, 190, 192–93, 195,
200–201, 213, 230–35, 258–62,
268, 294

P

Padovano, Anthony, 93–94, 190,
244–45, 247, 253, 256, 258, 261,
265–84, 295, 298–99, 303, 308
Padovano, Theresa Lackamp, 267,
284
Parks, Rosa, *xiv*
Patriarchy, 235–36, 260
Paul VI, Pope, 19, 23, 24, 27, 70,
123, 132, 287
Peña, Roberto, 251
Penaskovic, Robert, 200
Pfeiffer, Cynthia, 291–93
Pfeiffer, William, 254, 291–95, 303
Phoenix, 212–14, 217
Phoenix as symbol, 214
Pinto, Linda, 261, 308
Pius XII, Pope, 6
Pleasant, Ann, 156–57
Pleasant, Frank, 155–57, 212
Political action, 39, 82, 105–6
Powers, William, 306
Priestly Ministers/USA, 245–48,
250, 252, 254
Primeau, Ernest J., bishop, 23
Pro-Life movement, *xv*
Prophetic ministry, 72–73
Proteau, Janet. *See* Bonnike, Janet
Proteau.
Protestants, 154, 157, 175, 190, 201,
206, 228
Pucelik, Thomas M., 29–30, 37, 48

Q

Question of Conscience, A (Davis), 4
Quinn, Francis, bishop, 184, 199

R

Ratigan, James, 246, 251
Rausch, James S., bishop, 213
Registration of sacramental
actions, 194–95
Reid, Sr. Ursula, 114
Reiff, Maureen, 238
Reilly, Marita. *See* Grudzen, Marita
Reilly.
Reinstatement, 176, 223
Renewal Coordinating Committee
(RCC), 298
Rescript on dispensations, 171–72
Rienzo, Gregory, 215
Ritter, Fr. Bruce, 258–59
Ritter, Joseph Cardinal, 19
Rodriguez, Carlos, 127
Romero, Gilbert, 305
Roy, Henry, 143–44
Ruane, Joseph, 11, 212, 220, 239,
276, 306
Ruether, Rosemary Radford, 101,
106, 113–15, 149, 153–54, 223–36,
240, 253

S

Sacerdotalis Celibatus (encyclical), 23
Sacraments, 82, 187, 194, 201, 278
Schallert, Eugene, S.J., 16, 20
Scharf, Robert C., 189–90
Schillebeeckx, Edward, 3, 9–10,
189–91, 209, 229
Schlesinger, Paul, 191–92, 198, 238,
306
Schlesinger, Susana, 198, 238, 306
Schutzius, Mary Jane, 212, 224,
236–40, 306

Vatican Council II (cont.), 9, 12,
  14, 20, 39, 91, 93, 97, 109, 123,
  155–56, 168, 197, 204, 209, 227,
  244, 250, 265, 267, 269, 288, 301,
  303
Vocare, 296

W

Waller, James C., 185–86
Warner, Mary Alice, 158
*Why Priests? A Proposal for a New
  Church Ministry* (Küng), 268–70
Wilber, James, 173, 307
Wilber, Joan, 173
Woggon, H. A., 157
Women-Church movement, 225,
  234–38
Women in free ministry, 151–55,
  212–13, 223–40, 244, 260
Women as priests, 28, 130, 153–55,
  159, 167, 189–90, 200, 212–13,
  231–35, 252, 258–61, 275, 283
Women-Church Speaks
  Conference, 237–38
Women's liberation movement,
  xiv, xv, 4, 10, 151–52, 212–13,
  231–40, 244, 260
Women's Ordination Conference,
  233, 234–35, 253
Wood, Steven, 215
Woolever, Frank and Mimi, 211
Wright, John Cardinal, 156–57
Wuerl, Donald W., bishop, 281

Y

Yeltsin, Boris, *xiv*
Young Christian Students, 144
Young Christian Workers
  movement, *xv*, 144, 216

Z

Zehfuss, Mary Lou, 276, 287